STUDIES IN IMPERIALISM

General Editor: Andrew S. Thompson

Founding Editor: John M. MacKenzie

When the 'Studies in Imperialism' series was founded by Professor John M. MacKenzie more than twenty-five years ago, emphasis was laid upon the conviction that 'imperialism as a cultural phenomenon had as significant an effect on the dominant as on the subordinate societies'. With well over a hundred titles now published, this remains the prime concern of the series. Cross-disciplinary work has indeed appeared covering the full spectrum of cultural phenomena, as well as examining aspects of gender and sex, frontiers and law, science and the environment, language and literature, migration and patriotic societies, and much else. Moreover, the series has always wished to present comparative work on European and American imperialism, and particularly welcomes the submission of books in these areas. The fascination with imperialism, in all its aspects, shows no sign of abating, and this series will continue to lead the way in encouraging the widest possible range of studies in the field. 'Studies in Imperialism' is fully organic in its development, always seeking to be at the cutting edge, responding to the latest interests of scholars and the needs of this ever-expanding area of scholarship.

The cultural construction of the British world

MANCHESTER 1824

Manchester University Press

SELECTED TITLES AVAILABLE IN THE SERIES

WRITING IMPERIAL HISTORIES
ed. Andrew S. Thompson

MUSEUMS AND EMPIRE
Natural history, human cultures and colonial identities
John M. MacKenzie

MISSIONARY FAMILIES
Race, gender and generation on the spiritual frontier
Emily J. Manktelow

THE COLONISATION OF TIME
Ritual, routine and resistance in the British Empire
Giordano Nanni

BRITISH CULTURE AND THE END OF EMPIRE
ed. Stuart Ward

SCIENCE, RACE RELATIONS AND RESISTANCE
Britain, 1870–1914
Douglas A. Lorimer

GENTEEL WOMEN
Empire and domestic material culture, 1840–1910
Dianne Lawrence

EUROPEAN EMPIRES AND THE PEOPLE
Popular responses to imperialism in France, Britain, the Netherlands, Belgium, Germany and Italy
ed. John M. MacKenzie

SCIENCE AND SOCIETY IN SOUTHERN AFRICA
ed. Saul Dubow

The cultural construction of the British world

Edited by

Barry Crosbie and Mark Hampton

MANCHESTER UNIVERSITY PRESS

Published by MANCHESTER UNIVERSITY PRESS
ALTRINCHAM STREET, MANCHESTER M1 7JA, UK
www.manchesteruniversitypress.co.uk

British Library Cataloguing-in-Publication Data
A catalogue record for this book is available from the British Library

Library of Congress Cataloging-in-Publication Data applied for

ISBN 978 0 7190 9789 8 *hardback*

First published 2016

ISBN 978 1 5261 2713 6 *paperback*

First published 2018

Typeset in Trump Medieval by
Koinonia, Manchester
Printed in Great Britain by
TJ International Ltd, Padstow

Dedicated to the Memory of

Sir Christopher Alan Bayly (1945–2015)

'Death is not extinguishing the light;
it is only putting out the lamp
because the dawn has come.'
(Rabindranath Tagore)

CONTENTS

ILLUSTRATIONS

NOTES ON CONTRIBUTORS

Sir Christopher Bayly was Emeritus Professor of Imperial and Naval History at the University of Cambridge. He wrote extensively on the history of colonial India and on British imperial and global history. He was the author of numerous books including *The Birth of the Modern World: Global Connections and Comparisons, 1780–1914* (Wiley-Blackwell, 2004), and most recently, *Recovering Liberties: Indian Thought in the Age of Liberalism and Empire* (Cambridge University Press, 2011). Professor Bayly was a Fellow of the British Academy and Royal Historical Society and was knighted for services to history in 2007. At the time of his death in April 2015 he was Indian Ministry of Culture Vivekananda Visiting Professor at the University of Chicago.

John M. Carroll is Professor of History and Associate Dean of the Faculty of Arts at the University of Hong Kong. He is the author of *Edge of Empires: Chinese Elites and British Colonials in Hong Kong* (Harvard University Press, 2005) and *A Concise History of Hong Kong* (Rowman & Littlefield, 2007). His research interests include the history of Hong Kong and encounters between China and the West. Carroll is currently writing a history of the British in Canton before the Opium War.

Barry Crosbie is Assistant Professor of History at the Hong Kong Institute of Education. His work focuses on the cultural, social and political history of the British Empire in Asia, particularly in relation to Ireland's imperial involvement. He is the author of *Irish Imperial Networks: Migration, Social Communication and Exchange in Nineteenth-Century India* (Cambridge University Press, 2012) and is currently carrying out a book-length study of the impact of Irish colonial figures in Asian port cities as well as the reciprocal impact of Asia on Irish politics, culture and society.

Bronwen Everill is the author of *Abolition and Empire in Sierra Leone and Liberia* (Palgrave, 2013) and editor of *The History and Practice of Humanitarian Intervention and Aid in Africa* (Palgrave, 2013). Her articles have appeared in the *Journal of Global History*, the *Journal of Imperial and Commonwealth History* and *Slavery & Abolition*. She has held an Andrew Mellon Fellowship at Oxford University and taught at Warwick University. She is currently a Leverhulme Fellow at King's College London.

Mark Hampton is Associate Professor of History at Lingnan University in Hong Kong, where he is also Director of the Centre for Cinema Studies and Associate Dean of the Faculty of Arts. He is the author of *Visions of the Press in Britain, 1850–1950* (University of Illinois Press, 2004) and *Hong Kong and British Culture, 1945–1997* (Manchester University Press, 2016), and editor (with Joel H. Wiener) of *Anglo-American Media Interactions, 1850–2000* (Palgrave, 2007). He is a co-editor of the journal *Media History*.

NOTES ON CONTRIBUTORS

Philip Harling is Professor of History and John R. Gaines Professor of Humanities at the University of Kentucky. He is the author of *The Waning of 'Old Corruption': The Politics of Economical Reform in Britain, 1779–1846* (Oxford University Press, 1996) and *The Modern British State: An Historical Introduction* (Polity Press, 2001), as well as numerous articles. His current research focuses on the ethical dilemmas of British imperial governance, c. 1835–65.

Christopher Hilliard is Professor of Modern British History at the University of Sydney. He is the author of *English as a Vocation: The 'Scrutiny' Movement* (Oxford University Press, 2012), *The Bookmen's Dominion: Cultural Life in New Zealand, 1920–1950* (Auckland University Press, 2006), and *To Exercise Our Talents: The Democratization of Writing in Britain* (Harvard University Press, 2006).

Philippa Levine is Mary Helen Thompson Centennial Professor in the Humanities at the University of Texas at Austin and Co-Director of the Program in British Studies and the European Union Center of Excellence. Her books include *Prostitution, Race and Politics: Policing Venereal Disease in the British Empire* (Routledge, 2003). Her *Oxford Handbook of the History of Eugenics* (Oxford University Press, 2010), co-edited with Alison Bashford, won the 2011 Cantemir Prize. She is at present writing a book on colonial nakedness.

Tillman W. Nechtman is Associate Professor of History at Skidmore College in Saratoga Springs, New York. He is the author of *Nabobs: Empire and Identity in Eighteenth-Century Britain* (Cambridge University Press, 2010) as well as many articles on the eighteenth-century British experience in India. His current research focuses on smaller pieces of Britain's eighteenth- and nineteenth-century empire – locations like Gibraltar and Pitcairn Island.

Michelle Tusan is Professor of History at the University of Nevada, Las Vegas, where she teaches British history and writes about liberalism, humanitarianism and the media. She is the author most recently of '"Crimes against Humanity": Human Rights, the British Empire and the Origins of the Response to the Armenian Genocide' in the *American Historical Review* (February, 2014). Her books include *Smyrna's Ashes: Humanitarianism, Genocide and the Birth of the Middle East* (University of California Press, 2012) and *Women Making News: Gender and Journalism in Modern Britain* (University of Illinois Press, 2005).

Martin J. Wiener is Mary Gibbs Jones Professor of History at Rice University. He is the author of *English Culture and the Decline of the Industrial Spirit 1850–1980* (Cambridge University Press, 1982), *Reconstructing the Criminal 1830–1914* (Cambridge University Press, 1990), *An Empire on Trial 1870–1935* (Cambridge University Press, 2008) and several other books. He has received book prizes from the American Historical Association and the North American Conference on British Studies and has held fellowships from the Guggenheim Memorial Foundation, the National Endowment for the Humanities, the Woodrow Wilson International Center for Scholars, the National Humanities Center and the National Science Foundation. He is at present studying liberalism in the British Empire.

ACKNOWLEDGEMENTS

This book grew out of a three-day conference at Lingnan University in May 2011, co-organised by Mark Hampton and James Fichter and partially funded by Lingnan University's University Conference Fund, the British Council's Hong Kong office and Mr. Tam Kwong-lim. The editors are grateful to James Fichter, Grace Ai-Ling Chou and other members of the Lingnan University History Department who made this conference a great success and, above all, to Vincy Au and Ann Wong for handling the prodigious logistics that this conference entailed. The editors would like to thank the University of Macau for its generous support in assisting with the reproduction costs of the images found in Chapter One, Simon Case for his highly skilled editorial assistance, and both Simon Case and James Fellows for compiling the index. In addition, the editors would like to thank Zou Yizheng, Carol C.L. Tsang, and Penelope Ching-yee Pang, who helped to ensure that the conference ran smoothly and who co-authored a conference report published in the November 2011 edition of the British Scholar Society's newsletter. Finally, the editors are confident that they speak for all of the book's contributors in thanking the other ninety conference participants for their presentations, comments and conviviality.[1] The editors would also like to acknowledge the following libraries, museums and galleries for providing reproduction and image rights for several illustrations contained in this volume: Rijksmuseum, Amsterdam, The John Carter Brown Library, National Portrait Gallery, London, National Maritime Museum, Greenwich, Tate Gallery, London, National Gallery of Canada, Ottawa, Tasmanian Museum and Art Gallery, Bridgeman Art Library and the National History Museum, London.

Note

1 For a full list of conference presenters, see http://ln.edu.hk/history/conference/BritishConference.php (accessed 22 June 2014); for the conference report see Carol C.L. Tsang, Penelope Ching-yee Pang and Zou Yizheng , 'Empire State of Mind: Articulations of British Culture in the Empire, 1707-1997', http://britishscholar.org/publications/2011/11/01/november-2011/ (accessed 22 June 2014).

Introduction: the cultural construction of the British world

Barry Crosbie and Mark Hampton

This book examines the dissemination and exchange of ideas within the British world between 1763 and 1997. In particular, it is concerned with looking at the ebb and flow of concepts integral to the circulation of imperial culture, as well as the beliefs, practices and outcomes associated with them. In doing so, it builds on two key developments in scholarship since the turn of the century: first, the historiographical integration of domestic and imperial cultures, and second, the identification of a coherent, if precarious, 'British world' system straddling the nineteenth and twentieth centuries. The former, associated with historians such as Catherine Hall, Antoinette Burton, John MacKenzie and Andrew Thompson, has broken from a previous tendency to seal empire hermetically from metropolitan history. Far from being a phenomenon 'out there', the empire crucially shaped such 'domestic' events as the Second Reform Bill (1867) and the campaign for women's suffrage in the late nineteenth century. At the same time, imperial themes permeated what Thomas Richards has called the 'commodity culture' of Victorian Britain. The tendency of this 'new imperial history' has been not only to bring empire 'home' but also to decentre imperial culture; rather than ideas and institutions flowing from a metropolitan centre to a colonial periphery, they travelled in multiple directions, sometimes bypassing the British Isles altogether.[1] Indeed, contestations of what Stuart Ward has referred to as the 'minimal impact' thesis – the idea that metropolitan Britain remained impervious to developments happening in the periphery – have effectively demonstrated that Britain's domestic and overseas histories are in fact inseparable from one another. For Ward, as for an increasing number of scholars, empire was central not only in the construction of both metropolitan and colonial identities, but also in the manner in which imperial dimensions continue to influence Britain and many of its former colonial possessions today.[2]

The second major theme on which this collection builds is the 'British world' model, or more specifically upon John Darwin's reconception of this model as the 'Empire project'.[3] In Darwin's account, a British world system, based on migration, London's financial dominance and the Indian Army predominated from the mid-nineteenth to mid-twentieth centuries. This British world included, but was not limited to, the formal empire; indeed, formal annexation of territory often embodied a failure of the system to operate efficiently. Likewise, decolonisation was not coterminous with decline, but remained compatible with an effort to preserve the British world system by other means, in a changing geopolitical environment. By the end of World War II, British economic weakness and the loss of India's army forced the British world system to rely increasingly heavily on alliance with the United States, until, by the late 1960s, the system collapsed.

This book draws on both of these departures in imperial historiography; indeed, in many ways it integrates them by reconceptualising the British Empire as a 'system' foregrounded by imperial culture. It is based on the premise that the British world was held together by more than the material factors of demography, economics and military power: there was what the book terms a 'cultural British world' underpinning much of Darwin's system, one that we argue was structured around a complex series of multilateral networks based on leisure, family organisation, ideologies, legal cultures, religion and scientific practice.[4] Although this 'cultural British world' was a crucial factor in cementing Darwin's 'British world-system', their borders did not necessarily correspond, either geographically or chronologically. Cultural practices, institutions and ideas could, on the one hand, potentially expand beyond the borders of anything that could meaningfully be called a 'British world-system' and survive its demise, while, on the other hand, the 'world-system' could potentially extend to a given territory through financial or military power even in the absence of any meaningful British cultural penetration. What seems clear, however – and what the book argues – is that the borders of the 'cultural British world' and the 'British world-system' overlapped considerably, and that, by transcending the conventionally defined boundaries between metropolitan and colonial space, the cultural British world helped to ensure the system's cohesion by supplying the cultural sinews that served to reinforce the institutional, political and economic bonds of empire.

Moreover, this cultural world was not necessarily centred on conventional themes associated with investigations in the cultural history of the British world – such as sport, film, theatre and the media – nor was it strictly bound to the old colonies of white settlement that, along with the United States, became what James Belich has called the 'Angloworld'.[5] Rather, this book views the cultural British world as a much more inclusive, dynamic and mutually constitutive space that could penetrate areas in which the British never settled in large numbers and that accommodated traditional gender, racial, class and ethnic divisions. The book argues that a less familiar, though no less significant, range of cultural interactions and expressions fashioned between 'coloniser' and 'colonised' often served to support, reinforce and, at times, supplant more traditional cultural practices in linking British communities around the globe and in contributing to a shared sense of British identity during this period. Indeed, this was a British world in which the transmission and exchange of cultural practices were as much attributable to the forces of 'contestation' as they were to those of 'construction'. Such practices under investigation here, for example, include the contributions of elites (metropolitan and colonial) and their pressure groups in challenging traditional modes of legal and economic thought and, in turn, giving rise to new political cultures within the empire; the role of humanitarianism, anti-slavery movements and literary criticism in shaping national and imperial identities; the dynamics of imperial networking, careering and the role of 'regional' domestic cultures in shaping 'British' culture; and the importation to Britain from the empire of various material, scientific, legal and financial cultures in shaping metropolitan attitudes, thought and society. Moreover, by highlighting the close interplay between less 'popular' cultural themes and the empire's shifting economic and political imperatives in different geographical contexts and at different periods in time, this book advances a particular reading of 'empire as culture' in a way that does not downplay the crucial role of the empire's economic, diplomatic and political dimensions. Indeed, one of the wider aims of the book is to emphasise how cultural practices across the empire were never neatly bounded, isolated phenomena occurring within some sort of specially designated 'cultural space'; rather, they were frequently born out of the empire's diverse political, military and fiscal imperatives and, as such, ought to be integrated within a broader imperial institutional and economic context.

One of the principal aims of the book, then, is to anchor the volume firmly within the existing literature while at the same time laying the groundwork for a new research agenda that moves beyond conventional approaches to the study of 'empire and metropolitan culture'. Specifically, it seeks to advance an understanding of the conduits and directionality of cultural flows throughout the British Empire by demonstrating how a plethora of imperial cultures were constituted in the traffic of ideas, practices, habits and assumptions that permeated the 'British world-system' (a process largely downplayed within the existing historiography). These cultural practices were sometimes self-consciously adopted in the service of empire; in other cases, they simply constituted attempts to reproduce familiar practices abroad. In still other cases, 'British' practices were in fact cultural borrowings. Moreover, even if cultural practices supported the British world system, they were not necessarily contained by it. Many survived the demise of any convincing British world system – the prevalence of cricket in many former colonies is an obvious example – although with the rising predominance of American culture within late twentieth-century globalisation, the global penetration of Japanese, Chinese and other popular or mass cultures, and the resurgence of various national and regional cultures, such legacies could no longer in any meaningful sense help to constitute a 'cultural British world'.[6] Rather, at most, they remain isolated and selective legacies within distinctly non-British cultures. In this regard, what we are calling the cultural British world not only helped to cement the British world system, but was even to some extent coterminous with it and dependent upon it.

In its attempts to examine the integrative nature of a cultural British world, this book identifies the period in the immediate aftermath of the Seven Years' War as a logical point of departure. The 1760s, in particular, constituted what Tony Ballantyne has described as a 'globalising decade', a time when rival imperial states, fronted by Britain, embarked upon voyages of exploration and discovery, commercial expansion and territorial conquest. As nascent colonial powers began consolidating their newly acquired overseas possessions and negotiated a whole series of informal economic arrangements and treaties with non-colonised lands, associated warfare, scientific enterprise, as well as commercial, legal and administrative institutions fashioned new bodies of knowledge and cultural networks.[7] Within these networks, expatriates, settlers and indigenous peoples generated an entirely new system of global information gathering and exchange, often determining the movement of people, goods, ideas and capital moving back and forth across the British world in the process.[8] Built variously upon kinship structures, educational and religious institutions, ethnic as well as fraternal organisations, clubs and societies, these networks connected private, official and provincial interest in both the metropole and colonies, and constituted what Gary Magee and Andrew Thompson have described as the 'software of empire'. This 'software' ultimately enabled the operation of a vast system of mobility and exchange across the empire through which shared cultural practices and knowledge helped to tie the British world together.[9]

Indeed, at the heart of scholarly attempts to challenge the old historiographical certainties of class and nation, as well as to unsettle more traditional paradigms in imperial history such as 'metropole' and 'periphery', is the need to think of Britain and its empire as much more fluid, porous and mutually influencing sites than has previously been assumed. Since the early 1990s, scholars of the 'new imperial history' have made productive use of network theory in demonstrating how Britain's constituent parts each successfully generated, hosted and replenished dense interconnecting sets of social networks that played fundamental roles in the evolution of both the metropolitan union-state and its worldwide empire. Within this broader, more nuanced narrative, historians are increasingly moving away from a study of the simple bilateral relations involving 'metropole' and 'periphery', to the more complex multilateral relationships engendered through the webs of contact, dialogue and exchange that were fashioned directly among Britain's colonial societies . Moreover, within domestic British history, there is growing acknowledgement that previously accepted understandings of the origin and meaning of 'Britishness', as well as that of a largely Anglo-centred 'British' empire, need to be problematised and revised.

Following the publication of several regionally focused studies examining the distinct experiences of empire among the four primary ethnic groups that constituted 'British' in the nineteenth century – namely English, Irish, Scottish and Welsh – John MacKenzie, among others, has called for a 'Four Nations' approach to British imperialism.[10] While the domestic histories of England, Ireland, Scotland and Wales have long been viewed in regional and national contexts, the history of the British Empire (integral to the unfolding of the history in each of these locations) has until the early 2000s been treated separately. Traditional accounts of metropolitan-focused imperial history have tended to view the history of the British Empire almost exclusively from the perspective of England, situating London as the unparalleled, even hegemonic, imperial metropolis from where ideas, capital and power all flowed outward to the colonies in the periphery. Metrocentric versions of imperial history, as typified by Peter Cain and Antony Hopkins' seminal concept of the 'Gentlemanly Capitalist', can be most productive in highlighting the reality of the empire's dominant economic and political machinery in London, but the preponderance of literature on the history of empire to date that has effectively privileged England as the undisputed imperial centre belies not only the crucial role that Scotland, Ireland and Wales played in the empire and in the fashioning of 'British' imperial culture, but also that of indigenous peoples and 'colonial' institutions themselves.[11]

At the same time, while endorsing the 'decentring' of imperial culture embodied in the 'new imperial history', this book is emphatically concerned with *British* culture in the empire and along its edges. Frederick Cooper and Ann Laura Stoler have criticised the common formulation of an 'indigenous "response" or "resistance" to an imperialist initiative' as failing to 'capture the dynamics' of the encounter; we argue, in parallel terms, that the cultural British world was similarly dialectical.[12] Moreover, this was a cultural world that evidently encompassed parts of the empire outside of the colonies of white settlement; as such, the book ventures beyond Bridge and Fedorowich's call for 'the delineation of Britishness across the old Dominions' to examine regions of the empire where the English language was not necessarily a crucial determinant in defining 'British' culture.[13] Whether as migrants to settler colonies or outposts of informal empire, or short-term expatriates to the tropical colonies, Britons sought to recreate the institutions familiar from home: clubs, sport, educational systems and, where possible, family structures; at the same time, despite attempts to maintain social distance from their colonial subjects, these institutions adapted to specific colonial contexts.[14] Similarly, although Britons abroad may have interpreted their colonial experience through categories forged in metropolitan contexts, these categories were often shaped through the colonial encounter, and frequently by colonised peoples themselves. This point takes in not only political ideologies but also governing strategies, including, for example, the policing of venereal diseases.[15] In this regard, this book goes beyond the notion of 'mutual constitutiveness' to examine the agency of the subjects of empire in the making of British culture in what Richard Price refers to as the 'middle grounds'. Colonised people were, after all, instrumental in running the empire; and it was in the colonies, not in the metropole, that power relations were negotiated and empire was made. As Price has argued, the colonies, far from being passive and receptive sites of European imperialism, 'were places where various kinds of hybridities' flourished. Hybridity, he reminds us, 'whether it be a cultural, social, or sexual kind ... dilutes the power of the colonizer', thus giving rise to an imperial culture that was 'not entirely dependent on imperial largesse'.[16]

While the book places the agency of the subjects of empire in the fashioning of a cultural British world at its fore, it is, at the same time, very much concerned with placing such interactions in a broader, more comparative framework. As Antoinette Burton notes, empires and nations were ultimately porous constructs whose 'borders' were continually crossed by the migration of peoples, ideas and goods, rendering them 'precarious, unmoored, and in the end, finally unrealizable'.[17]

As such, any study of a cultural British world would in effect necessitate a comparative study that seeks to reposition the history of the British world within a wider global narrative. However, as Burton points out elsewhere, there is a danger that integrating the British Empire into global history can recast the whiggish British exceptionalism long familiar from domestic history. As a result, 'English democracy, English abolitionism, [and] the English civilizing mission' are credited as primary engines of globalisation, most notably (but by no means exclusively) in the work of Niall Ferguson. For this reason, Burton calls upon scholars to study the British Empire fully within the context of its interactions with other empires and with other colonial and national cultures: to 'write the British empire into world history in terms of its proportionality rather than its exceptionalism, in terms of its role in the co-production of imperial globality rather than its originary character, in terms of its limits rather than its inflated and ultimately self-serving image'.[18] The essays in this book very much support Burton's exhortation, placing the British world not as the driver of globalisation but as a fluid and often precarious 'system', engaging not only with small kingdoms and stateless tribes, but with such empires as the Qing, the Ottoman and the Mughal, as well as the newly emergent United States of America. It was, in part, through these interactions that a cultural British world began to emerge in the mid-eighteenth century and that it shared much in common with rivalling imperial powers and states. By connecting the colonial and post-colonial eras in ways that illuminate the continuities between each time period, the book offers readers insight into how historians can combine fresh archival material with the latest methodological and theoretical approaches to create complex and subtle assessments and understandings of colonial dynamics and culture.

This book is organised around eleven thematically related essays, each offering a timely rethink about the cultural interconnectedness of Britain's imperial past. In its examination of a series of new perspectives on the cultural dynamics of the British world, the book brings together a myriad of different methodological approaches and styles by individual authors. Throughout the book, detailed, individual case study-focused chapters are complemented by others that adopt a much broader, synthetic approach. In contrast, other chapters, in their attempt to highlight the complex, overlapping networks that defined this global system, seek to frame their work in more comparative and contrastive studies. Chapters One and Two offer sweeping examinations of Britons' cultural engagement with the indigenous peoples they encountered in their empire, through accounts that between them show markedly different attitudes toward colonial peoples. Philippa

Levine's chapter relates British representations of nakedness both to the changing character of imperialism and to changes in British domestic culture. In doing so, it traces the contrasting themes of the 'noble savage' and the 'naked native'. The former, more emblematic of the early modern travel writers' and painters' views, envisioned indigenes unsullied by the artifice of European civilisation, even if most agreed that some aspects of the civilising mission were essential. This openness to the merits of non-European peoples could underwrite missionary and educational efforts, including the imperial conquest that would facilitate such efforts. The shift to the 'naked native', on the other hand, paralleled the rise of a greater cultural pessimism about the possibilities for integrating imperial subjects into British civilisation. One could argue that this increasing pessimism on the part of Britons 'at home', in turn, shaped the attitudes of Britons in the empire, reinforcing the tendency, for example, to establish racially exclusive clubs and neighbourhoods, such as the Indian hill stations or Hong Kong's Peak.

In contrast to Levine's account of Western commentators casting 'natives' as foils for their rule, Christopher Bayly's chapter shows that British intellectuals could learn from Asians, in that way bringing the latter's voices directly into the British cultural tradition. In doing so, his chapter draws important connections between two separate bodies of historical scholarship, namely the 'new imperial history' and an emerging 'global intellectual history', to examine some of the ways in which British-born radicals and socialists based in Asian colonies sought to critique empire for its effect primarily on indigenous peoples and societies (as opposed to highlighting the effects that imperialism had on the British constitution). Through an examination of several key individuals, including James Silk Buckingham, Alan Octavian Hume and Phillip Spratt, Bayly explores how a common 'radical scepticism' among such people gave rise to a particular strain of 'liberal imperialism' within Indian politics that sought to drive anti-colonial thought and to push for reform in imperial governance from outside the metropolitan centre. Rather than simply impose their own beliefs and personal philosophies upon their Asian counterparts, these individuals sought to articulate and position their political concerns within a discourse grounded in themes that spoke directly to particular Hindu, Buddhist and Muslim sensibilities. Crucially, the melding of various strains of metropolitan and Indian intellectual thought in such ways enabled a mutually beneficial flow of ideas circulating across the globe during this period, at once facilitating the construction of specific Asian notions of anti-colonialism as well as promoting a 'benign form of orientalism' among a wider European and American audience. Significantly, while many of these British-born radicals were employed as colonial officials while in Asia, Bayly demonstrates that their motivations and desire for political reform within the empire extended beyond the traditional theme of political economy to include humanistic, religious, aesthetic and sexual concerns.

Chapters Three, Four and Five examine the place of political thought, including humanitarian ideals, in tying together the cultural British world. Yet, as Philip Harling, Michelle Tusan and Martin Wiener all show in various ways, the role of political thought was not straightforward. Harling and Tusan show, for example, that any attempt to import British humanitarian ideals, whether free trade and anti-slavery or human rights more broadly, could run into challenges on the ground, whether because of conflicting interest groups, conflicts between ideals and economic interests, or recalcitrant institutions.

Accordingly, Harling's chapter examines the Caribbean sugar industry in the years after 1846, when sugar duties were abolished and British 'free sugar' competed against the slave-produced sugar of Brazil and Cuba. Unfortunately, the removing of duties led to what Harling calls a 'free-trade crisis' in sugar monoculture in Trinidad and British Guiana, as sugar prices plummeted even as planters' expenses rose, for labour costs increased dramatically as slavery was abolished in the empire. As former slaves fled or sharply reduced their working hours, many British commentators interpreted this behaviour in racial terms as slothfulness. Ultimately, only the government-supported importation of indentured labour from India and Africa – a form of labour closer to slavery than its defenders would like to admit – saved the sugar industry. Harling sees this policy as a compromise of *laissez-faire* and humanitarian ideals, and accepts the broader argument that British attitudes toward empire in the second half of the nineteenth century were more authoritarian and racially exclusive than they had been in the early part of the century. Still, he shows that the humanitarian impulse never disappeared completely. Anti-slavery, in particular, was more than simply self-congratulatory justification; it remained central to how many British saw themselves and the purpose of their empire, and helped to check the worst imperial excesses.

Where Harling focuses on trade, Tusan examines humanitarianism in diplomacy, as well as the British expatriate networks on which this diplomacy depended. Her chapter traces Henry Layard's career as Ambassador in Constantinople as a case study of the role of diplomats and civil servants in promoting Britain's late nineteenth-century informal empire in the Near East. Pointing out that much of the existing scholarship focuses on travellers' narratives, Tusan shows that diplomats and civil servants built more sustained networks of political advocacy and humanitarianism. She examines a circle of expatriate supporters cultivated by Layard, whose philanthropy and political activism, particularly in response to the Bulgarian Atrocities (1876) and Russo-Turkish War (1877–78), helped to create a British humanitarian culture in the Ottoman Empire. This humanitarianism outlasted Layard's ambassadorship, for example in pursuing famine relief in the 1880s. Tusan argues that Layard and his fellow expatriates were largely unsuccessful in their attempts to reform Ottoman institutions. They did, however, cement the idea that Britain had a moral obligation to intervene in the Ottoman Empire, and, as a result, help to underscore the role of this new culture of diplomacy in the making of the British cultural world. In addition, Tusan's chapter reminds us that the British cultural world was not confined by the boundaries of empire.

Like Harling and Tusan, Wiener points to the complexity of the relationship between British political ideals and imperial governance; unlike the other two, though, Wiener's chapter points not to the difficulty of translating ideals into concrete political action, but to the question of imperial belonging. In particular, his chapter focuses on liberal political ideals, especially those concerning representation. He uses two late nineteenth-century case studies, Trinidad and Bengal, to argue that these ideals could, depending on context, serve either to defend British settlers' exclusive legal and racial privileges or inclusively to articulate the rights of colonial subjects. Denying both a whiggish narrative of a 'gradually and steadily expanding inclusion' of colonial subjects in the blessings of English liberty and the exclusionary narrative of British settlers securing their freedoms at the expense of all others, Wiener shows that British political culture was multivalent, offering a shared master-language whose meaning and scope could be contested.

The British world was, of course, not only an arena to imagine through metropolitan political categories; it was also an arena in which Britons (and especially those from the so-called 'Celtic periphery') could make careers and through their movement back and forth across the empire could influence the spread of specific forms of 'British' culture and values. In Chapter Six, Barry Crosbie examines the British world through the lens of nineteenth-century Ireland by demonstrating how Irish military, religious and professional networks in India all operated in ways that recognised the centrality of Ireland and Irish people in imperial power-brokering and in the construction of 'British' imperial identities and culture. Crosbie's chapter gives credence to historiographical emphasis since the turn of the century on developing an understanding of how Britishness (both at home and abroad) was shaped through the activities of various ethnic groups within the context of the wider British and Hibernian Isles (in this case, the Irish), whose own particular identities and cultural practices were frequently brought to bear upon colonial peoples and institutions. By foregrounding the centrality of Ireland to Britain's imperial mission in India through an examination of a wide range of 'Indo-Irish' connections and exchanges – including those at the level of scientific, religious and political thought – his chapter highlights the multifaceted and essentially pluralised nature of 'British' imperial culture by enunciating a sense of Irishness and Britishness which overlapped extensively, affording advancement and belonging to a group at once colonial and imperial.

Whereas the first six chapters of the book focus most heavily on the place of British political ideals, and Britons themselves, in the British world, the remaining chapters employ concrete case studies to expand upon one of the book's central themes, namely the decentring of the cultural British world. Chapters Seven, Eight and Nine focus principally on the realm of ideas, while Chapters Ten and Eleven examine how consumer culture across the British world was made tangible. All five chapters demonstrate the multi-directional character of intellectual exchange, with Britons selectively learning from the 'natives' they encountered, even as colonial subjects selectively borrowed from a useable British culture.

John Carroll's and Mark Hampton's chapters (Chapters Seven and Eight) are bookends to Britain's modern engagement with South China, with Carroll's examining the period before the British imperial expansion into China and Hampton's focusing on the period around its conclusion. Carroll's chapter examines the cultural engagement of British travellers in Canton prior to the Opium War. He argues that the typical scholarly focus on Sino-British political and diplomatic relations, as well as the eventual outbreak of war in 1839, has obscured a wide-ranging cultural engagement that can be seen in these travellers' accounts. Rather than using China purely as a mirror by which to define their own superiority, British traders and missionaries allowed their observations of Canton to challenge their previously held views of China. Moreover, they made precise distinctions between Chinese civilisation and Chinese manners, and between the Cantonese and inland Chinese. Although the later nineteenth century would see unequal treaties and extraterritoriality, these British travellers' attempts to 'sort out' China laid the groundwork for more productive Sino-British cultural interactions in the twentieth century. Through this analysis Carroll's chapter addresses the ways in which British popular knowledge about the world beyond the British Isles was being transformed during the early nineteenth century through first-hand accounts. In focusing on Canton, he revises the prevalent understanding of British attitudes toward China as something that needed to be 'opened up' (especially during a period in which British attitudes toward China were becoming critical), thereby making the case for seeing the diplomatic and commercial relationships between Britain and China through a cultural lens.

Hampton's chapter examines Hong Kong between 1945 and 1979 as an imagined space in which a British 'unbridled capitalism' could flourish even as Britain itself developed a welfare state 'consensus'. Drawing on political pamphlets, novels, memoirs, journalistic accounts, politicians' speeches and trade organisations' papers, it argues that Hong Kong was widely seen by expatriates as a place in which British values survived after having been quashed in a 'declining' Britain. At the same time, Hong Kong provided a foil against which neo-liberal think-tanks could highlight Britain's need to revive an enterprise culture. Hampton shows that, in fact, Hong Kong's status as a *laissez-faire* economy was overstated, as the government increasingly intervened in such fields as housing, public health, education and infrastructure. In addition, this meme depended on assumptions that the Chinese were compulsive workers uninterested in leisure, and that Hong Kong Chinese were politically apathetic, both of which collapsed in the late 1960s. Despite these tensions, this distinct idea of a Hong Kong Britishness provided a cultural legacy that survived the collapse of the 'British world'. At the same time, by preserving what were often called neo-Victorian economic ideals, Hong Kong constituted a model to which anti-Keynesian British politicians of the 1970s could point.

Where Hampton's chapter focuses on popular economic discourse in and about Britain's last major colony, in Chapter Nine Christopher Hilliard shows the selective borrowing of a British literary tradition outside the metropole, including in ways that could subvert the notion of a cultural British world. Hilliard examines the influence within the empire of the Leavisite literary critical movement, as exemplified by F. R. Leavis's journal *Scrutiny* and Q. D. Leavis's book *Fiction and the Reading Public*. He takes issue with a common assumption that Leavisite criticism was hegemonic in the mid-twentieth century, either in Britain or in the empire. Moreover, contrary to those who see Leavisite criticism as a vehicle for asserting metropolitan cultural dominance at the expense of colonial or native cultures, Hilliard shows that it acted in more complicated ways. Taking India and New Zealand as case studies, Hilliard shows that Leavisite criticism provided a tool for critics to evaluate their own emerging national literatures. In doing so, Hilliard provides an example of the way in which British culture helped to constitute a British world, not through top-down dissemination of specific values, but through cultural practices that were re-appropriated in local contexts.

In Chapters Ten and Eleven, Tillman Nechtman and Bronwen Everill demonstrate the ways in which colonial material and consumer culture operated both in the metropole and in the colonial context, in both cases helping to define national identity. Nechtman's chapter examines the manner in which late eighteenth-century nabobism and material culture combined to raise important questions among a domestic British audience about how empire impacted upon contemporary understandings and articulations of Britishness as well as what constituted 'British' culture. By showing how returning East India Company employees used material possessions as a means of narrating and documenting their experiences in India, Nechtman argues that their architecturally alien homes, pets, foreign objects, styles and fashions 'functioned on a more complex register' than simply 'being different' to the tastes of ordinary, everyday Britons. For the nabobs, their material possessions and attachment to South Asian cultural norms reflected their 'global biographies' and lives spent outside of Britain. Despite fierce opposition from a sceptical and hostile British public who understood their 'Indianness' as confirmation that their time abroad had 'changed them' and had rendered them 'less British', nabobs such as William Hickey, Francis Gillanders and David Hare ignored public criticism and, through the life-styles they led in Britain, forced domestic audiences 'to come face to face with the material reality of the South Asian empire'. Nechtman explores how, by building 'micro-Indias' across the British landscape in the form of South Asian-inspired homes and estates, the material culture of the nabobs contributed to the fashioning of a hybrid British identity that recognised the crucial role of the colonies and of indigenous cultural practices and objects in defining more clearly ideas of nation and empire at home.

While Nechtman's chapter focuses on the influence of Indian material culture on the metropole, Everill's chapter examines the role of material culture in shaping the colonial history of Sierra Leone, particularly in relation to how the growth of 'legitimate commerce' in the region in the 1840s helped to shape the lives of repatriated former slaves and influenced their relations with both the metropole and other West African states. She argues that through their participation in domestic political movements, their use of petitions and anti-slavery rhetoric and through their purchases and sales of imperial-produced goods and commodities, Sierra Leoneans played an important role in developing mid-Victorian ideals of modernity and citizenship.

These political and economic actions, in turn, helped to connect the mutually reinforcing processes of commerce and consumption across the British world at the time. As an important yardstick for measuring the relative success of Britain's imperial civilising mission throughout the empire, the experiment of introducing 'legitimate commerce' and new patterns of consumerism in nineteenth-century Sierra Leone had important implications for the emergence of Sierra Leonean identities as well as for the continuation of the British imperial project across colonial West Africa.

The essays in this volume are by no means exhaustive, nor do they offer a comprehensive treatment of the emergence and subsequent development of a 'cultural British world' between the mid-eighteenth and late twentieth centuries. But they do contribute in a rich variety of ways to an emerging body of work that seeks not only to 'bring empire home', but also to locate British history and culture within broader, more dynamic global contexts. No doubt some of the material presented in this book will feed back into lively debates on the heterogeneous nature of 'Britishness', and on the cultural construction of a British world that extended beyond the physical boundaries of both nation and empire, as well as those of racially exclusive, largely English-speaking settler societies. In this regard, David Lambert and Alan Lester have argued that any imagined 'imperial space' – such as the cultural British world under investigation here – should be seen neither as something that is constructed hegemonically from above nor rising reactively from below, but rather as an arena of mutually reinforcing mobility and exchange: 'the sphere of a multiplicity of trajectories ... coming together ... in specific ways and at a specific time'.[19] By reconceptualising the British Empire as a 'system' that transcends the conventionally defined boundaries between metropolitan and colonial space and that stresses both the centrality and heterogeneity of the cultural practices that reinforced the institutional, political and economic bonds of that system, it is hoped that this collection of essays will illustrate afresh the central importance of the empire-wide dissemination and exchange of ideas – the ebb and flow of concepts integral to the circulation of imperial culture and in the construction of the British world.

Acknowledgement

We are grateful to John Carroll, James Epstein, Philip Harling, Martin Wiener and the referees for Manchester University Press for their helpful suggestions and thoughtful comments on earlier drafts of this introduction.

Notes

1 Antoinette Burton (ed.), *After the Imperial Turn: Thinking with and through the Nation* (Durham, NC and London: Duke University Press, 2003); Catherine Hall and Sonya M. Rose, *At Home with the Empire: Metropolitan Culture and the Imperial World* (Cambridge: Cambridge University Press, 2007); Andrew Thompson, *The Empire Strikes Back: The Impact of Imperialism on Britain from the Mid-Nineteenth Century* (London: Pearson Longman, 2005); John M. MacKenzie, *Propaganda and Empire: The Manipulation of British Public Opinion, 1880–1960* (Manchester: Manchester University Press, 1988); Catherine Hall, *Civilising Subjects: Metropole and Colony in the English Imagination, 1830–1867* (Chicago: University of Chicago Press, 2002); Antoinette Burton, *Empire in Question: Reading, Writing, and Teaching British Imperialism* (Durham, NC: Duke University Press, 2011); Thomas Richards, *The Commodity Culture of Victorian England: Advertising and Spectacle, 1851–1914* (Stanford, CA: Stanford University Press, 1991). For a vigorous criticism of this historiographical trend, see Bernard Porter, *The Absent-Minded Imperialists: Empire, Society and Culture in Britain* (New York: Oxford University Press, 2006).

2 Stuart Ward (ed.), *British Culture and the End of Empire* (Manchester: Manchester University Press, 2001), p. 4. On the impact of decolonisation on metropolitan culture, see also Jordanna Bailkin, *The Afterlife of Empire* (Berkeley: University of California Press, 2012).

3 John Darwin, *The Empire Project: The Rise and Fall of the British World-System, 1830–1970* (Cambridge: Cambridge University Press, 2009). See also James Belich's magisterial *Replenishing the Earth: The Settler Revolution and the Rise of the Anglo-World, 1783–1939* (Oxford: Oxford University Press, 2009).

4 Gary B. Magee and Andrew S. Thompson, *Empire and Globalisation: Networks of People, Goods and Capital in the British World, 1850–1914* (Cambridge: Cambridge University Press, 2010).

5 Carl Bridge and Kent Fedorowich (eds), *The British World: Diaspora, Culture and Identity* (London: Frank Cass Publishers, 2003); Phillip Buckner and R. Douglas Francis (eds), *Rediscovering the British World* (Calgary: University of Calgary Press, 2005); Kate Darian-Smith, Patricia Grimshaw and Stuart Macintyre (eds), *Britishness Abroad: Transnational Movements and Imperial Cultures* (Melbourne: Melbourne University Press, 2007); Catherine McGlynn, Andrew Mycock and James W. McAuley (eds), *Britishness, Identity and Citizenship: The View from Abroad* (Bern: Peter Lang, 2011). The vast majority of the essays in these collections focus on the Dominions.

6 See, e.g., C. L. R. James, *Beyond a Boundary* (Durham, NC: Duke University Press, 1993); Simon J. Potter, *Broadcasting Empire: The BBC and the British World* (Oxford: Oxford University Press, 2012); Jeremy Tunstall, *The Media Were American: U.S. Mass Media in Decline* (New York: Oxford University Press, 2007).

7 Tony Ballantyne, *Orientalism and Race: Aryanism and the British Empire* (Basingstoke: Palgrave, 2002), p. 4.

8 See, for example, Barry Crosbie, *Irish Imperial Networks: Migration, Social Communication and Exchange in Nineteenth-Century India* (Cambridge: Cambridge University Press, 2012); Alan Lester, *Imperial Networks: Creating Identities in Nineteenth-Century South Africa and Britain* (London and New York, 2001); Zoë Laidlaw, *Colonial Connections, 1815–45: Patronage, the Information Revolution and Colonial Government* (Manchester and New York: Manchester University Press, 2005); Tamson Pietsch, *Empire of Scholars: Universities, Networks, and the British Academic World, 1850–1939* (Manchester: Manchester University Press, 2012); Christopher Prior, *Exporting Empire: Africa, Colonial Officials, and the Construction of the British Imperial State, c. 1900–1939* (Manchester: Manchester University Press, 2012).

9 Magee and Thompson, *Empire and Globalisation*, p. 16.

10 See, for example, Keith Jeffery (ed.), *'An Irish Empire'? Aspects of Ireland and the*

British Empire (Manchester: Manchester University Press, 1996); T. M. Devine, *Scotland's Empire, 1600–1815* (London: Penguin, 2005); and Aled Jones and Bill Jones, 'The Welsh World and the British Empire, c. 1851–1939: An Exploration', *Journal of Imperial and Commonwealth History*, 31 (May 2003), 57–81. See also, John M. MacKenzie, 'Irish, Scottish, Welsh and English Worlds? A Four Nation Approach to the History of the British Empire', *History Compass*, 6 (2008), 1244–63.

11 P. J. Cain and A. G. Hopkins, *British Imperialism, 1688–2000* (London: Routledge, 2nd edn, 2001).

12 Frederick Cooper and Ann Laura Stoler (eds), *Tensions of Empire: Colonial Cultures in a Bourgeois World* (Berkeley and Los Angeles: University of California Press, 2007), p. 6.

13 Bridge and Fedorowich, *The British World*, p. 8.

14 Dane Kennedy, *Islands of White: Settler Society and Culture in Kenya and Southern Rhodesia, 1890–1939* (Durham, NC: Duke University Press, 1987); Dane Kennedy, *The Magic Mountains: Hill Stations and the British Raj* (Delhi: Oxford University Press, 1996); Elizabeth Buettner, *Empire Families: Britons and Late Imperial India* (Oxford: Oxford University Press, 2004); Robert Bickers, *Britain in China: Community, Culture and Colonialism 1900–1949* (Manchester: Manchester University Press, 1999); Robert Bickers, *Empire Made Me: An Englishman Adrift in Shanghai* (London: Penguin, 2004); Patrick F. McDevitt, *May the Best Man Win: Sport, Masculinity and Nationalism in Great Britain and the Empire, 1880–1935* (Basingstoke: Palgrave Macmillan, 2004); Lanver Mak, *The British in Egypt: Community, Crime and Crises, 1882–1922* (London: I. B. Tauris, 2012). On the concept of settler colonialism more generally, see Robert Bickers (ed.), *Settlers and Expatriates* (Oxford: Oxford University Press, 2010); Lorenzo Veracini, '"Settler Colonialism": Career of a Concept', *The Journal of Imperial and Commonwealth History*, 41 (2013), 313–33.

15 Philippa Levine, *Prostitution, Race and Politics: Policing Veneral Disease in the British Empire* (New York: Routledge, 2003); Richard Price, *Making Empire: Colonial Encounters and the Creation of Imperial Rule in Nineteenth-Century Africa* (Cambridge: Cambridge University Press, 2008); Martin J. Wiener, *An Empire on Trial: Race, Murder, and Justice under British Rule, 1870–1935* (Cambridge: Cambridge University Press, 2009); Michelle Tusan, *Smyrna's Ashes: Humanitarianism, Genocide, and the Birth of the Middle East* (Berkeley: University of California Press, 2012); James Epstein, *Scandal of Colonial Rule: Power and Subversion in the British Atlantic During the Age of Revolution* (Cambridge: Cambridge University Press, 2012).

16 Richard Price, 'One Big Thing: Britain, Its Empire and Their Imperial Culture', in *The Journal of British Studies*, 45 (2006), 602–27, at 608.

17 Antoinette Burton, 'Who Needs the Nation? Interrogating "British" History', *Journal of Historical Sociology*, 10 (1997), 227–48.

18 Antoinette Burton, *Empire in Question*, pp. 277–9, 292.

19 David Lambert and Alan Lester (eds), *Colonial Lives Across the British Empire: Imperial Careering in the Long Nineteenth* Century (Cambridge: Cambridge University Press, 2006), p. 14.

CHAPTER ONE

Naked natives and noble savages: the cultural work of nakedness in imperial Britain

Philippa Levine

Clothing has received a great deal of attention from anthropologists, sociologists and historians, but its absence has sometimes been taken for granted, regarded more as a natural state than as a site of cultural meaningfulness. Yet a fascination with undress has a long history which we can trace through a remarkable number of historical sites; then and now this apparent 'state of nature' has been fraught with significance: legal battles have been fought over it, children have been removed from their families because of it, books and art works have been banned for promoting it. For an apparently natural state of affairs, the condition of nakedness has taken up a remarkable amount of legal, political, theological, social, economic and cultural space. I want, then, to consider nakedness not as a simple description nor as a state of being but as a contested historical marker with very particular and peculiar ties to modern imperialism.

Early modern European explorers – the Dutch, the Spanish, the Portuguese alongside the British – emphasised in their travel accounts the lack of clothing they encountered on their travels, a deficiency regarded as representative of a primitive state of nature. This may seem an obvious and perhaps even a trivial point. Images of naked 'primitives' litter the historical record, to be sure, but these representations have largely been taken for granted, assimilated and even normalised. Yet the tenacity both of a fascination with the state of unclothedness and of its seeming link to savagery and primitivism make this an area worth exploring. The colonial body was something which could be observed, scorned, desired, instructed, measured, made profitable, and while all of these activities could and did work also upon clothed bodies, nakedness as emblematic of the colonised, savage state prefaced, justified and defined colonial rule in important cultural and political ways which spoke alike to missionaries and planters, to theologians and politicians, to artists and scientists.

We may see this link between colonialism and nudity actively at work in the two tropes of the 'noble savage' and the 'naked native', both terms with which many Britons by the nineteenth century would have been familiar. These were not always wholly distinct imaginaries, of course. Eighteenth-century representations of Native Americans and of Pacific Islanders often veered wildly between these representations. In both individual and textual representations emanating from Europe, the 'savage' was almost always naked and quite often a cannibal too. In an engraving (Figure 1) by the Dutch artist Crispijn van de Passe dating from the early seventeenth century and now in the Rijksmuseum in Amsterdam, a naked princess receives the homage of multiple scalps while in a large pot beside her we have an amputated human foot and calf as well as a human hand. In Frances Barlow's rendition of an Indian warrior (Figure 2), appearing almost two centuries later in 1791, the scalp is still in the visual forefront, and our warrior is still in a state of undress. George Townshend's 1859 sketch (Figure 3) is very similar: an essentially naked Indian holds a scalp in one hand and a formidable weapon in the other. Thus we have a remarkably stable imagery over a period of 250 years, and one which had little truck with the idea of the nobility of the primitive.

1. *Amerika*, Crispijn van de Passe

2. *An Indian warrior entering his wigwam with a scalp*, Frances Barlow, 1789

Yet the Noble Savage, made famous by Rousseau and Montaigne in particular, was nonetheless a powerful image, and one among a number of representations available for Western consumption from the late eighteenth century. John Dryden's much-satirised play, *The Conquest of Granada*, first performed in 1670, is credited with the first appearance in English of the term Noble Savage, in a pretty speech by the hero Almanzor which included the line 'when wild in woods

3. *An Indian war chief, completely equipped with a scalp in his hand*, George Townshend, 1759

the noble savage ran'. The phrase, of course, conjured up a rather more idyllic version of 'nature' than that of the naked princess with her tub of limbs and her many animal companions.

A number of scholars have questioned the significance or the spread of the idea of the Noble Savage in the eighteenth century.[1] Robert

Berkhofer has argued that in the American context it gained more purchase in the nineteenth century, when dying-race theory began volubly to predict the demise of indigenous Americans unable to withstand the onslaught of 'civilisation'.[2] Kate Flint points to the growth of a 'nostalgia dependent on imminent extinction'.[3] Yet there was a considerable body of visual and literary representation, especially in the latter half of the eighteenth century, that invoked the possibility of a primitiveness not wholly without redeeming qualities, although as many constituencies rejected as embraced the idea.

Stephanie Pratt has argued that the 'American Indian was perceived as the quintessential Noble Savage from at least' the 1580s, when Montaigne's *Essais* appeared, although she identifies a critical shift in portrayal in the mid-eighteenth century towards an emphasis on violence and warcraft.[4] Troy Bickham likewise sees a tendency (a result of the recognition of the central role of Native Americans in determining the political future of America) to portray the Native American as warlike from the 1750s, downplaying the element of nobility.[5] Yet even with the growth of a tradition which emphasised the savage as a naturally violent (and perhaps cannibalistic) entity, the Noble Savage by no means disappeared from the colonial imaginary in the eighteenth and nineteenth centuries. British travellers in the Pacific region, in particular, deployed versions of this ideal, imbued with Christian nostalgia for a lost paradise of innocence. The region known in eighteenth-century parlance as the South Seas consolidated the well-worn connection between the primitive and the naked as European sailors and scientists explored the Pacific. James Cook's famous voyages in the 1760s and 1770s produced a plethora of literature and art which dwelt upon the alien customs and appearance of the peoples encountered on the journeys across the Pacific Ocean. Cook's own account of social practices in the Antipodes was clearly cognisant of the contours of the Noble Savage idea. His critique of Western materialism is not far from the surface in this passage:

> From what I have said of the Natives of New-Holland they may appear to some to be the most wretched people upon Earth, but in reality they are far more happier than we Europeans ... They live in a Tranquillity which is not disturb'd by the Inequality of Condition: The Earth and sea of their own accord furnishes them with all things necessary for life, they covet not Magnificent Houses, Houshold-stuff etc., they live in a warm and fine Climate and enjoy a very wholesome Air, so that they have very little need of Clothing and this they seem to be fully sencible of, for many to whome we gave Cloth etc., left it carelessly upon the Sea beach and in the woods as a thing they had no manner of use for.[6]

In Cook's journal entry, we have a healthy, happy, unclothed people untouched by materialist greed: nakedness becomes practically definitional here in a place where cloth seemed a mere irrelevance. The literature and art produced out of this new region of travel and exploration proved as enduringly popular with the British public as had that focused on the Native American. Plays, poems and exhibitions about the region burgeoned alongside travel accounts, paintings and engravings. The major cultural figures of the day seized upon the Pacific for new material. Byron's 1823 poem *The Island, or Christian and His Comrades* took as its focus the *Bounty* mutiny. Playwrights fashioned dramas and comedies from the encounters in the Pacific. Harriet Martineau penned a Pacific novel, *Dawn Island*, which appeared in 1845, and by the end of the nineteenth century the region was a favourite setting for the imperial adventure stories aimed at middle-class British boys. In all these variants Islanders were regularly depicted as naked or nearly so, a 'fact' that prompted a wide variety of responses. Inevitably, the naked body in this context was frequently read as an index of lustfulness and promiscuity; much of the popularity of the travel accounts after the three Cook voyages rested on allusions to the intimacies between his crews and the local women, routinely described as sensual and willing beauties. Where Cook himself saw an ennobling lack of interest in materialism, many saw an alarming brazenness which would damn these populations in the afterlife.

It was thus that the palm-fringed islands of the Pacific were among the earliest targets of the Protestant mission organisations gathering steam in a growingly imperial Britain. Shame, or more accurately its absence, became a critical and an urgent element in understandings of colonial and savage nakedness. This was by no means a new sentiment, of course. The fourteenth-century traveller Sir John Mandeville had observed that 'in Ethiopia and in many other countries [in Africa] the folk lie all naked ... and the women have no shame of the men'.[7] In 1613 the popular preacher Alexander Whitaker, writing about the Virginia colony where he had settled two years earlier, drew a direct and biblical link between the absence of clothing and the presence of sin. 'Let the miserable condition of these naked slaves of the divell move you to compassion towards them ... They live naked in bodie, as if their shame of their sinne deserved no covering.'[8] In these readings nakedness revealed not just parts better kept under wraps, but shame itself, a compelling narrative of cultural, theological and social incommensurability. For the eager missionaries who, from the late eighteenth century, made the trek to the Pacific, lack of shame was a problem to be solved, its presence an index of heathenism, underlining the deep link between nakedness and savagery, a link that kept whole populations from knowing the embrace of the Christian God. As Ruth Barcan points out in her perceptive study of nudity (one of the few theoretical pieces to take up this issue), 'clothing represented a form of salvation ... theologically and ideologically central to the colonizing project'.[9] Thus did James Wilson, one of the earliest of those sent to the region by the London Missionary Society, boast about inculcating bodily shame among Tahitian women.[10] Scholars who have written about those voluminous and flowery Mother Hubbards and mumus (popular purchases even today among tourists to Hawaii) owe Wilson and his ilk a debt for providing them with such rich materials. For missionaries, 'the clothing of the body was seen as quintessential to the salvation of the soul and an ultimate sign of conversion to the Christian faith'.[11] Culture, religion and politics, as the editors of this volume suggest in their introduction, were invariably linked in the colonial project.

Nakedness among men and among women was a source of fascination and of horror in the West, but it was women's bodies, and most particularly their breasts, which were the most drawn, sketched, painted and later photographed. Consider, for example, John Webber's *Portrait of Poedua* (1777) shown in Figure 4. The painting is famously deceptive, belying the circumstances in which it was produced and, relatedly, the background against which this idealised Pacific 'maiden' sat for Webber. Despite the idyllic background of the painting, Poedua sat for Webber in a cabin aboard HMS *Discovery* on Cook's third Pacific voyage (on which he was the official artist) while she was a hostage, brought aboard with her brother and her husband to force the return of two sailors who had jumped ship in late November 1777. Pregnant at the time of her captivity, Poedua is nonetheless painted as an idealised figure, her pert breasts suggesting youth and virginity at the same time as desirability. The serene gentility of her gaze offers the viewer no clue as to the coercive conditions under which this portrait – a genre closely associated at this time with the high-born and frequently the product of a commission – was painted. Poedua was, as the portrait's title indicates, from a powerful family, though one whose kidnapping by Cook's crew exposed the limits of their power in a colonising world. Her lineage may go some way to explaining the classically influenced drapery of the portrait, as might her pregnancy. In a nod to classical sculpture European nudes were commonly (although by no means exclusively) draped; it was a much less common motif in depictions of colonial nakedness, where full nudity might perhaps be read as confirmation of colonial power. In this instance, while nakedness remains central to the portrayal, there is nonetheless a dignity to it, even while the circumstances of its creation speak to colonial power structures.

4. *Portrait of Poedua*, John Webber, 1777

Yet, as a woman of Pacific origin, Poedua's breasts were a fundamental part of the package: their bareness marked her difference even as the backdrop, the drapery and her unruffled mien offer a different reading. Almost all the women whom Webber painted and sketched – in the South Seas, as in Australia – during the long voyage are bare breasted, some with an infant slung over their shoulder, suggesting the breast as sustenance as well as desirable.

Joshua Reynolds' celebrated portrait of Ma'i (or Omai as he was known by the British), Cook's interpreter on his second and third Pacific voyages, on the other hand, shows its subject fully clothed (Figure 5), as did other pictures made during Ma'i's visit to Britain in the 1770s. The portrait has Ma'i orientalised in a European idiom by the addition of a turban-like head dress and robes that are vaguely classical in form and shape, although art historians have recently suggested that they might be *tapa*, a cloth native to the Pacific. The expressly and recognisably 'Pacific' mark in the portrait comes from Ma'i's tattooed arms, prominently displayed in this otherwise classically posed figure.

In the fashionable circles in which Ma'i moved while he was in Britain, he was celebrated as a man of natural civility, a symbol of the good that British influence might effect. Georg Forster deplored the fact that Ma'i left England in 1776 not with the knowledge and skills the metropole might have offered, but with 'an infinite variety of dresses, ornaments and other trifles, which are daily invented in order to supply our artificial wants'.[12] Here, then, was the Noble Savage corrupted by the giddy frivolities of polite European society, and principal among its fripperies was clothing. One fantasy illustration of Omai's return home shows him astride a prancing horse, bedecked in a suit of armour given to him by the Earl of Sandwich (Figure 6).

The figure of the savage colonial was, thus, often a malleable one, sometimes noble, sometimes ludicrous (armour in the Pacific!), sometimes bloodthirsty. Ma'i was certainly marked foreign by his dress and his skin markings, but the poise of the portrait and his clothedness set his portrait apart from the more common depictions of the peoples of the Pacific. Anne Salmond has described the portrait, a favourite of Reynolds', as unequivocally depicting Ma'i as a Noble Savage.[13]

Poedua and Ma'i were, in one way or another, understood to be the elite of their communities; we can see an element of idealisation in portrayals of them which may reflect that hierarchy but which also speaks to the eighteenth-century 'moment' of the Noble Savage idea. Perhaps the most iconic of such representations is the Anglo-American painter Benjamin West's *The Death of General Wolfe* (1770) (Figure 7), in which a tattooed, scantily clad 'Indian' dominates the

5. *Portrait Of Omai,* Joshua Reynolds, c. 1776

6. *Journal of Captain Cook's last voyage to the Pacific ocean,* 1781. Royce, after Dodd, in John Rickman (2nd edn)

foreground of the painting.[14] This is no enemy, no foe, but a collaborator (at a critical moment in American history) capable of emotion – and of choosing the 'right' side. Still, the contrast between the display of so much skin and the formal clothing of the Europeans ranged across the canvas draws the eye to this figure, isolated from the crowd and rendered different in every way. In an earlier and less well-known painting, *General Johnson Saving a Wounded French Officer from the Tomahawk of a North American Indian* (1764–68), begun shortly after West moved to London, where he would end his days, the figure of the Native American is remarkably similar in placement, positioning and costume to that in *The Death of General Wolfe*, yet here that same figure's intent is to scalp the fallen soldier and not to mourn him.[15] Painted within a few years of one another, West's two canvases suggest a striking degree of ambivalence.

Nobility or civilisational potential, as this contrast suggests, was by no means the routine focus in cultural productions, textual as well as visual, about those living under colonial rule. Savagery and nobility were far more frequently dissociated than linked, while nakedness was principally a symbol of savagery. In the famous portrayal of the 'taming' of the Tasmanian Aborigines (Figure 8), breasts mark one of the few discernible differences between the men and the women – both wear

7. *Death of General Wolfe*, Benjamin West, 1770

beads around their necks, women as well as men sport short hair, the spear-carriers in the background seem sexually indeterminate. Even where the whole body was displayed nude, however, the penis was rarely visible, a convention which really did serve to make women's breasts central in visual representations of nakedness, for they thus became the principal sign of sexual difference. The work by George Angas in Figure 9, one of the first Australian artists to be exhibited outside Australia at the 1855 Paris exposition, is typical; Angas gets around the penis problem either with a minimalist covering or with a profile view, in stark contrast to the remarkable family group, shown in Figure 10, by an artist whom we know only as the Port Jackson painter. Depictions such as this are far less common than those which blur, minimise or simply do not include male genitalia.

Much, I think, was going on here. Clearly audience was an issue. Male viewers would have been regarded as more interested in looking at the naked female form, while it would have been unseemly to confront female viewers, allegedly prone to the modesty 'savages' so palpably lacked, with images of fully naked men. The leaf and the loin-cloth were useful and indeed suggestive props. Moreover, one powerful narrative of colonisation stressed the effeminacy of conquered peoples, a point that could be visually achieved by downplaying the

8. *The Conciliation*, Benjamin Duterrau, 1840

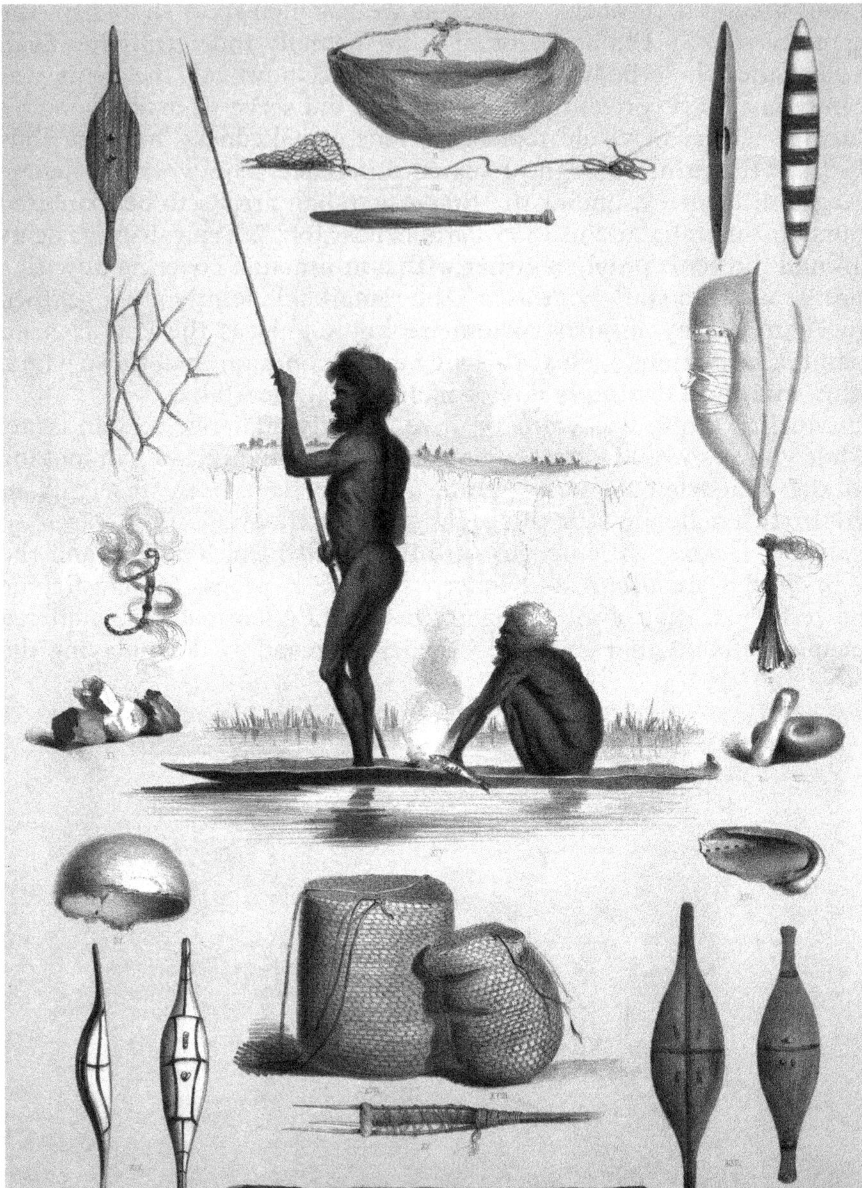

9. *The Aboriginal Inhabitants*, George French Angas, 1847

penis in favour of the female form. Given the popularity of images of warriors displaying their human war booty, we should not perhaps over-emphasise this angle, but there is certainly considerable evidence to suggest that conquest equated to emasculation. If the penis was a symbol of power, then the conquered colonised male was symbolically stripped of that authority. Male hairlessness, likewise, precipitated a questioning of true manliness. A number of early natural historians postulated that the effect of living in primitive conditions was that men lost their sexual desire, a factor contributing to the prophesied and fast-approaching extinction of 'backward' peoples.[16] Of course such attitudes competed with an opposing perspective of hyper-sexuality as the characteristic condition of savagery. Already extant in the eighteenth century, and common in discussions of the lives of Atlantic slaves, this view would come to dominate in the nineteenth century and offers an alternative explanation for the absence of views of male genitalia. Depictions of the hyper-sexual male would alarm male and female viewers alike, if for different reasons, although the fantasy of tropical sexual excess found a profitable outlet in an Orientalist pornography of dominating and overwhelming penises.

One of the most enduring and powerful themes which linked primitivism, nakedness and savage sexuality was found in depictions of dancing, an activity which found disfavour among some Protestant communities in the West at various moments.[17] Christopher Steiner notes the pervasiveness of such disapproval – beginning with Cicero,

10. *Port Jackson painter*

who associated dancing with 'inferior' foreigners – from the South Pacific to Africa and Mexico.[18] Invariably both textual and visual representations of 'primitive' dances and rituals feature men and women wearing little or no clothing, in contrast to the highly formal dress associated with the genteel dances so beloved among Western elites. Illustrations of 'savage' dance often emphasised a fondness for elaborate headgear, sometimes jewellery or weapons, but in such depictions the bodies remain largely unclothed and in this respect always worthy of comment and criticism. The ship's surgeon on Cook's third Pacific voyage in 1777 described witnessing a dance to awaken the war god 'Oro-taua. The young women, he reported, 'put themselves into several lascivious postures ... At certain parts they put their garments aside and exposed with seemingly very little sense of shame those parts which most nations have thought it modest to conceal.'[19] Missionaries in Jamaica, Catherine Hall tells us, recoiled in the 1820s from 'the scenes of dissipation and general wickedness' witnessed at the dance-heavy celebrations of Carnival.[20] A common missionary ruse was the pairing of a before and after scene in which manic and naked native dancing was replaced by sober order and clothed neatness. Fast-forward almost one hundred years and to another continent, but the sentiment is remarkably similar. Richard Meinertzhagen, a young officer in the King's African Rifles, stationed in Britain's East African Protectorate (later Kenya), attended a 'native dance' in June 1902. His description is worth quoting at length:

> In the afternoon the natives gave us a treat. A large party of young men and girls danced together for many a hot hour. To my mind the dance was most suggestive and immoral, but that did not make it any the less interesting ... In the dances I witnessed this afternoon the last phase is the bolting of the lady into the bush, hotly pursued by the young man. As both are almost nude, and as the girl is invariably caught and tripped up, the climax of a Kikuyu dance can best be imagined. It certainly could not be introduced into Belgravia, though modern dancing in England is sometimes little better than the savage displays in tropical Africa.
>
> The men dancers had their heads smeared with red earth saturated with sheep's fat, and were bedecked with beads and copper wire, which gave them the look of veritable little demons.[21]

The allusion to little demons is reminiscent of another military traveller's account. Charles Chaillé-Long, an American by birth, was General Gordon's chief of staff in Khartoum and travelled extensively in Africa and the Middle East, publishing an abundance of travel literature before his death in 1917. His revealingly titled volume of 1876, *Central Africa: Naked Truths of Naked People*, not surprisingly gives over a good deal of space to the naked body. Figure 11 is a fairly typical

11. *Central Africa: Naked Truths of Naked People,* Charles Chaillé-Long

example of the book's illustrations, reminding us once more of the visual dominance of the female breast. And Chaillé-Long too saw a direct link between fearsome dancing and 'naked peoples'.

> One may see the Dinka, Chillouk, and Nouers, forgetting their savage rivalries, engaging in dance and song around the fire at night; their gyrations and contortions of body keep perfect time to an inimitable melody, wild and weird, as they move in circles accompanied by their 'bints' in puris naturabilis. These people, whether male or female, do not affect any dress whatever, regarding it as a sign of weakness. In the flickering torch-light, reflected upon their black bodies and hideous faces, they look like demons dancing in some mad bacchanalian scene in Orcus [Orcus, of course, being a god of the underworld].[22]

As would Meinertzhagen almost three decades later, Chaillé-Long deployed the trope of the demonic to describe naked African dance, explicitly pitting dangerous maniacal hedonism against the grace of Christianity. Yet Meinertzhagen was, as Elspeth Huxley notes in her preface to his *Kenya Diary*, a man who 'killed abundantly and killed for pleasure'. He described himself as having 'no belief in the sanctity

12. *Every dog has his day – or black devils amusing themselves with a white Negro driver*, George Cruikshank, 1818

of human life'.[23] And Chaillé-Long was, to all intents and purposes, a mercenary, so the use of religious imagery on the part of men with no particular spiritual zeal is arresting. Theirs was a cultural use of a theological position, as was George Cruikshank's who, in a satirical print from 1818 (Figure 12), has black devils dancing merrily as they burn a representative of African slavery alive. His devils are inspired both by medieval illustrations of the devil and by the racial ideologies of the African slave trade. Cruikshank, as Figure 13 from the same year, shows, was himself steeped in racial stereotypes. In *Puzzled*, which pokes fun at the trans-Saharan expedition of the African Association, which unsuccessfully sought to reach central Africa from the north, the Africans are naked grotesques and the cannibal motif lurks in the skulls atop the spears of the royal bodyguards. In both these Cruikshank prints the viewer is left in no doubt: savagery and nakedness are synonymous. Nakedness is a behaviour, a sign, a state of affairs.

There is, then, clearly more to this connection than – if you will pardon the pun – meets the eye, and there is a wealth of material on which to draw. There can be no doubt that the very presence of

13. *Puzzled which to Choose!! Or, The King of Tombuctoo offering one of his daughters in marriage to Capt – (anticipated result of ye African mission),* George Cruikshank, 1818

nakedness (we might even call it the act of nakedness) invoked sexuality, and still does today. Sexuality in turn invoked gender relations, whether in terms of desire, reproduction or Christian notions of sin. This was, indeed still is, difficult terrain, but it was also always a site where difference could be explored, classified, deplored or applauded. Sexual difference and gender difference lay at the heart of the Genesis story but so, too, did nakedness. As I have argued elsewhere,[24] nakedness is a constant concern in the Bible: Genesis 2:25 ('and they were both naked, the man and the wife, and were not ashamed') is, of course, swiftly replaced by the search for bodily covering in Genesis 3:7. From then on, the trope of nakedness does a good deal of work in the Old and in the New Testament, explicating and developing the related concepts of shame and sin. It would simply not have been possible for early modern European travellers, steeped in such a theology, not to have remarked upon the unabashed nakedness of non-Christian peoples. Nakedness really did quite literally equal heathenism, for Christians knew well the meaning and consequences of going uncovered. Difference had powerful political consequences at home and beyond, and if explorers 'discovered' anything it was surely that human cultures were remarkably diverse, a discovery that pushed some heretically in the direction of polygenesis.

Philip Deloria has argued that the representation of colonies as wild and primitive helped to justify the imposition of strong imperial authority.[25] He is surely right, but this articulation of cultural difference is perhaps more complicated, and I think that attention to the long-standing trope of nakedness helps us to appreciate both this justification and the mechanisms by which it was born. Representations of nakedness inevitably offered mixed messages. In the idealised beauty of bare-breasted women lay not just desire but availability (in short, conquest), but that fantasy of heterosexual flawlessness was constantly undercut by fear, disgust and anxiety, for that same desirable naked body was shameless and wanton, sometimes fatal and, of course, represented the central original sin of temptation.

And if that was not enough to worry about, colonial nakedness overturned the new gender norms emerging in Britain which de-emphasised women's sexuality and insisted on an increasingly covered body. While 'native' women were immodest, the men were either feminised, as evidenced by their acceding to colonial rule, or rudely barbarous by virtue of such traits as cannibalism or brutality towards women. Their indifference to the nakedness of women was puzzling and their own nakedness made masculinity overall quite vulnerable. Yet at the same time the obstinacy of 'primitive' peoples in the matter of dress – some remained stubbornly naked, others wore Western clothing wrongly –

proved, as anthropologists began to argue in the nineteenth century, that they were relics of an older epoch, frozen in time and unable to change and adapt to modern environments. The Noble Savage of the eighteenth century, chimerical as that image may have been, had potential, as some of the portraits analysed in this chapter imply. It was the reason why Joseph Banks and Robert Fitzroy brought 'savages' back to Britain to 'civilise' and educate them for missionary purposes. It was the reason why Macaulay could advocate an English education among the Bengal elite. Over time, though, and despite the insistent rhetoric of the civilising mission, a more pessimistic belief in a fundamental incommensurability emerged in British thought, a position that, in many ways, paralleled the representational shift from Noble Savage to naked native. By the middle of the nineteenth century, the naked native was by far the more common of these two images. The Noble Savage did not disappear, but was increasingly represented as disappearing, that is, on the verge of extinction, because, rather than holding out the prospect of improvement and progress, such beings now proved the theory of incommensurability through their inability to withstand the onslaught of modern civilisation. The clamour of voices pronouncing the ineluctable, certain disappearance of those unable to adapt to the modern world reached its apogee in the mid and late nineteenth century, strengthened by evolutionary theory. The Noble Savage became less a prospect than a myth, a museum piece linked to the new anthropology of salvage. But nakedness lived on: images of the bare-breasted, grass-skirted dancing woman, the spear-carrying man clad only in a loin-cloth, made their way into school textbooks, popular magazines and postcards sent from exotic holiday destinations. These are, even today, not unfamiliar images, sanitised for modern sensibilities to be sure. But the work that they do and the desires that they conjure have their origin in a history where to be naked was to be within the reach of colonialism's grasp. Whether as Noble Savage or as naked native, the naked body, the absence of clothing, were profoundly powerful symbols of difference understood physically as well as culturally, intellectually as well as economically: material proof of the need for a firm colonial hand.

Notes

1 See, for example, Troy Bickham, *Savages Within the Empire: Representations of American Indians in Eighteenth-Century Britain* (Oxford: Oxford University Press, 2005).

2 Robert F. Berkhofer, *The White Man's Indian: Images of the American Indian, from Columbus to the Present* (New York: Alfred Knopf, 1978), p. 88.

3 Kate Flint, *The Transatlantic Indian, 1776–1930* (Princeton: Princeton University Press, 2009), p. 12.

4 Stephanie Pratt, *American Indians in British Art, 1700–1840* (Norman: University of Oklahoma Press, 2005), p. 6.
5 Bickham, *Savages Within the Empire*, p. 82.
6 J. C. Beaglehole (ed.), *The Journals of Captain James Cook on His Voyages of Discovery, vol. 1: The Voyage of the Endeavour 1768–1771* (Cambridge: Cambridge University Press, 1968), pp. 395–9.
7 A. W. Pollard (ed.), *The Travels of Sir John Mandeville: The Version of the Cotton Manuscript in Modern Spelling*, (London: Macmillan, 1915), p. 109.
8 Quoted in Berkhofer, *The White Man's Indian*, p. 19. See too, Jennifer Morgan's discussion of the absence of shame in Jennifer Morgan, '"Some Could Suckle Over Their Shoulder": Male Travelers, Female Bodies, and the Gendering of Racial Ideology, 1550–1770', *The William and Mary Quarterly*, 54 (1997), 167–92.
9 Ruth Barcan, *Nudity: A Cultural Anatomy* (Oxford and New York: Berg, 2004), pp. 158–9.
10 Patty O'Brien, *The Pacific Muse: Exotic Femininity and the Colonial Pacific* (Seattle: University of Washington Press, 2006), p. 99.
11 Susanne Küchler and Graeme Were, 'Introduction', in Susanne Küchler and Graeme Were (ed.), *The Art of Clothing*, (London: UCL Press, 2005), pp. ix–xxx, xxiii.
12 Harriet Guest, *Empire, Barbarism, and Civilisation: James Cook, William Hodges and the Return to the Pacific* (Cambridge: Cambridge University Press, 2007), p. 157 quoting Georg Forster, *A Voyage Around the World* (Honolulu: University of Hawai'i Press, 2000), vol. I, p. 11.
13 Anne Salmond, *Aphrodite's Island: The European Discovery of Tahiti* (Berkeley: University of California Press, 2010), p. 394. See too Guest, *Empire, Barbarism, and Civilisation*, p. 69.
14 For an interesting reading, see Vivien Green Fryd, 'Rereading the Indian in Benjamin West's "Death of General Wolfe"', *American Art*, 9 (1995), 72–85; for a specific discussion of nakedness in the painting, see p. 84.
15 Jonathan Conlin offers a detailed and convincing reading of the painting in 'Benjamin West's *General Johnson* and Representations of British Imperial Identity, 1759–1770. An Empire of Mercy?' *Journal for Eighteenth-Century Studies*, 27 (2004), 37–60.
16 Gustav Jahoda, *Images of Savages: Ancient Roots of Modern Prejudice in Western Culture* (London: Routledge, 1999), p. 15.
17 Christopher B. Steiner, 'Travel Engravings and the Construction of the Primitive', in Elazar Barkan and Ronald Bush (eds), *Prehistories of the Future: The Primitivist Project and the Culture of Modernism* (Stanford, CA: Stanford University Press, 1995), pp. 202–25, at p. 417, n. 15.
18 Steiner, 'Travel Engravings', p. 211.
19 David Samwell in J. C. Beaglehole (ed.), *The Journals of Captain James Cook on His Voyages of Discovery, vol. 3: The Voyages of the Resolution and Discovery* (Cambridge: Cambridge University Press, 1968), p. 978.
20 Catherine Hall, *Civilising Subjects: Metropole and Colony in the English Imagination, 1830–1867* (Chicago: University of Chicago Press, 2002), p. 179.
21 Richard Meinertzhagen, *Kenya Diary (1902–1906)* (New York: Hippocrene Books, 1983), p. 22.
22 Charles Chaillé Long, *Central Africa: Naked Truths of Naked People. An Account of the Expeditions to Lake Victoria Nyanza and the Makraka Niam-Niam, West of the Bahr-El-Abiad. (White Nile).* (London: S. Low, Marston, Searle & Rivington, 1876), p. 228.
23 Meinertzhagen, *Kenya Diary*, p. v.
24 Philippa Levine, 'States of Undress: Nakedness and the Colonial Imagination', *Victorian Studies*, 50 (2008), 189–219, at 191.
25 Philip Joseph Deloria, *Indians in Unexpected Places* (Lawrence, KS: University Press of Kansas, 2004), p. 29.

CHAPTER TWO

British radicals in Asia and the persistence of empire c. 1820–1950

C. A. Bayly

This chapter examines the role and significance of British radicals and socialists in the politics of colonial India. It also briefly touches on Ceylon, the Malay world and the Middle East to frame some connections. It attempts to insert a new term between two related bodies of work in the first decade of this century. Firstly, I hope the chapter is timely because of the publication in 2010 of Robert Bickers's edited volume, *Settlers and Expatriates*, an additional part of the *Oxford History of the British Empire*.[1] This is a volume which considers issues of identity, race and gender which are very much to the fore in contemporary world history. It builds on the work of scholars such as Peter Marshall, Dane Kennedy and Elizabeth Buettner.[2]

Secondly, there is an emerging tradition of what has been called global intellectual history that has been concerned with liberal imperialism and radical scepticism about empire. On the one hand, Jennifer Pitts and Karuna Mantena have examined the shift from the constructive, interventionist imperialism of the early nineteenth century to the conservative stance epitomised by Henry Maine later in the century.[3] On the other hand, Miles Taylor, Gregory Claeys, Edward Moulton, Mira Matikkala, Bernard Porter and Stephen Howe have studied the anti-colonial, or at least the anti-authoritarian thread as it developed from Joseph Hume in the 1820s to British socialists in the mid-twentieth century.[4]

This chapter, however, focuses mainly on British people who worked in Asia for significant periods and critiqued empire for its effects on colonised people. It is less concerned with domestic politicians and intellectuals who stressed the danger that imperialism posed to the British constitution. Radicals such as James Silk Buckingham in the 1820s, or Alan Octavian Hume in the 1880s or Phillip Spratt in the 1930s were significant for several reasons. Firstly, they provided intellectual and, in the case of Spratt, real ammunition which helped indigenous public figures to construct their own anti-colonial arguments and practice. Equally, these expatriates absorbed ideas and influences from Asian intellectuals, which they forged into a benign form of orientalism and purveyed to the European and American public. In both ways, they helped to keep liberal imperialism on the defensive and, along with Asian nationalists and domestic 'imperial sceptics', pushed forward modest changes in imperial governance.

Later generations of anti-colonial nationalists have sometimes criticised these expatriate radicals for lack of true commitment to Asian self-rule. Hume, for instance, considered as one of the founders of the Indian National Congress, acknowledged the fact that he was creating a 'safety valve' for Indian opinion in order to bring into being a more humane empire. And it is true that figures such as Hume, William Wedderburn and Henry Cotton helped to promote reforms which, paradoxically, contributed to the striking longevity of the British Empire. They acted, in the contemporary political language of social Darwinism, to perpetuate the organism of empire through struggle and evolution. Indeed, it was no accident that some of the most effective critics of empire were or had been colonial civil servants. Their attitude to empire was not only sceptical, but also ambivalent. Yet the emphasis that these men and women put on the free press, Asian access to juries, indigenous political representation, the division of executive and judicial powers and local economic protection did at least strengthen political reformers in Britain's Asian colonies and help to inform their liberal, even democratic principles.

A study of these figures also holds up a mirror to the development of the major themes in the intellectual history of Britain and the wider British world. For these expatriate radicals were not simply exponents of political economy. It is striking that humanistic, religious, aesthetic and even sexual themes motivated many of them in their assaults on colonial governance. I will consider three broad periods: the 'moment' of intellectual history between Waterloo and 1848; the years between the founding of the Indian National Congress in 1885 and the coming of the First World War; and, finally, the socialist 'moment' of the 1930s and 1940s.

From liberal constitutionalism to the shadow of Chartism

Before the wars of the revolutionary and Napoleonic period the concept of 'radicalism' among British expatriates in Asia is even more ambivalent than it would be in the nineteenth century. Private traders attempting to work within the East India Company's aegis, such as

William Bolts, the Anglo-Dutch Bengal merchant, resorted to the language of freedom of commerce and the Englishman's liberties. As Linda Colley has shown, Philip Francis appealed to habeas corpus and the right of trial by jury against the obduracy of the Company.[5] In her study of that wide-ranging trading and political family, the Johnstones, which was scattered across the world from Florida to Bengal in the 1760s, Emma Rothschild writes of the confusion of the public and the private, of the state, the Company and the family.[6] The Johnstones in Bengal fell out with Clive and the growing political power of the Bengal government. But this was mainly because they were, remarkably, even more deeply implicated in the Indian web of present giving, land grabbing and exactions on the country trade than Clive himself.

In these colonies, the law was a miscellany of fragments and postures used in familial and political conflicts. Even at the later time of the dispute between Warren Hastings and Philip Francis considered by Colley, it is not clear that Francis's 'radicalism' amounted to much more than a set of libertarian sentiments directed against the growing power of the Governor of Bengal and his purported 'Mughal constitution.' The conflict at this period and, for decades beyond, was about the best way to profit from, and find advancement within, state and empire, rather than about their morality or existence. Radicals were basically errant and difficult insiders.

James Light and Stamford Raffles, for instance, worked within the East India Company's monopoly, but often rejected its authority. They both continued this tradition of libertarian insolence into the age of the revolutions. In 1787 Light made an agreement with the Sultan of Kedah for the establishment of the free port of Penang without the authority of the Company, let alone the British state. Raffles famously ignored the order to return Singapore to the Dutch in 1819, supported by the growing body of advocates of free trade in Calcutta and a small number of early Indian 'liberals', such as Rammohan Roy.

As the Company's military-fiscal despotism in India and beyond grew more intrusive and sure of itself, the language of authority, and thus of radicalism itself, changed, responding not only to events in Britain and India but to the wider ideological changes unleashed by the French and Iberian revolutions. Governor-General Wellesley deported newspaper editors from Calcutta whom he termed 'Jacobins'. Later Company officials tried to insist that British expatriates in Calcutta, Madras or Bombay were the equivalent of indentured servants, or subject to discipline under the equivalent of a ship's captain. Sir John Malcolm, arguing fiercely against freedom of the press, asserted '[w]e could give to the Brahmins and others of the instructed classes of India, no weapon which they would know better how to use than a free press'.[7] Equally, those who demanded free colonisation, free trade and the licence to deal with Indian magnates and labourers as they wished invoked the language of English liberties, laced with the garnish of international constitutional liberalism. James Silk Buckingham, perhaps the first comprehensive critic of British colonial rule in India, compared Governor Adam's press restrictions to the despotism of the Ottoman Sultan, the reactionary Pope and the 'beloved King of Spain'.[8]

Even before Buckingham began his campaign of obstruction in India, however, another key figure in British and imperial radicalism had illustrated this shift from legally garnished factionalism to a new, more class-based set of ideological positions which reflected a harder difference between Left and Right. This was Joseph Hume,[9] who came from a relatively poor background but had shone in medical studies at the University of Edinburgh. Attached to an East Indian Regiment during Lord Lake's wars of conquest against the Marathas in 1802–3, he prospered as an interpreter, having mastered 'native tongues', and then as commissary general, where his knowledge of the properties of gunpowder made him a fortune. Returning to Britain like any eighteenth-century nabob, he entered Parliament as a Tory through the 'rotten borough' of Weymouth in 1812 and married the daughter of an East Indian director.

This inauspicious start for the key figure of early nineteenth-century British transnational radicalism was rapidly erased as Hume fell out with his patron, Spencer Perceval, on issues relating to sinecures and workers' rights and was dropped at the subsequent general election. Here ideology triumphed decisively over patronage, a premonition of the new face of British politics. Following a period of reflection and social observation, Hume once again entered Parliament in 1828, now as a radical influenced by James Mill, Jeremy Bentham and Francis Place. This was no mere theoretical conversion. Hume worked to establish schools for working people and tried, alongside Buckingham, to end the flogging of seamen and the poor treatment of Indian lascars. His early Indian experience made him a powerful opponent of the Company in Parliament and around the country. Like many radicals of this period he also paired the release of Greece from 'Ottoman tyranny' with the abolition of the East India Company. Hume's career in regard to Greek independence was somewhat tarnished, though, by the financially dubious consequences of the Greek Loan which came to light in 1826. Yet he pushed relentlessly for the freeing of Asian trade and for Indian and mixed-race rights until his death in 1855.

Robert Montgomery Martin's career displayed similar features. An Irish Protestant of middle-class but impecunious origins, he went to Australia, worked as an assistant surgeon and then moved to

Calcutta in 1828, where he became a supporter of Rammohan Roy and Dwarkanath Tagore. For a time he edited the Indian liberals' *Bengal Herald*. He was the most prominent early exponent in Bengal of what I have called 'statistical liberalism'. His statistical and historical studies of the British Empire, especially its taxation systems, were a critical resource for contemporary radical politicians interrogating the East India Company, including Hume, and also for later historians. On his return to Britain, Martin moved from early support of O'Connell's movement to a resolute Unionist position. But he had already added an important strand to Anglo-Indian liberalism in the subcontinent itself. His Bengali clerk's son was Keshub Chunder Sen, a dominant figure in the Brahmo Samaj and a resolute critic of Western morality.

This whole group of early nineteenth-century radicals paired social and parliamentary reform in Britain with free trade and an end to 'despotism' in the British and Ottoman empires. Another key figure here was Leicester Stanhope, a member of a middling Dublin aristocratic family, who entered the army in 1799 and served in India, becoming a supporter of the liberal Governor-General Lord Hastings and a proponent of the freedom of the Indian press. In 1823 he went to Greece as an agent of the English Greek Committee and became an associate of John Bowring, Bentham's literary executor, industrialist and, later, in 1854, Governor of Hong Kong, following his key role in the origins of the Opium War with China.

There are several general points of significance about the radicals of this period. Firstly – and this will be clear throughout the chapter – heterodox religion played an important part in their intellectual formation. Buckingham was a Methodist lay preacher before he joined the navy and began to agitate for the rights of slaves, British sailors and lascars. He was also a temperance zealot. Other radicals in Asia, and across the empire, were Unitarians, notably John Bowring. This was significant, for Rammohan Roy, Buckingham's closest colleague, called himself a 'Hindu Unitarian' and pitched his case for the reform of the Company to Unitarian and reformist audiences in Britain and, by extension, in the United States, as Lynn Zastoupil has shown.[10] For his part, Joseph Hume appears to have been a free-thinker in the style of his namesake, David Hume, and he had developed an early interest in Indian religion. Almost all of these publicists argued for freedom of religion and Catholic emancipation.

Secondly, many radicals throughout the colonial period were of Scottish or Irish origin, whether from failing aristocratic, middle-class or artisan origins. Of course, it is true that Scots and Irish were over-represented in the colonial world more generally, including among the administrators. Buckingham's bête noire, the Reverend James Bryce, was a Scots Presbyterian who took government office in Calcutta, 'out-Torying the Tories' as the *Calcutta Journal* put it.[11] Still, colonial radicalism tended to reflect distaste for the status quo in Britain: the dominance of London, political corruption, military-fiscal gigantism and religious discrimination.

Thirdly, a complex of issues of significance in both Britain and India tied the composition of grand juries to press freedom and the authority of the writ of habeas corpus outside Britain. Buckingham offended the Company's government with criticism of its commercial despotism, published in his newspaper, the *Calcutta Journal*. The Company's government tried to prosecute its opponents in the courts or simply to imprison them and expel them from India. Buckingham himself was removed from India by the government, as was his successor, the Anglo-Indian Sandford Arnot, after a period of imprisonment was ended by a writ of habeas corpus. Reform of the jury, therefore, became the first key issue of political representation for both Indians and expatriate Britons. Hindus were supposedly incapable of taking an oath and could not serve as jurors. British radicals, for their part, believed that the courts were too close to the political authorities to sustain English liberties. Both groups helped to advance the cause of legal reform that was enacted in the East India Juries Act of 1825. This made it possible for Indians, Malays and Chinese to sit on juries, though actual implementation took much longer. These changes mirrored the Jury Acts in England, which allowed jurors to decide matters of law as well as of fact.

The connection between radicals and Hindu political and social reformers continued after Rammohan Roy's death in Bristol in 1833. The radical and friend of the Irish 'Liberator' Daniel O'Connell, Colonel James Young, who had been head of the agency house Alexander and Co., had worked with Indian and Eurasian liberals against press restrictions and for the Jury Bill in the mid-1820s.[12] Young was responsible for introducing Dwarkanath Tagore, Rammohan's moral successor, to John Brougham, the radical and free trader, when he visited Britain in the 1840s. Young wrote that Dwarkanath was 'my own, very particular and old friend, at the head of everything liberal in India'.[13]

A fourth feature of this early radicalism was the role that people of mixed race played in arguing for rights, something which again linked them to early Indian, Ceylonese or Malay radicals. Mixed-race people in India founded newspapers and organised petitions to Parliament demanding their rights as British subjects around the time of the Reform Bills. They proclaimed their loss of what they actually referred to as 'civil rights', to which both Europeans and Indians were entitled. By this they meant access to civil and military offices, from which

Lord Cornwallis had excluded them in the 1790s.[14] Prominent among Calcutta Eurasians was J. W. Ricketts, businessman, philanthropist and founder of the Parental Academic Association that admitted Indians into its debates. At this period, Eurasians acted as intermediaries between European radicals and the new Indian public men. Henry Derozio, the poet, was typical of this group, as was John Sandys, the Eurasian who took over editorship of the *Calcutta Journal* after both Buckingham and Arnot had been deported from India.[15] Derozio, Sandys and the others represented a thread of Eurasian radicalism that re-emerged periodically until the 1880s, when some leaders of the community, especially those connected with the railways, championed the Indian National Congress.

Finally, this early radicalism was, at least in theory and argument, a transregional and transnational discourse. Indian newspapers noted the campaign of Australian settlers for freedom of the press and examples of oppression on the China coast. Radical Indian journals compared the Company's government unfavourably with the Crown colony of Ceylon, where so-called Dutch Burgers, mixed-race people and some Ceylonese sat on juries. The Ceylonese, by contrast, noted that Indians held considerable local power as subordinate magistrates. The authorities were also thinking transregionally. In the 1830s, for instance, the government of the Straits Settlements complained about the 'licence of the press' in Calcutta, irritated by the Bengal newspapers' attacks on territorial expansion around Penang. Most striking, British radicals, Eurasian spokesmen and the first generation of Indian public men were closely observant of events in the Portuguese and Spanish worlds, where, from 1808 onward, constitutional revolutions in Lisbon and Madrid found echoes in places such as Goa, Diu, Daman and Macao. A Portuguese tract on constitutional government in the Portuguese empire, written by Bernardo Peres da Silva, a Goan Brahmin Christian, was well known in Bombay and closely paralleled the arguments that Rammohan Roy was making about the 'ancient Indian constitution'.[16] Liberal British officials secretly supported da Silva's armed revolt against the royal reactionaries in Goa.

Yet here the ambivalence of expatriate and creole radicalism becomes clear again. Many of the proponents of free trade and enemies of the Company's despotism among British expatriates, Portuguese *luso descendentes* and Indian magnates wanted a free opium trade to China and were prepared to support the use of force against the Qing Empire to achieve this.

There are many historical studies of Rammohan Roy and his coevals, especially by historians of religion. Meanwhile, Buckingham is emerging from historical obscurity. But the age of Chartism and the revolutions of 1848, in India at least, have not received the same degree of attention. Miles Taylor wrote of the consequences of 1848 for the empire as a whole. He noted in passing the agitation in Ceylon, where the Irish Protestant radical Christopher Elliott was engaged in a campaign to abolish the labour services demanded of the local population and extend the franchise to a substantial body of Ceylonese subjects.[17] But India itself was not unaffected by these events. The sight of French citizens of Pondicherry travelling to the Paris constitutional assembly of 1848 caused a stir in Calcutta. But even before this, Chartist agitations, the campaign against American slavery and hostility to the Company's foreign wars in Afghanistan had transformed the earlier constitutional liberalism into something more radical, acutely aware of class and more systematically anti-colonial. One of these intellectual shifts, the Chartist critique of British society and discovery of the 'working man', was directly signalled by the appearance in India in 1843 of the British radical spokesman George Thompson (1804–78). Thompson helped to institutionalise a new range of political associations in alliance with young Indians who increasingly distanced themselves from the landholding system of which many had been beneficiaries.

George Thompson was in many ways a younger version of Buckingham. He emerged as an opponent of slavery in Liverpool and later became an associate of Joseph Hume in the National Parliamentary Reform Association. He visited the United States on several occasions to agitate against slavery and was considered by John Bright to have been 'the liberator of the slaves in the English colonies'.[18] An MP, prophetically from Tower Hamlets in East London, though never directly a Chartist agitator, he emphasised the need for Indians to organise to bring their grievances to the attention of the British electorate. This was because, as he said, it was the British people that 'make Parliament'. Thompson viewed the Indian associations as the equivalent to the electoral reform societies with which he had worked in the 1820s in Britain. He himself appears to have been a Unitarian, 'devoted to the Being who was maker of all men'.[19]

Even before leaving England, Thompson had savaged the Government of India's revenue policy in a speech to working people at Paisley. He denounced it as 'a system of taxation more impolitic, oppressive and injurious than anywhere in the world'.[20] The Mughal system, where the state took a share of the actual produce, in his view at least, had been replaced by an inflexible money payment which bled the country dry, impoverished the peasantry and benefited only the money-lender. Even Britain itself got little out of the system because it 'crippled and paralysed our trade with India' by reducing this 'defenceless people [the Indians] to poverty'.[21] In the speeches during his tour, Thompson and his Indian hosts dwelt on the nature of representative government, the importance of 'combination', the diffusion of information in India and Britain and the unity of mankind. Many of Thompson's themes echoed those of the Chartists in Britain, especially their hostility to monopoly and privilege, but also their view of the police as a system of 'oppression'. This new generation of public men, British radicals and Indians, began to summon up powerful visions of the future, of a prosperous, industrial India with an improved and educated populace. Thompson himself orated on the need for 'an Indian Sheffield, and Indian Birmingham'.[22] It was a theme, an 'imagined future' in the style of Reinhart Koselleck, taken up in almost the same year by the Bengali reformers Bholanauth Chunder and Dakshinaranjan Mukhopadyay.[23]

Nevertheless, expatriate radicalism was a mixed phenomenon, which arose as much from British commercial aspiration as from any coherent anti-colonialism. While both detested the Company's monopoly, British and Indian radicals soon came to disagree on the wisdom of European colonisation and unrestricted free trade. For instance, Loftus Longueville Clarke, a Supreme Court barrister and member of a long-resident family, argued that the true enemies of the Indian people were the 'myrmidons of the East India Company', not the European planters. The real object of the continuing ban on colonisation was, in his words, 'to prevent the Briton from infecting Indians with their love of liberty and stop the contagion of freedom'.[24] But here the contagion of freedom seemed to mean free trade and free European settlement. Longueville Clark was involved with Dwarkanath Tagore in the Bengal Coal Company, for instance, in attempts to secure rights on the estates of the Raja of Burdwan.[25] While they opposed the Company and the big landholders, most Indian liberals already rejected the notion of unrestricted freedom of trade, while at least until the 1880s European radicals continued to press for it. So in this first phase of expatriate radicalism, the demand for the extension of English liberties worldwide merged with demands for free trade, free colonisation, the rights of Eurasians and the ripples of the Iberian and French revolutions.

Congress, British radicals and the Raj

This chapter now moves on to the period between about 1880 and 1914. The critical event that framed this period was, of course, the brutal suppression of the 1857–59 rebellion. This was accompanied by the expansion of a racialist expatriate community in India and the beginning of British liberal moves to institute local self-government, mainly for reasons of economy. Both British radicals and Indian liberals, again, portrayed the campaign against the mutineers as part of a history of despotism. *Reynolds News*, for a further century the key medium of British radicalism, compared the suppression of the Rebellion to repression in Bourbon Naples and Ireland.[26] Indian intellectuals compared it to the reaction after the English Civil War and the French Revolution. The only possible future, both groups argued, involved the extension of representation to Indians, a new political economy that protected the peasant and a moral rearmament of the empire. Here I want to capture the moral sentiments that lay behind late Victorian British radicalism in India and beyond. Gregory Claeys has pointed to the role of a British version of August Comte's positivism in this story.[27] The religion of humanity was posed to move the world from the age of exploitative colonialism to a cooperative future, purged of violence. An Indian expatriate such as Sir Henry Cotton was indeed strongly influenced by positivism.

Yet several other forms of humanistic religiosity played an equally important part in British colonial radicalism and these throw light on wider intellectual history. They included what I call counter-orientalism, Theosophy, romantic socialism, an early version of 'gay' self-assertion and 'Christian Fulfilment Theology'.

By the 1870s British liberals generally articulated their ideologies without fear of popular revolt; the Chartist riots were well behind them. But in India, 'the liberalism of fear' persisted, constantly reinforced by memories of 1857 and explosions such as the Deccan riots of the 1870s. Indians themselves were chary of pointing too vigorously to the disaffection of the masses. But British Indian radicals such as A. O. Hume (son of Joseph Hume) and William Wedderburn, both former Indian Civil Service officials and founder members of the Indian National Congress, had no such constraints. They could claim that alerting the public to coming mutinies was their way of saving the empire. Hume, a radical liberal, Theosophist and survivor of the Rebellion, wrote of the last years of Lord Lytton's viceroyalty in the 1870s in this 'counter-orientalist' vein. He reported of a vast web of communication across the subcontinent, of 'legions of quasi-religious orders', with disciples corresponding with their gurus about the state of the popular mind: 'what goes on under the surface'.[28] These networks revealed an impoverished population 'convinced that they would starve and die'. They would resort to crime and violent action 'in order to do *something* and to stand by each other'.[29] For Hume, the Congress he founded was to serve as a lightning rod, or rather 'safety valve', to avert this catastrophe. The move was intended to parallel British liberals' favourable turn towards an expansion of the electorate following the terrors of 1848.

Theosophy itself was a critical affective influence on this late nineteenth-century radicalism in India. However exotic a plant Theosophy might now seem, it drew on strong antecedents in nineteenth-century thought. It represented a kind of relativising cosmopolitanism that appealed to nationalists and internationalists alike at a time when the exclusive claims of orthodox religions were coming under increasing scrutiny in Britain, Ireland and beyond. Comte had postulated the transformation of the human spirit through phases of moral and intellectual evolution. Giuseppe Mazzini had written of 'messiah peoples' and the constant rebirth of great souls. Theosophy located the critical moment of this process in India. Annie Besant, Irish and Indian nationalist, began to develop a theory of politics and international relations from the Bhagavad Gita, in a way that was comparable with the thought of her Indian coevals, such as Aurobindo Ghose and Bipin Chandra Pal. Besant held that the rise and fall of nations was brought about by 'karmic revenge'.[30] Both India and Britain suffered from malign karma, the one for her colonial genocide, the other for 'the sin of untouchability'. Mobilising India against British imperialism through Congress and the Home Rule Leagues would release both peoples from this eternal curse, Besant argued.[31] Similar arguments were made by another Irish woman activist, Margaret Noble, alias Sister Nivedita, who had become a devotee of Swami Vivekanand. Before her early death, she had been active in promoting Indian home rule in the company of Ananda Coomaraswamy, the Anglo-Ceylonese radical, and Rabindranath Tagore, arguing that the 'spirit of the East' was superior to Western commercial greed.

By the mid-1890s or 1900s, many of the British founders and co-workers with Indian nationalism and social reform, Theosophists or not, had moved from a liberal to a 'soft' socialist stance. A. O. Hume's farewell speech to India in 1894 had concluded that nothing would be done for India 'until our [i.e. British] working men put forth in earnest the power vested in them and put into power a true democratic ministry'.[32] Sir Henry Cotton foresaw a 'United States of India' in which labour was protected from the sort of abuse that was daily evident in the Assam tea plantations. Edward Carpenter[33] and Ananda Kentish Coomaraswamy, the Anglo-Ceylonese, both romantic socialists, denounced the destruction of Indian industries by the evils of British capitalism. Carpenter wrote of ancient India as 'wisdom land', comparing it with the 'cheap and nasty puffing, profit mongering, enterprising, energetic business' which was to be seen in the 'queer broil' of places such as Bombay and Calcutta. Here the 'highest concept of life and religion' was the General Post Office.[34]

Carpenter was a remarkable figure, a gay orientalist, who had idolised the Vedanta since an early encounter with Walt Whitman and the Bhagavad Gita. As a middle-class proponent of the movement Towards Democracy, he identified with both the British and Indian working class, but though he attended a meeting of the Second International, he was more at home with humanist anarchists than with the scientific Marxists, as his most recent biographer, Antony Copley remarks.[35] In both Ceylon and India, he was entranced with the notion that male sexual liberation and human spiritual progress were one and the same. The stylised *lingams* and *yonis* (male and female sexual organs) adorning Hindu temples seemed to prove to him that there had been a better life before modern capitalism and the oppressive impact of Christian moralising. This life would assert itself again in the future. Gender studies and post-colonial writers have indicted Carpenter for 'colonial' sexual predation, on the one hand, and denying female sexuality, temple *yonis* notwithstanding, on the other. Yet he represents a curiously British turn to radical spiritualism and a reaction to Victorian moral conventions. Indian liberals and radicals enlisted him in their assault on Western civilisation and reactionary Indian government. This form of gay colonial liberationism was re-embodied in several later expatriate radicals, such as E. M. Forster and Tom Driberg.

During his sojourn in Ceylon, Coomaraswamy, for his part, had refurbished Buckingham's old radical theme of the merits of local government by pointing to the *gansabhava*, the village council. His descriptions of village life in the island lauded the institution as the only way to preserve watercourses and wells, local industry and indigenous life more generally.[36] But to Coomaraswamy, 'Ceylonese are Indians', and his admonition referred as much to the *panchayat* or local councils of the subcontinent. Coomaraswamy told an audience in Madras that 'people who lived up to their own ideals, had their own arts and industries, and who like the Japanese had their own industries would be respected and not succumb to imperialism'.[37] This was not a doctrine of class struggle, but of small-scale enterprise and cultural authenticity. India, he said would not benefit from large industries such as those that had created the slums of Bombay and Calcutta. Aesthetics and production had to come before profit. Coomaraswamy eventually abandoned Britain for the United States in 1916, denouncing the use of Indian soldiers in an imperialistic war. Yet he was an important transitional figure in India itself. He stands as a middle term between the old Indian liberals, Ruskin, Morris, Tolstoy and Gandhi himself.

The final 'affective' context for British colonial radicalism in this period was Christian Fulfilment Theology, or more broadly Christian spiritual relativism. This tended to postulate the spiritual equality of all humans and consequently began to consider the need for political equality. Not all Christian expatriates of this mode of thinking argued for Asian liberation. Others, such as Edward Thompson, Methodist missionary and father of the celebrated historian, favoured dominion status within the empire for the Asian colonies, but only really promoted it as writers. Yet the radicalism of a few was more direct. I will consider the epochal link between Charles Freer Andrews and Mohandas Gandhi. This friendship helped to empower one of the major national liberation movements of the twentieth century through a kind of half-conscious mutual recognition, what Bakhtin might have called a 'dialogic slippage'. Appropriately, perhaps, for this chapter, it arose indirectly from a Cambridge connection.

In 1909 the Cambridge Mission to India in Delhi and St Stephen's College were among the few institutions to provide higher education in a city. They also organised dispensaries, inspected schools and worked with women's education. By 1909 major changes were in train. Despite pervasive racism, Indians were already coming to the fore in the professions. Sushil K. Rudra, son of a Bengali Brahmin convert, had become vice-principal of St Stephens. Rudra, already a moderate nationalist, initiated a series of events that were to bring Gandhi back from South Africa to India and transform the Indian national movement.

Rudra decided that the college needed new blood. He approached the Cambridge Brotherhood, requesting that Charles Freer Andrews, fellow, college lecturer and chaplain of Pembroke College, should be invited to become principal of St Stephens. This Andrews did in 1904. Andrews, himself from a family of messianic dissenters, had become an Anglican in the university. He always believed firmly that India was a sacred trust committed by God to Great Britain. But having worked among the poor in East London as a young priest, he was also deeply aware of the injustices of imperial rule; he campaigned successively against the abusive conditions of indentured labour in Fiji, Mauritius and British Guiana. He wrote diatribes against the opium trade to China and championed the rights of Indians in South Africa. He argued that Indians should hold high office in their own country. Later in his life, in the 1920s, he moved to Canada, where he became a spokesman for Indians, mainly Sikhs, whom white Canadians were trying to debar from settlement.

Retreating swiftly from his High Church Anglican beliefs when he reached India, Andrews became sympathetic to Christian Fulfilment Theology. As I implied, this held that Hinduism, or for that matter Buddhism or Sikhism, could provide the seed-bed for Christianity: Christ represented the fulfilment of the seed of belief that lies in all.

This was a radical departure from the rigid evangelical positions of the mid-nineteenth century. But it surely picked up on the relativistic spiritualism and anthropological awareness of the tradition of Robertson Smith and E. G. Browne, respectively an Arabist and a Persianist, which Andrews had encountered at Cambridge.

In the meantime, Andrews rapidly developed connections with India's nationalists. This was the period of the so-called extremist movement and the upsurge of assassinations of British officials as the imperialist policies of the Viceroy, Lord Curzon, reaped their consequences. Indian leaders were imprisoned and transported. Yet in 1907 and 1908 the students of St Stephens had rapturously welcomed the radical Punjabi leader, Lala Lajpat Rai. In response, Andrews sought help from the Indian liberal and social reformer, G. K. Gokhale. Gokhale visited South Africa and made contact with a young lawyer, Mohandas Gandhi, leader of the Natal Indian Congress. Andrews himself was to visit South Africa in 1913 and was deeply impressed by Gandhi's doctrine of non-violence (*ahimsa*), which he tried to class as a version of Christ's doctrine of 'turning the other cheek'. It was Rudra and Andrews who invited Gandhi to return to India, while Andrews later contributed greatly to the spread of the myth of the Mahatma across the world.

Much of the writing about Andrews (and, for that matter, Gandhi) exudes Christian sentimentality. Andrews is Deenabandhu, 'friend of the poor', 'the Apostle of Jesus to Delhi', survivor of 'The ordeal of love'. His connection with Gandhi becomes almost a personal atonement for the evils of British imperialism. Not everyone saw him this way, however. The socialists Sidney and Beatrice Webb visited Delhi in 1912, following meetings with anti-colonialists in China and Japan. The couple met and immediately disliked Andrews: he was 'a somewhat smooth and disingenuous ecclesiastic', they sneered, 'bent on the redemption of Indians through Christianity'.[38] Andrews was full of 'malicious slanders' against Indians and the Indian character. The Webbs admired radical nationalists such as Lajpat Rai. But they also disliked Andrews's moralising. Indeed, his drive to secure rights for Indians across the world was, in part, an effort to counter what he saw as cultural and sexual degeneration that occurred when Indian men were debarred from migrating with women. Indeed, Andrews echoed – in a non-scientific way – many of the fashionable eugenic ideas of the era. The Webbs had little time for liberal reformism, particularly in a Christian guise. But the incident also points to the internal differences within expatriate radicalism.

British radicals, socialism and the empire in the twentieth century

This chapter ends with a brief discussion of the final transformation of British colonial radicalism, after 1900, towards what was apparently a hard socialist form of anti-colonialism, but one that was actually still inflected with this pervasive moralising humanism. A transitional figure here was the socialist and Arabist, Henry St John Philby, another Cambridge product, who emerged from its relativising and critical atmosphere in the first decade of the twentieth century. Philby left Cambridge for service in India at the end of 1908, but spent the critical period of his career after 1914 in what was to become Saudi Arabia as an agent of the Indian government there. He later became a Muslim and worked against British interests in the region.

As he tells us in his autobiography, Philby had started his undergraduate career as a conservative in religion and politics. He even spoke at the Cambridge Union defending the British authorities in Egypt, who had recently executed several Egyptian villagers on charges that all Egyptian nationalists and the several Egyptian undergraduates in Cambridge regarded as grossly unjust. This was to be a key moment in the rise of popular Egyptian nationalism. But Philby's experience in the university itself pushed him rapidly towards a gentleman's version of socialism. One influence here was his mentor, the professor of Persian, E. G. Browne, author of *A Year Amongst the Persians.* Browne himself represented an emerging tradition of scholarship on the Arab world and the East which created a more nuanced understanding both of the Bible and of Islam. Browne had also long been an advocate of Persian independence. He sponsored Persian students in Cambridge. He denounced the Anglo-Russian agreement of 1907 that carved up the country into spheres of influence. In 1909 he staged a public campaign urging the British government to support Persian liberals when the Shah suppressed the new constitutional assembly. Browne also informed Philby's career in a more precise way. Tiring of his usual lectures on Persian one year, Browne breezily subjected his students to an elementary course in Arabic. Socialism and Arabic were the two forces that propelled Philby, a decade later, into the service of Ibn Saud of Arabia.[39]

As British relations with the Ottomans soured after the Young Turks seized power in Istanbul in 1908, the British began to seek allies on the fringes of the Ottoman domains. The eastern reaches of Arabia were critical to British India. They bordered the Persian Gulf, the route to Basra and the south Persian oilfields, soon a key resource for the Royal Navy. An Indian political officer, the evocatively named Captain

William Shakespeare, travelled to meet Ibn Saud. This contact became an alliance and ultimately turned into a flow of money and arms that powerfully aided the rise of the Saudis. It helped to overthrow the rival Hashemite dynasty, Britain's former ally in the region, which had been advised by the Oxford graduates T. E. Lawrence and Gertrude Bell. Despatched by the India Office in 1918 to aid the Saudis, Philby had become convinced that Britain was betraying the Arabs. Thereafter, he worked ceaselessly to promote the cause of Saudi independence and Arab statehood.

In 1924, Ibn Saud occupied the holy sites of Mecca and Madina and began reorganising the pilgrimage in accordance with his purist form of Islam. This was a key moment in the political evolution of the contemporary world. For the Arabian Wahhabis were ideological conservatives, but social radicals. They were deeply hostile to all forms of ritual and spiritual authority associated with the mystical Sufi orders. They aimed to purge Islam of 'innovations' and take the faithful back to the days of the Prophet. Yet they were spiritual egalitarians and their king was merely the first among the faithful. They built model villages and worked to settle the wandering Bedouin to a productive and godly life-style.

It was this simplicity which appealed so much to Philby. He applauded what he took to be the Wahhabi socialistic ethos, claimed that Ibn Saud was a socialist 'democrat' and ultimately converted to Islam himself: this is a classic case of the 'misrecognition' of ideas to which I also alluded to in the case of Andrews. Philby now supported the king against British influence and became instrumental in the discovery of oil in Saudi Arabia. Philby probably did more to constrain the power of the British Empire than his notorious son, the Cambridge spy Kim, ever did.

Earlier modes of British or Anglo-Irish radicalism persisted during and after the First World War; notable here was Margaret Cousins, an Irish nationalist and suffragette, who on being released from prison in 1913 moved to India with her husband and established a series of organisations for Indian women, especially the Indian Woman's Association, which first met in 1914. She later became a close ally and devotee of Mohandas Gandhi and was imprisoned in 1932 for agitation during his civil disobedience movement. Yet it was experience of the Great Depression and the Second World War that finally turned British expatriate radicals towards conspiratorial anti-colonialism and brought them into the socialist international. A representative figure here was Phillip Spratt, product of a lower middle-class Baptist family, who was converted to Communism at Cambridge and was sent to India in 1927 by the British branch of the Comintern to establish underground cells there. Along with most other members of the Indian Communist Party he was arrested, tried in the notorious Meerut Conspiracy case of 1929 and imprisoned, not once but twice.

Yet here we sense that ambivalence about pure political activity and the appeal of radical humanism. As he says in his startlingly titled autobiography, *Blowing up India*, while in prison Spratt became disillusioned with the cynical instrumentalism of the Comintern and its hostility to Gandhi's civil disobedience movement. He read Gandhi's works and was impressed by the concept of 'soul force'. But, like his colleague M. N. Roy, Spratt felt impelled to support the Allied cause during the Second World War and broke, in turn, with Congress. After the war both men founded the Indian Radical Humanist movement, moving far away from 'scientific' Marxism.

This story was repeated more than once among young British Communists who worked with the Indian Left on the Burma Front during the Second World War. They included Sidney Bolt, author of the nicely titled 'Pseudo Sahib', and the great Urdu scholar, Ralph Russell. These men and their like passed information to Indian Communists while denouncing what they saw as the feeble British war effort, as compared with the heroic socialist resistance of the USSR to the Nazis. W. C. Smith, the Cambridge-educated Canadian teacher resident in Lahore, spread leftist propaganda and denounced the feudals of the Punjab before and during the war.[40]

Yet in all these men varieties of spiritual humanism ultimately triumphed and the idiosyncratic nature of British colonial radicalism was revealed anew. Russell became an expert on the Sufi poets in London University. Smith translated the idealist Muslim prophet of Pakistan, Muhammad Iqbal, and ultimately became a Christian professor at Harvard University. A final example of this ambivalent and idiosyncratic British leftism was Tom Driberg, columnist of the radical *Reynolds News*, socialist MP and friend of Louis Mountbatten.

Driberg had been brought up in India, where his father was a civil servant in Assam. In 1945 and 1946, Mountbatten, then Supreme Allied Commander, Southeast Asia, sent Driberg to Burma and Malaya to promote good relations with Aung San and other nationalists who were embattled by the Tory Governor of Burma. He played a small but significant part in the process of decolonisation in the region, confirming Mountbatten's own desire to avoid a rear-guard colonial war of the sort the French were embarking on in Indochina. Yet Driberg's *Times* obituary thirty years later was to state, with unusual candour for this newspaper, that he had been 'a journalist, an intellectual, a drinking man, a gossip, a high churchman, a liturgist and a homosexual'.[41] To add to this eclectic range of interests, many at the time also hinted that he had worked for the KGB.

Conclusion

James Mill once stated that he had no need to carry out an 'ocular investigation' of India. The expatriate radicals I have been discussing all had resorted to such an ocular investigation for longer and shorter periods of time. This, and their closer connection with emerging Asian opinion, meant that their ideas and political projects differed subtly from those of domestic critics of empire who did not move overseas. They were at one and the same time members of, and irritants to, expatriate societies in Asia, reflecting some of their values and rejecting others. Though there have been many individual studies of these people, there have been few attempts to examine their changing ideas over the long term.

There is a good reason for this. British expatriate radicals certainly did not constitute a coherent political tradition in either a Pocock-Skinner or a Koselleck-like tradition. They were mainly mavericks, if not 'nutters', to use Tony Blair's own description of the way the British public viewed the former prime minister and his spiritually informed politics. They throw a good deal of light on the unorthodox backwaters of British intellectual history. Most of these colonial radicals adopted a broadly anti-statist and anti-corporate concept of political economy, supported by detailed local information. But this varied sharply over time. It ranged from a desire for freedom of trade and European colonisation in the 1820s to its exact opposite, socialism and protectionism, by the 1920s. One thing they did have in common, however, was a broad, heterodox spiritual sensibility, whether this was expressed as Christian non-conformism, Theosophy, spiritualised socialism or even gay sexuality.

What, then, was their broader significance? Most of them imagined a reformed empire or even a socialist *ecumene*, rather than free Asian nation-states. From one perspective, their criticism, by nudging domestic opinion towards reform, even indirectly helped to perpetuate empire. A good number of them had been officials, became officials or remained in contact with the Indian and other colonial bureaucracies. Yet, by virtue of their nationality and heterodoxy, they also gave strength to anti-colonialism. They co-authored with Asian public men a language of political resistance, economic development and cultural superiority that profoundly influenced the international discourse of liberal humanism and communitarian socialism over the nineteenth and twentieth centuries.

Notes

1 Robert Bickers (ed.), *Settlers and Expatriates: Britons over the Seas. Oxford History of the British Empire Companion Series* (Oxford: Oxford University Press, 2010).
2 See, for example, P. J. Marshall, *'A Free Though Conquering People': Eighteenth-Century Britain and its Empire* (Aldershot: Ashgate, 2003); P. J. Marshall, *The Making and Unmaking of Empires: Britain, India and America*, c. 1750–1783 (Oxford: Oxford University Press, 2005); Dane Kennedy, *Britain and Empire, 1880–1945* (London: Routledge, 2002); Elizabeth Buettner, *Empire Familes: Britons and Late Imperial India* (Oxford: Oxford University Press, 2004).
3 Jennifer Pitts, *A Turn to Empire: The Rise of Imperial Liberalism in Britain and France* (Princeton: Princeton University Press, 2005); Karuna Mantena, *Alibis of Empire: Henry Maine and the Ends of Liberal Imperialism* (Princeton: Princeton University Press, 2010).
4 See Miles Taylor, *The Decline of British Radicalism* (Oxford: Clarendon Press, 1995); Gregory Claeys, *Imperial Sceptics: British Critics of Empire 1850–1920* (Cambridge: Cambridge University Press, 2010); Edward C. Moulton, 'Alan Octavian Hume and the Indian National Congress: A Reassessment', *Journal of South Asian Studies*, 8 (1985), 5–23; Mira Matikkala, *Empire and Imperial Ambition: Liberty, Englishness and Anti-Imperialism in Late Victorian Britain* (London: I. B. Tauris, 2011); Bernard Porter, *Critics of Empire: British Radicals and the Imperial Challenge* (London: I. B. Tauris, 2008); and Stephen Howe, *Anticolonialism in British Politics: The Left and the End of Empire, 1918–1964* (Oxford: Clarendon Press, 1993).
5 Linda Colley, 'Gendering the Globe: The Political and Imperial Thought of Philip Francis', *Past and Present*, 209 (2010), 117–48.
6 Emma Rothschild, *The Inner Life of Empires: An Eighteenth-Century History* (Princeton: Princeton University Press, 2011).
7 Sir John Malcolm, *The Political History of India (1784–1823)*, 2, ed. K. N. Panikkar (1826, Delhi: Associated Publishing House, 1970), pp. 167–8.
8 'Letters to Sir Charles Forbes, Bart., MP, on the benefits of a free press to the natives of India', *Oriental Herald*, 2, July–August 1824, p. 534.
9 Joseph Burnley Hume, *Joseph Hume. A Memorial* (London: John W. Parker & Son, 1855).
10 Lynn Zastoupil, *Rammohan Roy and the Making of Victorian Britain* (Basingstoke: Palgrave, 2010).
11 *Bengal Hurkaru*, 5 December 1829.
12 *Calcutta Review*, 11, January–June 1849, pp. 73–8.
13 Blair Kling, *Partner in Empire* (Berkeley: University of California Press, 1976), p. 171.
14 Petition of Indo Britons to the House of Lords, 29 March 1830, *India Gazette*, 6 September 1831.
15 Sandford Arnot, *A Sketch of the History of the Indian Press During the Past Ten Years, with a Disclosure of the True Causes of its Present Degradation, etc...* (London, 1829), p. 21.
16 See C. A. Bayly, *Recovering Liberties: Indian Thought in the Age of Liberalism and Empire* (Cambridge: Cambridge University Press, 2011), ch. 3.
17 Miles Taylor, 'The 1848 Revolutions and the British Empire', *Past and Present*, 166 (2000), 146–80.
18 *Dictionary of National Biography* (1917), 19, p. 691; George Jacob Holyoke, *Sixty Years of an Agitator's Life* (London, 1892), 1, p. 98; B. B. Majumdar, *History of Political Thought from Rammohun to Dayananda (1821–84)* (Calcutta: The University of Calcutta, 1934), pp. 170–5.
19 G. Thompson, *Addresses Delivered at Meetings of the Native Community of Calcutta and on Other Occasions by G. Thompson* (Calcutta: Thacker & Co, 1843), p. 5.
20 G. Thompson, speech at Paisley, 20 November 1838, *Bombay Times*, 29 May 1839.
21 G. Thompson, speech at Paisley, 20 November 1838.

22 Thompson, *Addresses*, p. 167.
23 *Bengal Spectator*, 15 October 1842.
24 Cited in Thompson, *Addresses*, p. 65.
25 Kling, *Partners in Empire*, p. 108.
26 Eugenio Biagini, 'The Politics of "Italianism"; Reynolds's Newspaper and the Radical Critique of Liberal Imperialism in mid-Victorian Britain.' Unpublished paper in author's possession.
27 Claeys, *Imperial Sceptics*.
28 William Wedderburn, *Allan Octavian Hume: Father of the Indian National Congress* (1913, reprint New Delhi: Pegasus, 1974), p. 79.
29 Wedderburn, *Allan Octavian Hume*, p. 81.
30 Annie Besant, *Why I Became a Theosophist* (London: Freethought Publishing Co., 1889).
31 Annie Besant, *Autobiographical Sketches* (London: Freethought Publishing Co., 1885).
32 Frederick C. Charles, 'English Socialists and India', *Bengalee*, 2 January 1907.
33 The fullest recent study of Carpenter is Antony Copley, *Gay Writers in Search of the Divine. Hinduism and Homosexuality in the lives and Writings of Edward Carpenter, E. M. Forster and Christopher Isherwood* (New Delhi: Yoda Press, 2006).
34 *Bengalee*, 2 January 1907.
35 Copley, *Gay Writers in Search of the Divine*.
36 James Brow, 'Utopia's New-found Space: Images of the Village Community in the Early Writings of Ananda Coomaraswamy', *Modern Asian Studies*, 33 (1999), 67–86.
37 Coomaraswamy's speech to the Madras Mahajana Sabha, *Bengalee*, 29 January 1907.
38 Sidney and Beatrice Webb, *Indian Diary*, ed. N. G. Jayal (Delhi: Oxford University Press, 1987), p. 150.
39 Henry St John Philby, *Arabian Days, An Autobiography* (London: Robert Hale Limited, 1948).
40 Wilfrid Cantwell Smith, *Modern Islam in India. A Social Analysis* (London: Victor Gollancz, 1946).
41 Francis Wheen, *Tom Driberg. His Life and Indiscretions* (London: Chatto & Windus, 1990), p. 2.

CHAPTER THREE

Sugar wars: the culture of free trade versus the culture of anti-slavery in Britain and the British Caribbean, 1840–50

Philip Harling

One might well say that Britain lost its soul to its sweet tooth in 1846. For in that year of the cheap sugar loaf as well as the cheap bread loaf, the House of Commons by a comfortable majority slated for execution the protective duties that had long given British Caribbean sugar a huge advantage in the home market. Before 1833 those duties had of course protected a slave-based system of production. But after emancipation they were seen to protect the 'great experiment' in free-labour sugar from the slave-made sugar of Cuba and Brazil, which was cheaper to produce and taking an ever-growing share of the world market. So widely felt was the need to safeguard British West Indian ex-slaves and planters from direct competition with slave sugar in 1833 that MPs rejected the Radical free-trader Joseph Hume's motion for sugar-duty equalisation by a ten-to-one margin. Only thirteen years later almost twice as many MPs voted for as against the Sugar Duties Bill that Lord John Russell's Whig-Liberal ministry introduced as soon as it took office. While for many years foreign sugar had laboured under a whopping duty, by this measure all sugar, regardless of source, was scheduled to enter Britain at a nominal rate from 1851 forward. Planters and their Tory allies mounted a spirited rear-guard attack on the Sugar Act, but managed to stave off full equalisation only until 1854. When the Tories briefly returned to power in 1852, they made it clear that they would do nothing to reverse free trade in sugar. British West Indian sugar had lost its protected status for good.[1]

Most of the scholars who have closely examined the Sugar Duties Act conclude that it was not just one of the last nails in the coffin of the old colonial system[2] and not just the moment when sucrose consumption became a national pastime.[3] It was also a symptom of abolitionism's political decline,[4] and the trigger for an economic decline throughout the British Caribbean that lingered most painfully in Jamaica. The Sugar Duties Act was a short-term disaster for virtually all of the West Indian colonies because sugar prices plummeted in its wake, pushing many planters, already heavily in debt, over the brink.[5] Over the next decade or so Barbados recovered because its high population density afforded ex-slaves with few alternatives to plantation labour. Trinidad and British Guiana also recovered because the immigration of indentured workers ultimately more than compensated for ex-slaves' flight from the sugar estates. But in Jamaica, where flight from the estates was especially dramatic, political divisions and, especially, high levels of debt ruled out large-scale immigration as a viable solution to the plantation labour shortage.[6] So while by the 1860s sugar production had not only rebounded from the depression of the late 1840s but far exceeded pre-emancipation levels in Barbados, British Guiana and Trinidad, in Jamaica production had fallen by 60 per cent between 1835 and 1865.[7] The free-sugar economy there was manifestly failing to compete, while the only thing that seemed to save other large colonies was an indentured-labour regime that looked suspiciously like slavery to many humanitarians.[8] In the meantime, the Caribbean economic crisis provoked a steep decline in British sympathy toward emancipees, as white opinion targeted the putative indolence of ex-slaves as its chief cause.

Thus the Sugar Duties Act plays a prominent role in accounts that chronicle the growing white disenchantment with freed blacks in the British Caribbean generally and Jamaica in particular.[9] These accounts, in turn, inform Catherine Hall's more recent and broadly influential account of the decline of humanitarianism and the rise of racialised metropolitan resentment toward the freed people of Jamaica.[10] Hall's account, in its turn, bolsters a well-established scholarly tendency to argue for a relatively sharp mid-century shift in British perceptions of the empire, a shift that was accelerated by such scarifying episodes as the Morant Bay rising, the Maori Wars, and the Indian Rebellion. That shift saw the crumbling of an early Victorian emphasis on the universal improvability of humankind, and its replacement by a later Victorian emphasis on the explicitly racial inferiority of subject peoples, their limited (or even non-existent) capacity to climb up the civilisational ladder and their unfitness for self-government in the foreseeable future.[11]

My argument here is not that this declensionist account of mid-Victorian humanitarianism is inaccurate, or that free trade in sugar does not merit a prominent place in that account. Indeed, there are three points about the story of free trade in sugar that bolster the declensionist account. The first is that the Colonial Office and colonial governors were convinced that *laissez-faire* shock therapy was the only way to discipline workers and planters alike into competitiveness, and that any pain this caused in the short term was simply in the providential order of things. The second point is how thoroughly official opinion came to equate ex-slaves' desire for some measure of autonomy from the plantation system with indolence and waywardness, and how thoroughly the Colonial Office and its minions came to embrace labour discipline as by far the most urgent solution to the West Indian crisis. The third point is that the imperative to shore up the plantation economy led these same proponents of *laissez-faire* to commit the imperial government to the sponsorship of assisted immigration as a chief solution to high labour costs. A fourth and final point I wish to make, however, is that notwithstanding its ruthless approach to the West Indian crisis, the Russell government did not entirely abandon its commitment to humanitarianism. Indeed, it staunchly and successfully defended its commitment to slave-trade suppression even when that commitment was seriously challenged in the wake of the Sugar Duties Act. The leaders of the Whig-Liberal government welcomed free trade in sugar, but they refused to abide a free trade in slaves.[12] This fact does not in itself rebut the pessimist narrative of the 1840s and 1850s, but it adds some nuance to it. Thus, in the end, this is an economic story that had deeply significant but ambiguous cultural implications. To the minds of virtually all British observers at the time, the 'British world' of the mid-nineteenth century was a world dedicated to the advancement of global free trade as a civilisational imperative. It was also a world that was supposed to remain dedicated to the promotion of global anti-slavery as a civilisational imperative. But reconciling these imperatives with each other proved to be an extremely awkward balancing act.

The Sugar Duties Act provoked an economic crisis in the British Caribbean. The bottom dropped out of sugar prices in its wake, greatly compromising planters' ability to pay wages that had skyrocketed in the face of post-apprenticeship labour shortages triggered by ex-slaves' flight from the estates. Planters' woes were greatly exacerbated by the financial crash of 1847–48 that claimed many banks both in London and in the colonies. Heavily leveraged planters went to the wall as their debts were called in. Those who survived found it next to impossible to get credit.[13] Planters sought a return to protection as the obvious solution to their troubles. But they extracted few concessions from the Russell government – the postponement of equalisation from 1851 to 1854, lower duties on rum and a low-interest £500,000 loan to promote immigration and capital improvements to be divvied up among the larger sugar colonies.[14] A bitter and desperate plantocracy now turned on the imperial government as the chief author of its woes. But the Russell administration did not budge in the face of the planters' recriminations. Its point-man for the West Indian crisis was the third Earl Grey (Viscount Howick until the death of his father, the former prime minister, in 1845). Grey was an ardent political economist and doctrinaire free trader. He was utterly convinced that putting a final end to protective duties was the only way to lower high prices and wages and thus make West Indian sugar competitive in the long run.[15] Indeed, Grey insisted that protection had been at the root of the economic crisis in the British Caribbean because it had artificially raised sugar prices, which in turn had artificially raised workers' wages to a point that ex-slaves could afford to work fewer days and shorter hours on the sugar estates. '[I]t is by reducing both prices and wages to their natural amount', he affirmed, 'that I hope to see the cost of production brought back to its due proportions, and a sound basis established for that energy, enterprise, and improvement by which the cultivation may be again rendered remunerative.'[16] Grey was resolute in his insistence that planters must no longer 'indulge in the visionary expectation that their former protection can possibly be re-established. Such an expectation could only lead to disappointment.'[17] Planters simply needed to weather the storm rather than 'yield[ing] to the panic of their present situation'. Looking back on the crisis, Grey insisted that while free trade may have been a bitter pill, it was simply for their own good that he had forced the plantocracy to swallow it.[18]

Even many of Grey's colonial governors who viewed the crisis from much closer to the ground remained remarkably detached from the wreckage that free trade left in its wake. Almost half of all Jamaican estates were either sold off or wound down between 1844 and 1854,[19] while in British Guiana the number of estates under staple production fell by over 40 per cent between 1838 and 1853.[20] Representatives of the imperial government shed few tears for the planters who had gone under. 'Proprietors without capital, without energy, without method, without resources of any kind, held two-thirds of the property of the island,' President Edward Dacres Baynes wrote from Montserrat. '[I]s it possible that any country could thrive in such hands? The island has at length been happily delivered from these dead weights.'[21] This notion that retributive justice had been meted out to the improvident tasted of the Christian political economy that influenced so many British public men in the 1830s and 1840s.[22] But no less prominent in imperial statesmen's response to the West Indian crisis was a defiantly optimistic faith in the providential blessings of economic growth and social comity that free trade was bound to bring so long as Britain did not permit its Caribbean charges to stray from the true path. 'It is hard for men to give up what they have considered their own,' Lord Harris, the Governor of Trinidad, conceded in pondering the collateral damage done by free trade in sugar. Still, 'matters are now as nearly as possible at their worst; artificial assistance will do little or nothing. Those who have energy, enterprise and capital may still continue to cultivate the soil ... and a natural state of things be produced which will place matters upon a more wholesome footing.'[23]

This potent blend of retributive providentialism and free-trade optimism was a marked feature of the Russell government's approach to free trade in the Caribbean, and indeed was even more conspicuous in its response to the infinitely graver Potato Famine crisis that was overwhelming Ireland at this very time.[24] Peter Gray has shown that its response to the Great Famine was dominated by a trio of 'liberal moralists' – Sir Charles Wood and Charles Trevelyan at the Treasury and Wood's brother-in-law, the third Earl Grey himself. In the famine they saw the providential destruction of incompetent landlords and hapless cottiers and a chance to replace the backward potato economy for which they stood with a pasture-oriented export market based on the hyper-efficient English model. They also showed a tight-fistedness and a dogged faith in the power of free markets to allocate resources in famine conditions that undoubtedly cost Irish lives. The struggle in the West Indies was not a matter of life and death on a vast scale, as it was in famine Ireland. But free trade created real turmoil in the British Caribbean in the late 1840s, and the imperial authorities, firm in their rectitude, were not inclined to let this bother them. Indeed, from their Olympian perch it seemed they could scarcely discern the bitterness of the struggle to uphold the sugar monoculture in the wake of free trade. That struggle pitted planters who were desperate to increase sugar production at lower costs against emancipated slaves who sought to escape the estates to the fullest possible extent. The flight from plantation labour – already dramatic in the years after the abolition of apprenticeship in larger colonies with relatively low population densities – now seemed a dire threat to planters who were fighting to preserve their estates. Now that protection was no longer an option, they felt a desperate need to secure steadier labour at lower wages from ex-slaves who sought to maximise their autonomy by minimising their dependence on sugar work. In the fight to secure a more disciplined plantation workforce, frustrated planters equated this quest for autonomy with indolence, ignorance and recalcitrance. The Colonial Office and colonial governors, sharing the planters' imperatives, tended to view the ex-slaves in the same negative light.

Once apprenticeship came to an end in the late 1830s, many ex-slaves were able to enjoy a much greater measure of freedom by squatting on uncultivated land or by purchasing it, which they managed to do (often collectively) despite frequent legislative and less-formal efforts to block land sales to them.[25] The growth of smallholdings was most dramatic in larger, less densely populated colonies – notably Trinidad, British Guiana and especially Jamaica, where by the mid-1840s two-thirds of ex-slaves formerly resident on plantations had moved away from them.[26] Most freed people sought to balance estate work against provision-gardening on their smallholdings, minimising the former and maximising the latter in a moral economy through which they sought optimal autonomy and the dignity and self-esteem that came with it. Since labour was scarce, ex-slaves were able to command higher wages for it, which in turn made such labour even scarcer by giving ex-slaves greater wherewithal to avoid it.[27]

The rationality of freed people's desire to escape the sugar estates to the fullest extent possible, so obvious to us, was not entirely lost on imperial and colonial authorities at the time.[28] But a far more common reaction was to bemoan the ostensible laziness, waywardness and bad faith of freed people who could not be trusted to work regularly because high wages gave them the means to avoid it. As Douglas Hall pointed out,[29] the 'myth of the lazy Negro' was fully on display in planters' testimony before Lord George Bentinck's Select Committee on Sugar and Coffee Planting even before Thomas Carlyle published his infamous portrait of 'Quashee'.[30] In this Caribbean variation of the capitalist's lament,[31] workers who sought to maximise their freedom on the job and from the job were damned for their stubborn indolence. (It is worth noting here the contrast with the post-Second World War Hong Kong Chinese workers described by Mark Hampton in Chapter Eight of this volume, who were praised for their putative addiction to incessant labour. This was a vastly different British world from the one I describe here, but one no less dedicated to free trade as an organising principle, and no less inclined to the racial stereotyping of colonised workers.) Thus one planter complained that '[s]ome of them will work two days in the week, and others will be idle the whole week, and work the whole of the next week'.[32] Another lamented that whereas 'in Cuba they work 18 hours a day, and every day in the week, at crop time', on his own estate in Antigua 'you could not get anything like the work you wanted out of them; some days they would work five or six hours, and some days more or less'.[33] A Jamaican planter complained of his workers' addiction to holiday-making, concluding that 'I do not know any population in any part of the world that I have visited more at their ease than the negro population of Jamaica.'[34] Planters were frustrated that they had precious few means to coax more work out of ex-slaves, since, as one owner of broad acres in British Guiana lamented, 'there is no such thing as poverty in that country, and it is quite impossible that it can exist, because any man can support himself by putting a few plantain roots into the ground'. 'The only hold we have on the negro', he concluded, 'is, the desire for the comforts of civilized life.' While that desire was strong in the heady days just after emancipation, 'I am afraid the effects of the last few years have been rather to diminish his desire for ... luxuries'.[35] Thus the planters who came to Westminster to testify in the depths of the crisis of the late 1840s had come to view as a curse the relative self-sufficiency and self-fulfilment of the ex-slaves who enjoyed access to the land. Their contentment was a bane, because that contentment seemed to depend on little beyond a subsistence that was all too easily secured without much recourse to plantation work.

To the planters, colonial officials and imperial governors who saw the British Caribbean through a 'sugared lens',[36] any alternative to sugar monoculture was, almost literally, unthinkable. We will never know how far market gardening might have emerged as a viable option in colonies such as Jamaica, Trinidad and British Guiana, because market gardening counted for nothing in the official mind. What mattered was the production of sugar and (to a lesser degree) coffee for the export market by relatively large and hence (it was assumed) more efficient units of production. It was a Victorian commonplace that peasant smallholdings stood in the way of agricultural progress, so their development was stymied in places where it might have done powerful social and political and indeed probably even economic good – stymied even much closer to home in Ireland, never mind Jamaica.[37] Not until the *fin de siècle* did British or colonial authorities see smallholdings as anything more than a nuisance, and in the mid-Victorian British Caribbean they saw them not just as a nuisance but as a dire threat to the sugar monoculture. In line with these assumptions, planters warned that if the plantation system was permitted to erode much further they would have no choice but to leave, in which case 'the retrogression of the inhabitants ... must be fearfully accelerated',[38] they 'must relapse into a state of savagery',[39] they must 'subside into a state of comparative barbarism'.[40] Planters had seen the post-sugar apocalypse, and it looked like Haiti. Thus, in line with the broader themes of this volume, it is worth stressing here that the 'British world' of the mid-nineteenth century was a world bound together by free trade and the production of cash crops for a global market. These were economic shibboleths, but of course they were thought to have profound cultural consequences. To metropolitan and colonial authorities alike, free trade was the only path to civilisational progress, while peasant self-sufficiency inevitably led to crushing poverty and regression down the civilisational ladder.

In order to prevent this nightmare scenario from becoming reality, the Caribbean plantocracies took decisive measures to keep freed people working in sugar and to thwart their efforts to make for themselves a life apart from the estates. Legal efforts to block the development of an independent peasantry were ubiquitous, and most potent where the planters had the strongest hold on the levers of government, notably British Guiana and Trinidad. Planters used a powerful arsenal to stymie an alternative peasant economy – restrictions on land purchase, the tightening of legal controls over freedom of movement away from the estates[41] and a fiscal system that shifted virtually the whole tax burden onto the labouring population.[42] The Colonial Office rarely stood in their way, and often abetted them.

Perhaps the most dramatic means by which planters sought to shore up the sugar hegemony was through an attack on workers' wages, and in this attack they were strongly encouraged by the Colonial Office. Planters had already made significant efforts to rein in wages even before passage of the Sugar Duties Act,[43] for during the initial flight from the estates in the years after the abolition of apprenticeship in 1838, workers' wages had risen sharply, while sugar production plummeted. Those efforts became more desperate in the late 1840s, when the survival of the plantation system seemed to depend on lower wages and a more reliable pool of labour. Wages fell 20 to 50 per cent throughout the British Caribbean in the decade after 1846, with the sharpest cuts coming in the late 1840s. Planters' attacks on wages provoked sporadic violence, especially in British Guiana, where the early months of 1848 were marked by strikes and incendiarism. But the Guyanese workers were quickly brought to heel, and the wage cuts continued apace.[44]

While wage reductions helped, the *deus ex machina* for the planters was the immigration of enough coolie labour to drive and keep wages down and thus to make sugar estates profitable. The Colonial Office helped to provide them with the cheap labour they sought, facilitating the indentured servitude of thousands of immigrants every year from the late 1840s forward in the most notable abdication of its humanitarian authority in the transition to a free-trade British Caribbean. Planters in the West Indies and Mauritius had already experimented with the importation of indentured workers from India in the late 1830s, in order to cope with the exodus of blacks from the plantations that resulted from the end of apprenticeship. But the Colonial Office had called a halt to it out of concern that high mortality and oppressive working conditions made indentured servitude look too much like slavery. But economic pressures quickly got the better of the imperial government's paternalism. Indentured immigration to Mauritius resumed in 1843. After several years of fitful experiments, indentured immigration to Trinidad and British Guiana took off in the late 1840s as the preferred antidote to the labour crisis. Over the next three-quarters of a century indentured servitude was a salient fact of life from Natal to Queensland. This was a highly coercive and discriminatory labour regime – a 'blurring of the line between bondage and slavery'[45] – to which almost half a million workers had been subjected by the time it came to an end after the First World War, the majority of them in Mauritius, British Guiana or Trinidad.[46]

More than anything else, it was indentured immigration, aided and abetted by the imperial government, which saved the sugar monoculture in Trinidad and British Guiana from the free-trade crisis of the late 1840s. In a further tarnishing of the Colonial Office's humanitarian credentials, it helped the planters to meet that crisis by arranging for the transfer of thousands of Africans rescued from slave ships by the Royal Navy to these and a handful of other West Indian colonies, where they worked as indentured labourers on the sugar estates. The navy had been intercepting slavers in the Atlantic ever since the abolition of the British slave trade in 1807. Most of the Africans thus 'recaptured' were sent to Sierra Leone or St Helena. For decades, a good many of these liberated Africans had been recruited into the African Corps and the West India regiments. By the latter 1840s the Colonial Office was making a vigorous effort to recruit recaptives to immigrate to the sugar estates. Not surprisingly, it remained a challenging business to persuade Africans who had just been forcibly taken from their homes and subjected to the terrors of the slave ship to set sail once again and move yet another world away. But the recruitment effort met with some success nevertheless. Over the full history of government-sponsored immigration of recaptives, from 1841 to 1867, some 36,000 Africans were shipped to the West Indies.[47] In British Guiana and Trinidad these recaptives played a significant role in forcing wages down and coaxing ex-slaves back to more-regular estate labour, even before the influx of Indian immigrants from the 1850s forward. The indentured system could not have been put in place without the active support of an imperial government that saw no future without sugar for the British West Indies, and that was quite willing to compromise its *laissez-faire* and humanitarian credentials to ensure that future.

For all its ruthlessness in pursuing free trade in sugar, however, the Russell government did not completely drop humanitarianism from its imperial agenda for the West Indies. In the wake of the Sugar Duties Act Britain's long-standing commitment to slave-trade suppression came under serious political assault. That assault would very likely have succeeded had Russell and Palmerston, outspoken defenders of the British government's anti-slavery tradition, not offered staunch resistance to it. Britain's anti-slavery reputation at home and abroad rested to a significant extent on its efforts to suppress the Atlantic slave trade through armed force. Between 1810 and 1864 Royal Navy cruisers captured over 1,200 slave ships and liberated some 150,000 slaves. While the number of cruisers detached to the African Squadron that did the vast bulk of the slaver-catching varied considerably over time, it reached a peak of twenty-four vessels by the late 1840s, employing a sixth of the navy's total strength and costing British taxpayers some £750,000 a year.[48] The Russell government's problem was that the Brazilian slave trade (declared illegal in a bilateral treaty with Britain in 1830) reached its peak in the late 1840s – on the order of 50,000–60,000 slaves a year – despite the unparalleled vigour of British coercion. The Sugar Duties Act was providing a fillip to the Brazilian slave trade, as sugar output responded to the opening of the British market. Brazilian slavers were formidably organised, abolitionist sentiment in Brazil was merely nascent, much of Rio's elite was deeply implicated in the illegal slave trade and the Brazilian government seemed disinclined at best to lift a finger against it.[49] Critics were now arguing that the Squadron was such an abject failure that it needed to be wound up entirely.[50]

William Hutt, Radical free-trade MP for Gateshead, emerged as the leading critic of the African Squadron. In March 1850 he forced a show-down on the cruisers by moving a resolution asking that the government withdraw from all its treaties that required force to suppress the slave trade. Hutt argued that the British state had spent some £25 million on a coercive system that had manifestly failed, and that it was past time to end this 'reckless disregard of expenditure' and let the laws of supply and demand kill off the slave trade in their own good time.[51] Seconding Hutt's motion, Henry Baillie taunted the government that naval suppression was not only an abject failure but rank hypocrisy, in light of the Sugar Duties Act, by which Britons were benefitting as never before from slave sugar, and hence from the Brazilian slave trade. It was high time, Baillie concluded, to 'declare to the nations of the world that in England free trade was at length triumphant and that the slave trade must proceed'.[52]

When Russell stood to answer Hutt and Baillie, the outcome was in doubt. An influential section of the press was now staunchly opposed to the African Squadron, notably the *Times* and the *Economist*.[53] Exeter Hall was of no assistance, as the Quaker-dominated British and Foreign Anti-Slavery Society was committed to strict pacifism, and thus was dead-set against the cruisers.[54] Russell and Palmerston had long insisted that the obverse of free trade in sugar had to be a vigorous suppression policy.[55] But they could no longer assume that the Whig-Liberal rank and file shared their faith in suppression as a necessary accompaniment to free trade, or indeed even their hatred of the slave trade. Russell's and, especially, Palmerston's hatred for it was real enough. A notoriously carnal gentleman of the old school who was named co-respondent in a divorce case while serving as prime minister at the age of seventy-eight,[56] Palmerston ('Lord Cupid') would seem the least likely of British public men to speak the language of providentialism and atonement. Yet he frequently did so in pronouncing judgement against the slave trade. 'Great Britain [was] the instrument in the hand of Providence' for its suppression, he insisted, and it was 'in vain ... to endeavour to resist the consummation of that which is written in the book of fate'.[57] For Palmerston, slave-trade suppression was a mission from God, a mission, moreover, that, in the ubiquitously arrogant view of his day, the people at the top of the civilisational ladder owed to those at the bottom.

While Lord John Russell was not as habitually outspoken as Palmerston on the evils of the slave trade, on the morning of the division on Hutt's motion he made it perfectly clear to the 160 Whig-Liberal MPs whom he gathered at 10 Downing Street that he and Palmerston would resign if it passed. He offered three reasons why they needed to stop Hutt, and why he and Palmerston would resign if they did not. First of all, if the Squadron were removed and the slave trade allowed to proceed 'totally unchecked and unrestricted', then:

> Brazil would receive vast multitudes of slaves, and ... such an increased cultivation, that our colonies would be quite unable to sustain the competition.... It would [then] be said that while we permitted and almost encouraged the Slave Trade in favour of Brazil, it were unjust and unfair to deprive our own colonies of African labour procured by the purchase of slaves in Africa to be set free in Jamaica and Trinidad.

This line of reasoning would, secondly, lead to the resumption of slavery in the British Caribbean. The reason why emancipation there was practicable in the first place, Russell argued, was because 'our slaves long settled in our colonies had attained a very considerable degree of civilisation'. This would not be true of a vast flood of newcomers. 'Great masses of Africans, arriving wild and savage in the West Indies, would require to be kept in order by laws of restraint and coercion which would amount in fact, though not in name, to a restoration of slavery. Thus the motion which is to be proposed to you leads, by logical and almost necessary steps, to the restoration of the British Slave Trade and Slavery.' Finally, Russell concluded, the long Whig tradition of anti-slavery obliged them to stand fast against Hutt's motion.[58]

Russell's threat of resignation was enough to defeat Hutt by 232 votes to 154. Palmerston and Russell wasted no time in following up this victory with an all-out assault on the Brazilian slave trade. In the spring of 1850 they authorised the Admiralty to attack suspected slave ships in Brazilian waters and even to send landing parties to destroy barracoons on shore. British warships quickly set upon slavers wherever they found them. The Brazilian government, itself not immune to the abolitionist sentiment that had lately been making headway in Brazil, knew there was little it could do to stop the Royal Navy. Faced with the prospect of a full-blown blockade, it pushed through a new anti-slave-trade law in September 1850 and set about enforcing it.[59] Once the Brazilians started actively cooperating with the British, the slave trade tailed off remarkably quickly, and was virtually extinct by 1853.[60] Thus Palmerston's and Russell's aggressive policy was amply vindicated by the results. Even the *Economist*, which for years had habitually attacked the Squadron on free-trade and cheap-government grounds, acknowledged that coercion had worked brilliantly in Brazil.[61] In 1858 Hutt, nothing if not persistent, proposed yet another motion against the cruisers. This time he lost by a ten-to-one margin, and Palmerston did not miss the chance to remind MPs that British naval intervention had made a pivotal difference in Brazil.[62] Palmerston lived long enough to see coercion vindicated once again in the closing of the Cuban slave trade, quickly choked off once the American as well as the British navy was committed to the interception of slavers by the Washington Treaty of 1862.[63]

In drawing attention to Palmerston and Russell's humanitarian motives, one must be careful to avoid reverting to the whiggish late-Victorian scholarly world of Lecky, for whom the British war on slavery and the slave trade ranked '"among the three or four perfectly virtuous pages comprised in the history of nations"'.[64] Slave-trade suppression was not 'a policy animated by purely philanthropic motives'.[65] One important motive for the naval blitz of 1850 was clearly pragmatic – to try to mitigate some of the immense damage that free trade in sugar had inflicted on the British Caribbean. While, moreover, the Brazilian campaign was indeed justifiable on humanitarian grounds and in conformity with existing treaties, it nevertheless provided one of but too many examples of how, as Sidney Herbert put it, '"Palmerston c[ould] never resist shaking his fist in the face of anyone he is not afraid of."'[66] The other examples were far less justifiable. Even if the Brazilian intervention was a uniquely virtuous episode in the annals of Palmerstonian gunboat diplomacy, it did precious little to mitigate the free-trade shock therapy that the Russell administration had prescribed for the West Indies. Over the next several years, as the sugar economy came back slowly (as in Trinidad and British Guiana) or scarcely at all (as in Jamaica), there was indeed a perceptible hardening of racial attitudes. This hardening of attitudes, in turn, *did* help to provoke the antagonisms that made thinkable the brutal violence with which Governor Eyre suppressed the Morant Bay rebellion in 1865, an episode that epitomised the decline of humanitarianism and fellow-feeling in the mid-Victorian empire.

Nevertheless, humanitarianism did not completely die out. If it had, Hutt's motion would have passed and a de facto free trade in slaves along the lines prophesied by Russell would likely have followed. If it had, Governor Eyre would have been universally lauded as an imperial hero for his draconian suppression of the Morant Bay uprising. He was not. The likes of Carlyle and Dickens hailed him as such, but John Stuart Mill, Thomas Henry Huxley and their colleagues on the Jamaica Committee sought to have him brought up on murder charges. Eyre was feted by his supporters when he returned to England, but he was also burnt in effigy by a throng of his detractors. The Jamaica Committee never managed successfully to prosecute Eyre for murder or anything else. But Eyre never received another government appointment and it took eight years and a change of government before he was granted his pension.[67]

To equate the argument between Eyre and Mill as 'the narcissism of minor differences'[68] is to trivialise the major tensions between authoritarianism and humanitarianism in British perceptions of empire; neither ever managed to sweep the other from the field. Authoritarianism tended to prevail from the late 1850s, but humanitarianism never faded away. (This is a point strongly reinforced in a very different context by Michelle Tusan in the next chapter of this volume). Without the importance of humanitarianism to Britons' perceptions of themselves, it is impossible to understand the abiding commitment to anti-slavery, as seen in the huge British readership for *Uncle Tom's Cabin* and in Harriet Beecher Stowe's visit to England in 1853,[69] in the phenomenal popularity of Livingstone's *Missionary Travels* (1857)[70] and in the sporadic but persistent British efforts to suppress the East African slave trade from the 1860s forward.[71] Admittedly, anti-slavery was very frequently a device by which Britons could congratulate themselves on being better than everybody else.[72] Admittedly, the consequences of 'sudden' emancipation in the West Indies convinced British authorities that they should move much more slowly to de-legalise slavery in Africa, as they had done in India.[73] Admittedly, anti-slavery in the *fin-de-siècle* heyday of empire could be used as a convenient justification for conquest, as it was by Frederick Lugard in his assaults on the Sokoto Caliphate.[74] But it is still worth remembering that anti-slavery as an ideal to which Britons felt the need to live up lingered on for decades after 1850.[75] None of this is meant to fundamentally challenge the pessimist story of humanitarianism in the mid-Victorian British Empire. It is simply to note that this is a complicated story, and that, at the very least, the humanitarian impulse never completely faded away.

Acknowledgement

Many thanks to Richard Huzzey and Mark Hampton for their perceptive and helpful comments on earlier drafts of this essay.

Notes

1 Seymour Drescher, *The Mighty Experiment: Free Labor versus Slavery in British Emancipation* (New York and Oxford: Oxford University Press, 2002), pp. 138–4; Robert Livingston Schuyler, *The Fall of the Old Colonial System: A Study in British Free Trade 1770–1870* (London: Oxford University Press, 1945), pp. 138–40, 151–2; C. Duncan Rice, '"Humanity Sold for Sugar!" The British Abolitionist Response to Free Trade in slave-Grown Sugar', *Historical Journal*, 13 (1970), 402–18.

2 See esp. Eric Williams, *Capitalism and Slavery* (New York: G. P. Putnam's Sons edn, 1966), chs 8–9; Anthony Howe, *Free Trade and Liberal England, 1846–1946* (Oxford: Oxford University Press, 1997), ch. 2.

3 Sidney Mintz, *Sweetness and Power: The Place of Sugar in Modern History* (New York and London: Penguin Books,1986), esp. pp. 72–3, 118–19, 129–34, 143, 186. Sugar accounted for nearly one in every five calories of the English diet by 1900 (p. 6).

4 For an especially influential account of which see Catherine Hall, *Civilising Subjects: Colony and Metropole in the English Imagination, 1830–1867* (Chicago and London: University of Chicago Press, 2002), ch. 6.

5 William A. Green, *British Slave Emancipation: The Sugar Colonies and the Great Experiment 1830–1865* (Oxford: Oxford University Press, 1976), pp. 402–3; Douglas Hall, *Free Jamaica 1838–1865: An Economic History* (New Haven, CT: Yale University Press, 1959), p. 1; Williams, *Capitalism and Slavery* p. 153.

6 Philip Curtin, 'The British Sugar Duties and West Indian Prosperity', *Journal of Economic History*, 14 (1954), 157–64.

7 Green, *British Slave Emancipation*, p. 245.

8 Drescher, *The Mighty Experiment*, esp. ch. 10; Seymour Drescher, *Abolition: A History of Slavery and Antislavery* (Cambridge and New York: Cambridge University Press, 2009), pp. 277–83; Howard Temperley, *British Antislavery 1833–1870* (Columbia: University of South Carolina Press, 1972), ch. 6.

9 Philip Curtin, *Two Jamaicas: The Role of Ideas in a Tropical Colony 1830–1865* (New York: Atheneum, 1970); Hall, *Free Jamaica*; Green, *British Slave Emancipation*; Thomas C. Holt, *The Problem of Freedom: Race, Labor, and Politics in Jamaica and Britain, 1832–1938* (Baltimore and London: Johns Hopkins University Press, 1992).

10 Catherine Hall, *Civilising Subjects* (2002).

11 See, e.g., Ronald Hyam, *Britain's Imperial Century, 1815–1914: A Study of Empire and Expansion* (Basingstoke: Palgrave Macmillan, 3rd edn, 2002), ch. 2; Niall Ferguson, *Empire* (New York: Basic Books, 2002), ch. 3.

12 Richard Huzzey has deftly explored the awkward ideological balancing act between Free Trade and anti-slavery as it was carried out in the late 1840s and early 1850s – not only in Whig-Liberal circles but well beyond. Richard Huzzey, *Freedom Burning: Anti-Slavery and Empire in Victorian Britain* (Ithaca and London: Cornell University Press, 2012), esp. chs 3–5. See also Huzzey, 'Free Trade, Free Labour, and Slave Sugar in Victorian Britain', *Historical Journal*, 53 (2010), 359–79.

13 Douglas Hall, *Five of the Leewards 1834–1870: The Major Problems of the Post-Emancipation Period in Antigua, Barbuda, Montserrat, Nevis and St Kitts* (St Lawrence, Barbados: Caribbean Universities Press, 1971), pp. 96–7; Donald Wood, *Trinidad in Transition: The Years After Slavery* (Oxford: Oxford University Press, 1968), pp. 121–3; K. O. Laurence, *Immigration into the West Indies in the Nineteenth Century* (Aylesbury: Caribbean Universities Press, 1971), pp. 20–1; Howe, *Free Trade and Liberal England*, pp. 52–3.
14 Green, *British Slave Emancipation*, pp. 233–40.
15 Holt, *The Problem of Freedom*, pp. 205–6.
16 Parliamentary Papers (hereafter PP) 1847–48 (399), p. 4: 3rd Earl Grey to Sir Charles Edward Grey, 14 April 1848.
17 PP 1847–48 (167), p. 356: 3rd Earl Grey to Sir Charles Edward Grey, 30 October 1847.
18 3rd Earl Grey, *The Colonial Policy of Lord John Russell's Administration* (2 vols, London: Richard Bentley, 1853; repr. New York: Kraus, 1972), vol. 2, p. 303.
19 Green, *British Slave Emancipation*, p. 249.
20 Alan H. Adamson, *Sugar Without Slaves: The Political Economy of British Guiana, 1838–1904* (New Haven and London: Yale University Press, 1972), pp. 46–7, 160.
21 PP 1851 (1421), pp. 114: report of Edward Dacres Baynes (Montserrat), 31 October 1850.
22 Boyd Hilton, *Age of Atonement: The Influence of Evangelicalism on Social and Economic Thought, 1795–1865* (Oxford: Clarendon Press, 1988), pp. 36–70; Peter Mandler, 'The Making of the New Poor Law *Redivivus*', *Past and Present*, 117 (1987), 131–57; Peter Mandler, 'Tories and Paupers: Christian Political Economy and the Making of the New Poor Law', *Historical Journal*, 33 (1990), 81–101.
23 PP 1847–48 (749), pp. 322–3: report of Lord Harris (Trinidad), 19 June 1848.
24 Peter Gray, *Famine, Land, and Politics: British Government and Irish Society, 1843–1850* (Dublin: Irish Academic Press, 1999); Cormac Ó Gráda, *The Great Irish Famine* (Dublin: Gill and Macmillan, 1989), esp. pp. 437–49; Cormac Ó Gráda, *Black '47 and Beyond: The Great Irish Famine in History, Economy, and Memory* (Princeton: Princeton University Press, 2000), esp. pp. 43–4, 77–83.
25 B. W. Higman, 'Small Islands, Large Questions: Post-Emancipation Historiography of the Leeward Islands', pp. 8–31, at p. 9; Karen Fog Olwig, 'Cultural Complexity after Freedom: Nevis and Beyond', pp. 100–23, at p. 100; Jean Besson, 'Land, Kinship and Community in the Post-Emancipation Caribbean: A Regional View of the Leewards', pp. 73–100, at p. 92, all in Karen Fog Olwig, *Small Islands, Large Questions: Society, Culture and Resistance in the Post-Emancipation Caribbean* (London: Frank Cass, 1995).
26 Holt, *The Problem of Freedom*, pp. 144–7, 166–7.
27 D. Hall, *Free Jamaica* (1959), pp. 167–8; Brian L. Moore, *Race, Power and Social Segmentation in Colonial Society: Guyana after Slavery, 1838–1891* (New York and London: Gordon and Breach Science Publishers, 1987), pp. 34–6; Besson, 'Land, Kinship and Community', p. 78; J. R. Ward, *British West Indian Slavery, 1750–1834: The Process of Amelioration* (Oxford and New York: Oxford University Press, 1988), pp. 248–50; Curtin, *Two Jamaicas* (1970), p. 121.
28 Kenneth N. Bell and W. P. Morrell (eds), *Select Documents on British Colonial Policy 1830–1860* (Oxford: Clarendon Press, 1928), p. 412: Lord John Russell to Governor Henry Light of British Guiana, 15 February 1840.
29 D. Hall, *Five of the Leewards*, pp. 99–100.
30 See, e.g., C. Hall, *Civilising Subjects*, pp. 349–52.
31 See, famously, E. P. Thompson, 'Time, Work Discipline, and Industrial Capitalism', *Past and Present*, 38 (1967), 56–97.
32 PP 1847–48 (206), pp. 26–7: testimony of Henry Barkly.
33 PP 1847–48 (167), p. 289: testimony of William Codrington.
34 PP 1847–48 (167), p. 8: testimony of Lord Howard de Walden.
35 PP 1847–48 (206), pp. 27–8: testimony of Henry Barkly.
36 C. Hall, *Civilising Subjects*, p. 83. See also D. Hall, *Five of the Leewards*, pp. 128, 149; Holt, *The Problem of Freedom*, pp. 264–5.

37 See esp. Curtin, *Two Jamaicas*, pp. 110–19; Holt, *The Problem of Freedom*, pp. 278–81, 335–6, 347–8; and Riva Berleant-Schiller, 'From Labour to Peasantry in Montserrat after the End of Slavery', in K. F. Olwig (ed.), *Small Islands, Large Questions: Society, Culture and Resistance in the Post-Emancipation Caribbean* (London: Frank Cass, 1995), pp. 53–73, pp. 53–4.
38 PP 1847–48 (167), p. 59: testimony of Thomas Price.
39 PP 1847–48 (184), p. 127: testimony of Charles Marryat.
40 PP 1847–48 (184), p. 97: testimony of Matthew James Higgins.
41 D. Hall, *Five of the Leewards*, pp. 45–6, 153; Adamson, *Sugar Without Slaves*, pp. 32–3, 57–8; Moore, *Race, Power and Social Segmentation*, pp. 36–41, 111–13; Wood, *Trinidad in Transition*, p. 94.
42 Moore, *Race, Power and Social Segmentation*, pp. 114–16. See also Adamson, *Sugar Without Slaves*, pp. 76–9, 244, 262–3; Susan Lowes, '"They Couldn't Mash Ants": The Decline of the White and Non-White Elites in Antigua, 1834–1900', in K. F. Olwig (ed.), *Small Islands, Large Questions: Society, Culture and Resistance in the Post-Emancipation Caribbean* (London: Frank Cass, 1995), pp. 31–53, p. 33.
43 See, e.g., O. Nigel Bolland, 'Systems of Domination after Slavery: The Control of Land and Labor in the British West Indies after 1838', *Comparative Studies in Society and History*, 23 (October 1981), 591–619, at 591–2.
44 Moore, *Race, Power and Social Segmentation*, p. 41. See also D. Hall, *Five of the Leewards*, pp. 113–24.
45 Drescher, *The Mighty Experiment*, p. 216.
46 K. O. Laurence, *Immigration into the West Indies*, pp. 7–8; David Northrup, 'Migration from Africa, Asia, and the South Pacific', in Andrew Porter (ed.), *The Oxford History of the British Empire, vol. 3: The Nineteenth Century* (Oxford and New York: Oxford University Press, 1999), pp. 88–101, at pp. 88–92; Marina Carter, *Servants, Sirdars and Settlers: Indians in Mauritius, 1834–1874* (Delhi: Oxford University Press, 1995), pp. 24–5.
47 Northrup, 'Migration from Africa', pp. 90–1; Johnson U. J. Asiegbu, *Slavery and the Politics of Liberation 1787–1861: A Study of Liberated African Emigration and British Anti-Slavery Policy* (New York: Africana Publishing Corporation, 1969), esp. chs 3–6; Green, *British Slave Emancipation*, pp. 265–76; Laurence, *Immigration* (1971), pp. 13–15; Wood, *Trinidad in Transition* (1968), pp. 74–80; Monica Schuler, 'The Recruitment of African Indentured Labourers for European Colonies in the Nineteenth Century', in P. C. Emmer (ed.), *Colonialism and Migration; Indentured Labour before and after Slavery* (Dordrecht: Martinus Nijhoff, 1986), pp. 125–61, esp. pp. 128–37; Monica Schuler, *'Alas, Alas, Kongo: A Social History of Indentured African Immigration into Jamaica, 1841–1865'* (Baltimore and London: The Johns Hopkins University Press, 1980), chs 1–2.
48 Christopher Lloyd, *The Navy and the Slave Trade: The Suppression of the African Slave Trade in the Nineteenth Century* (London and New York: Longmans, Green, 1949), pp. 199, 275–7; Reginald Coupland, *The British Anti-Slavery Movement* (London and New York: Oxford University Press, 1933), p. 161.
49 Leslie Bethell, *The Abolition of the Brazilian Slave Trade: Britain, Brazil and the Slave Trade Question 1807–1869* (Cambridge and New York: Cambridge University Press, 1970), pp. 260–90.
50 For the politics of the African Squadron, see Bernard Semmel, *Liberalism and Naval Strategy: Ideology, Interest, and Sea Power during the Pax Britannica* (Boston: Allen & Unwin, 1986), ch. 3. For more general accounts, see Raymond Howell, *The Royal Navy and the Slave Trade* (New York: St. Martin's, 1997); W. E. F. Ward, *The Royal Navy and the Slavers: The Suppression of the Atlantic Slave Trade* (New York: Pantheon, 1969).
51 *Hansard*, 3rd ser., vol. 109, cols 1093–110 (19 March 1850). Quotation from col. 1108.
52 *Hansard*, 3rd ser., vol. 109, cols 1115–16 (19 March 1850).
53 See, e.g., *Times*, 6 March 1850, p. 5; *Economist*, 29 December 1849, p. 1450. See also *Leeds Mercury*, 26 January 1850, p. 3; *Nonconformist*, 20 March 1850, p. 230; *Glasgow Herald*, 22 March 1850, p. 1; *Liverpool Standard and General Commercial*

Advertiser, 2 April 1850, p. 8; Sir Henry Huntley, *Seven Years' Service on the Slave Coast of Western Africa* (2 vols, London: Thomas Cautley Newby, 1850), vol. 1, pp. 301–2.

54 The National Archives (TNA), Foreign Office 84/616, fols 64–9: Thomas Clarkson to the Earl of Aberdeen, 7 March 1845; Elizabeth Isichei, *Victorian Quakers* (Oxford: Oxford University Press, 1970), pp. 233–4; Temperley, *British Antislavery* (1972), ch. 9, esp. pp. 179–81; Rhodes House Library, British and Foreign Anti-Slavery Society papers, C112/8: Joseph Sturge to John Scoble, 8 September 1848.

55 This was consistent with the pro-Free Trade but anti-slavery position that had become prominent by the late 1840s, as Richard Huzzey has pointed out. Huzzey, 'Free Trade, Free Labour'. Indeed, Palmerston and Russell might well be considered its most prominent exponents.

56 The case was, alas, dismissed. Jasper Ridley, *Lord Palmerston* (London: Constable, 1970), pp. 528–9.

57 Quoted in Lloyd, *The Navy and the Slave Trade*, p. 235.

58 TNA, PRO 30/22/8D, fol. 91 (Lord John Russell papers): printed copy of Russell's speech, 19 March 1850.

59 Bethell, *The Abolition of the Brazilian Slave Trade*, pp. 312–15, 336–41.

60 Drescher, *Abolition*, p. 291; William Law Mathieson, *Great Britain and the Slave Trade 1839–1865* (London and New York: Longmans, Green, 1929), p. 131; Temperley, *British Antislavery*, pp. 181–3.

61 *Economist*, vol. 9, no. 412, p. 785 (19 July 1851).

62 *Hansard*, 3rd ser., vol. 151 cols 1320–1 (12 July 1858).

63 Lloyd, *The Navy and the Slave Trade*, pp. 179–82; Temperley, *British Antislavery*, p. 257.

64 Quoted in Lloyd, *The Navy and the Slave Trade*, pp. xii–xiii, from Lecky's *History of European Morals*.

65 *Pace* Lloyd, *The Navy and the Slave Trade*, pp. xii–xiii.

66 Quoted in Ridley, *Lord Palmerston*, p. 589.

67 Bernard Semmel, *Jamaican Blood and Victorian Conscience: The Governor Eyre Controversy* (1st American edn, Boston: Houghton Mifflin, 1963), esp. chs 3–5; R. W. Kostal, *A Jurisprudence of Power: Victorian Empire and the Rule of Law* (Oxford: Oxford University Press, 2008).

68 C. Hall, *Civilising Subjects*, pp. 435–6.

69 Huzzey, *Freedom Burning*, p. 21.

70 See esp. Claire Pettitt, *Dr. Livingstone, I Presume? Missionaries, Journalists, Explorers, and Empire* (Cambridge, MA: Harvard University Press, 2007). See also Andrew C. Ross, *David Livingstone: Mission and Empire* (London and New York: Hambledon Continuum, 2002).

71 Lloyd, *The Navy and the Slave Trade*, pp. 259–71; Suzanne Miers, *Britain and the Ending of the Slave Trade* (New York: Africana Publishing Company, 1975); Sir Reginald Coupland, *The Exploitation of East Africa 1856–1890: The Slave Trade and the Scramble* (Evanston, IL: Northwestern University Press, 1967), part 1; R. J. Gavin, 'The Bartle Frere Mission to Zanzibar, 1873', *Historical Journal*, 2 (1962), 122–48.

72 See esp. Jonathan Parry, *The Politics of Patriotism: English Liberalism, National Identity and Europe, 1830–1886* (Cambridge: Cambridge University Press, 2006).

73 See, e.g., Richard Roberts and Suzanne Miers, 'The End of Slavery in Africa', in Suzanne Miers and Richard Roberts (eds), *The End of Slavery in Africa* (Madison and London: University of Wisconsin Press, 1988), pp. 3–68; Martin A. Klein, 'Introduction: Modern European Expansion and Traditional Servitude in Africa and Asia', in Martin A. Klein (ed.), *Breaking the Chains: Slavery, Bondage, and Emancipation in Modern Africa and Asia* (Madison and London: University of Wisconsin Press, 1993), pp. 3–37; Martin A. Klein, *Slavery and Colonial Rule in French West Africa* (Cambridge and New York: Cambridge University Press, 1998); Suzanne Miers and Martin A. Klein, 'Introduction', in Suzanne Miers and Martin A. Klein (eds), *Slavery and Colonial Rule in Africa* (London and New York: Routledge, 1999), pp. 1–15.

74 Paul E. Lovejoy and Jan S. Hogendorn, *Slow Death for Slavery: The Course of Abolition in Northern Nigeria, 1897–1936* (Cambridge and New York: Cambridge University Press, 1993).

75 See esp. Huzzey, *Freedom Burning*, chs 6–7.

CHAPTER FOUR

At home in the Ottoman Empire: humanitarianism and the Victorian diplomat

Michelle Tusan

> What is to be the consequence to civilization and humanity if British interests are to be the rule for British agents all over the world, and are to be for them the measure of right or wrong?[1]

W. E. Gladstone posed this question in the House of Commons in April 1877 upon hearing of Austen Henry Layard's appointment as Ambassador to Constantinople. The elevation of the adventurer-turned-politician to top diplomat worried Gladstone. He believed that Layard would do little to promote civil and legal reform in the Ottoman Empire, a cause that the former prime minister argued should comprise a centrepiece of British diplomacy.

Gladstone personally had led the campaign to denounce what came to be known as the 'Bulgarian Atrocities' not long before Layard's appointment.[2] Starting in late summer 1876 the public read reports in the press of the mass slaughter of Bulgarian Christian minorities by Ottoman soldiers on the eve of the Russo-Turkish War (1877–78). Advocates of the Bulgarian cause at home believed that Britain ought to take responsibility for the thousands of victims of the humanitarian disaster unfolding in the Ottoman Empire.[3] Part of the obligation of empire, Gladstone argued in his widely read pamphlet 'Bulgarian Atrocities', was to protect persecuted minorities in the British Empire's informal sphere of influence.[4] Others, like then Prime Minister Benjamin Disraeli, dismissed Gladstone's advocacy work as 'coffee house babble', sending Layard to Constantinople with hopes that his reputed ties with Ottoman officials would sort things out and quiet the controversy over the question of Britain's obligation to protect the interests of minority populations living under Ottoman rule.[5]

But the humanitarian question continued to loom large long after the 1876 massacres, mediating the British Empire's relationship with the Ottoman Empire and its Christian minority subjects and the European

Great Powers. The responsibility of defending what Gladstone called the cause of 'civilization and humanity' abroad was entrusted to a new generation of Victorian diplomat trained to represent British interests abroad in part through engaging in the communities in which they lived. Gladstone immediately wrote to Layard about the duties of Britain's top diplomat, calling it a 'matter of honour and duty' to seek the 'liberation of the distressed provinces from tyranny' by making the Ottoman Empire reform how it ruled its non-Muslim subjects.[6] Layard responded by trying to reassure Gladstone that though they might differ on how to secure protection for Ottoman subjects, 'our object is the same – to obtain for the Turkish Empire just and good government'.[7]

The steady expansion of Britain's footprint in the Near East after the end of the Crimean War in 1856 made it possible to put humanitarian diplomacy in relation to the Eastern Question into practice. Fresh from victory over its Russian rival in the Crimea, Britain dramatically expanded its civil service in the Ottoman Empire. In addition to the Ambassador's residence in Constantinople, a network of sixty-two consular outposts in the Ottoman Empire grew through the 1860s as part of a highly specialised Levant Consular Service to employ around 350 consuls, vice consuls and consul generals, many of whom brought wives and children to join them.[8] Philanthropists and missionaries eager to assist with the humanitarian crisis also began to settle in the region in larger number.[9] Unlike travellers, whose experiences have dominated work on Britain and the Ottoman Empire, Victorian diplomats, civil servants and aid workers resided for many years here, serving in both official and unofficial capacities that included writing, political advocacy and humanitarian activities.[10] These new residents did not only see themselves as agents of empire, supporting British imperial might abroad. Rather, they were embedded in a series of overlapping networks that spread philanthropic and humanitarian ideals within and across the British Empire's informal imperial border with the Ottoman Empire that included the defence of the rights of Bulgarian and, later, Armenian minority populations.

Humanitarian diplomacy took on a clearly defined character in the Ottoman Empire as a result of the Bulgarian crisis. However, a similar experience characterised by the sometimes intimate involvement in local affairs came to define the lives of other consuls in the second half of the nineteenth century, particularly in regions where the British exercised only informal influence. Across Asia, Africa and the Middle East the consul increasingly maintained a presence as the eyes and ears of British foreign policy and imperial interests. This role was achieved as a result of the professionalisation of the service during the mid-nineteenth century, which better facilitated the ability of the consul to collect information about conditions on the ground and cultivate relationships with businessmen, philanthropists, travellers and missionaries who resided in and around regions under the jurisdiction of the British consulate.[11] In this way, the consul emerged at the centre of a new culture of hands-on diplomacy intended to further imperial aims and objectives through humanitarian engagement.

This chapter examines the personal and professional network that grew up around Austen Henry Layard in the Ottoman Empire in the wake of the humanitarian and diplomatic crisis of the late 1870s. The extended reach of Britain's informal empire in the Near East created new opportunities and obligations for the consuls, diplomats and philanthropists who understood themselves as part of a cultural British world. Layard and his circle made themselves at home in the Ottoman Empire, bringing with them an elevated sense of Britain's role in the region. Some found professional opportunity in this moment, while others saw little by way of personal gain. Their presence also affected the communities in which they lived. In the provinces and cities of the Ottoman Empire where these networks thrived, a particular set of ideals and institutions grew up whose apparent purpose did not necessarily mirror intended results. Taken together, the experiences of Layard's circle offer a view of informal empire from the inside; a project that cast humanitarianism as a core element of Britain's engagement with other nations and empires.

The new Ambassador

News of the Bulgarian Atrocities and the subsequent Russo-Turkish War put a spotlight on British power at the Sublime Porte, the seat of Ottoman government. Britain's Ambassador to the Ottoman Empire emerged during the crisis at the centre of a humanitarian aid network that facilitated the distribution of hundreds of thousands of pounds donated by the public for relief work. The tenure of Sir Henry Layard, as he came to be known, as Ambassador from 1877 to 1880 offers a look at how these networks intersected, grew and came to reflect British priorities in the Ottoman Empire during the late nineteenth century.

Layard's interest in the Ottoman Empire came from reading *Arabian Nights* as a child. Descended from a family of Huguenots, he was educated in Florence, France and Geneva, mainly as a result of his father's search for a cure for his asthma away from the damp English climate. He finished his formal education in England and entered his uncle's solicitor's office in London in 1834, a job he quickly came to dislike. Eager to escape the drudgery of his work as a clerk, he took an overland journey to Ceylon with an acquaintance to join an uncle who thought life as a barrister in the colonies might suit him better.

Travelling through the Ottoman Empire made Layard keenly aware of the privileges afforded to men like him in the Near East. 'All European strangers are supposed to be consuls', he observed.[12] Twenty-two years old and eager for adventure, Layard traversed the continent with relative ease, picking up Persian and Arabic language along the way. He soon abandoned plans to work as a barrister and decided to make the Near East his career instead. Facilitating a connection with the Royal Geographic Society, he explored 'a new route through Asia Minor' in order 'to visit parts of it which had hitherto not been explored by previous travellers'. Mapping western lands of the Ottoman Empire quickly became his new calling. He recorded his experiences, 'carefully mapping' his route which enabled him 'to lay down a fairly trustworthy map of the country through which we journeyed and which I afterwards sent, with a memoir to the Royal Geographic Society'.[13] These efforts, along with his work 'correcting' the map of Montenegro, earned him the Gold Medal from the Society in 1849.

Layard found the Ottoman Empire the ideal place to build his reputation as a gentleman adventurer and, later, politician. In the mid-1840s, thanks to the patronage of British Ambassador Stratford Canning, he began excavation work near Mosul, where he made claims on the Assyrian treasures that today reside in the British Museum. The connection with Canning, coupled with the popular success of his series of books on Nineveh, resulted in his appointment by Lord Palmerston as a paid attaché at £250 a year in the late 1840s. He then launched a brief political career back in England in Parliament, marked by controversy and culminating in an ultimately unsuccessful campaign against what he viewed as the maladministration of the Crimean War.[14]

Layard turned his ambition toward the diplomatic service. He again left England for the Ottoman Empire, in the hopes of obtaining a post with the help of Ambassador Canning, his former patron. However, a position in the diplomatic service did not come easily for this ambitious, untitled adventurer, who waited for years under Canning's encouragement for an official appointment. Layard persevered, ultimately leading to his appointment as Disraeli's Ambassador at Constantinople in the late 1870s. Dubbed the 'first Liberal Imperialist' by his biographer, he believed Britain should 'maintain the Turkish Empire in its present state until the Christian population may be ready to succeed the Mussulman [sic]'.[15] 'My conviction', Layard declared, 'is that it is possible to do so, and that this policy is the only hope of a favourable solution to the Eastern Question.'[16] British diplomacy regarding the Eastern Question, he believed, needed to take into account the position of Christian minorities in the Ottoman Empire. As a Huguenot he was encouraged by the growth of Protestantism among the peoples of Turkey, notably the Armenians and Greeks, and hoped 'that ere long this religious movement will bring about a political one and that we shall [see] the Protestant Christians of this country hold a very high and honourable position'.[17]

These foreign policy and humanitarian objectives regarding the Eastern Question could not be achieved by destabilising the current Ottoman regime. The British, Layard believed, instead should lead by example. After a visit to India in the wake of the 1857 mutiny, Layard asserted: 'Are we to hold the Bible in one hand and the sword in the other? If so what can we say to the Turks and other nations who would oppress Christians?'[18] He believed the popular agitation against the Bulgarian Atrocities, which he called one of England's 'periodic lunacies', would undermine efforts to exert informal influence over the Ottoman government.[19] After reading Gladstone's pamphlet, 'Bulgarian Horrors and the Question of the East', which would go on to sell over 200,000 copies, he wrote to a friend, 'you cannot drive three million Turks out of Europe into starvation and hopeless misery. The wild humanitarian cry about Turkey will lead to serious mischief. It is grievous to see a man like Gladstone turned into a mere vulgar pamphleteer.'[20] Layard, in a direct rebuke to the former prime minister, responded to Gladstone's campaign in an article in the *Quarterly Review* where he argued that Turkey should expire of its own accord rather than be driven to extinction by military might or condemned by public opinion.

Well before Layard took his post as Ambassador at Constantinople in March of 1877 he had taken steps to realise his ambition to influence Ottoman politics and culture from the inside. In 1856 he helped to establish the European-modelled Ottoman Bank in order to develop the 'material resources' of the Ottoman Empire.[21] He also supported philanthropic projects: 'I was anxious to promote the establishment of schools amongst the indigent Christian and Jewish populations of the Turkish capital – a matter with which Lady Canning took a very lively interest. We were able to open some schools in the poorest quarters of the city, and eventually one was founded for the education of children of the better classes without distinction of faith, it being meant for Christians and Mohammedans alike.' Such projects he believed would curry favour with the Sultan , who later supported these schools.

He also backed institutions focused on educating Christian minorities, such as the American missionary-run Robert College. In these schools, minorities with few rights and privileges 'acquired their knowledge of the institutions, laws, and customs of civilised countries and those principles of political freedom'. For Layard, the spread of liberal democratic institutions and values was in part responsible for helping to forge an independent Bulgaria after the Russo-Turkish War and what he called 'the independence of the Bulgarian race'.[22] The continued exposure of liberal values to the top levels of government and Anglo-centric education, in Layard's line of thinking, would result in the inevitable transition of the Ottoman Empire from despotism to democracy.

Education, however, was not enough. Layard believed that 'personal influence' would smooth the path to internal reform in Ottoman administration, particularly when it came to humanitarian issues related to the protection of minorities. In discussing his tenure at Constantinople in an interview in the *Contemporary Review*, Layard emphasised 'how exceedingly important it is for the English representative at Constantinople to maintain a personal influence over the Sultan'.[23] Here he claimed to follow the example of Canning, who he believed succeeded in resolving the grievances of Christian and Muslim subjects by appealing to the leadership at the Sublime Porte. 'So often can influence, well acquired and well directed, be exercised in the great cause of humanity, without distinction of persons or of creeds!' Layard declared. 'This is but one of the many instances in which Sir Stratford Canning has added to the best renown of the British name.'[24]

The Bulgarian Atrocities revealed the limits of Layard's embrace of humanitarian diplomacy in practice. In a September 1876 letter to Lord Derby he chronicled a long list of interventions by British officials on behalf of both Muslim and Christian subjects. In another letter dated two days earlier to Canning himself, now Viscount Stratford de Redcliffe, he called for punishment for those who had perpetrated the atrocities, while at the same time urging that the government should 'approach the Turkish question in a wise, moderate and statesman-like spirit and not with passion and exaggerated sentiment'. Nothing, however, was done to help mitigate the Bulgarian crisis. He defended his refusal to take decisive action to stop the massacres: 'A false step on the part of England at the crisis might be irretrievable and might be even fateful to the future of this country.'[25] By that time, all Layard could do was watch as the drama unfolded in a war that some blamed him for doing little to help avoid. As Gladstone would later remind him, the Ottoman subjects he claimed to protect through wielding informal influence over the Sultan suffered most.

Philanthropy and diplomacy

Even before the signing of the Treaty of Berlin in 1878 that ended the Russo-Turkish War codified Britain's obligation to defend Ottoman Christians by including special provisions for their care, a group of supporters had grown up around the Ambassador who believed that Britain had a legitimate role in Ottoman internal affairs, particularly when it came to the issue of protecting religious minorities.[26] This network came necessarily to rely on Layard's tacit and, at times, active support of its projects. Emily Anne Beaufort (1826–87) became central to Layard's circle. In 1862 she married Percy Ellen Algernon Frederick William Sydney Smythe, later the eighth Viscount Strangford (1825–69). The two shared a deep interest in Ottoman culture and politics, which connected them to the British diplomatic mission in the Near East.[27] Her husband's sudden death from a brain haemorrhage and the absence of an heir left her free to pursue her own projects in the Ottoman Empire, while giving her access to his income and her own sizeable fortune.[28]

The crisis years of the mid-1870s proved the perfect opportunity for Lady Strangford to further cultivate her interest in Ottoman affairs. Strangford enrolled in a four-year nurses' training course in England. In 1874, she published 'Hospital Training for Ladies' and waited for a call to use her new-found skills and wealth. Her work with the order of St John's Eastern War Sick and Wounded Fund led her to open her own fund to help destitute Bulgarian Christians. On 15 August 1876, almost at the very moment when atrocity reports began to filter back to England, she started the Bulgarian Peasants Relief fund, pledging to raise £10,000 to build houses for the homeless and provide emergency relief. Internecine conflicts complicated relief efforts, so Strangford decided to go to Bulgaria to administer the aid herself.

The Bulgarian Atrocities spawned a number of these humanitarian aid organisations in the Ottoman Empire. Almost a dozen large and small aid organisations had raised over £250,000 by the end of the Russo-Turkish War.[29] These organisations would not have been able to operate if it had not been for the help of civil servants, administrators and diplomats working in the region. Titled philanthropists like Lady Strangford had the advantage. Her connection with the official bureaucracy through her late husband, including the Ambassador's residence in Constantinople, meant that she had access to a network of goods and services that facilitated her projects and made them well known at home. By the time her fund wound up in the late 1870s, she and her four English doctors and eight English nurses had established six village hospitals (Figure 14). A flour mill, five sawmills and numerous local workers provided materials for a relief scheme that included food aid,

14. 'Lady Strangford visiting her Hospital at Carlovo, near Philippopolis', 1877

housing and tens of thousands of items of clothing and blankets.[30] One former president of a bank closed by the government after the insurrection that provided the excuse for the massacres in Bulgaria began a new career working as a tailor in a village several hours' walk away, where he and his thirteen employees filled Lady Strangford's orders.[31]

The impression lent by Lady Strangford's diary that she kept during the year and a half she spent in Bulgaria is one of a self-appointed ambassador to aid the Ottoman Empire's deserving poor. Comparing a local village to a 'Whitechapel Slum', the world that she mapped in her journal represented a paternalist humanitarian vision. In Bulgaria, her own religious and moral certitude bolstered her sense of duty as a member of the aristocracy. She recognised that she had little in common with the Bulgarians themselves and worked hard to control the level of contact with the largely peasant population that she served. 'You can form no idea of how difficult it is to find anything to say', she confided in her diary after one particularly difficult interaction with Bulgarians seeking her assistance. 'I sit in anguish of mind thinking what shall I say next?' Confident in the superiority of Anglo-Protestant values, she felt certain that the Bulgarians who belonged to the Eastern Orthodox faith, when waiting for her to receive them at the home of a zealous American missionary, must have felt ill at ease passing for the first time under 'the threshold of Protestantism'.[32]

Strangford represented herself in her writing as armed with little more than a guide book, a Turkish dictionary and a will to see her projects through. In reality she had a large entourage of local and English people that included doctors, nurses and servants who assisted her with her projects. The amount of travel that she did was astounding, as evidenced by how well she was known throughout the district and the reverent treatment shown to her by Turkish dignitaries and the people in the villages she visited. She was also well known among Britons travelling in the region, many of whom stayed with her and took advantage of her resources, political connections and hospitality.

Upon arriving in Philippopolis, Bulgaria Strangford put herself at the centre of relief efforts. 'Dear Lady Strangford', wrote American Consul Eugene Schuyler:

> Can you not do something for the poor people at Perustitsa in the way of distributing clothing and blankets? I was there yesterday and found the misery of some of the people extreme. They were almost frozen ... It seems that Perustitsa is so near to Philippopolis that it has been neglected by all the committees of Relief. Our committee here has done something for the widows and orphans which is all it undertakes to do. I shall bring the subject of Perustitsa before the Central committee as soon as I return to Constantinople. But meanwhile people are suffering.[33]

Strangford's personal visits to these districts and offers of assistance from her fund made her an obvious choice for such appeals. She must have left an unforgettable impression on those who witnessed her frequent tours. Her large entourage included her 'dragoman', or interpreter, 'a carriage', 'two good horses', 'a good coachman' and 'a native carriage' for her luggage and a small battalion of soldiers for protection. Such pomp Strangford believed was necessary in facilitating her work: 'the Bulgarians like it, because it is to do honour to "their lady" and friend and they feel it a protecting link between them and the government'.[34] Indeed, on several of these tours the large crowds that came out just to have a 'look at her' mistook her for the queen of England, an impression she did not entirely dispel.[35]

The amount of money and publicity associated with Strangford's project meant that conflicts inevitably arose. Upon her arrival, the *Daily News* correspondents responsible for breaking the Bulgarian Atrocities story paid her an unwelcome visit. She feared that they would criticise her following Layard's lead and refusing to blame the Ottoman government for the massacres. Realising the importance of good publicity for raising money for her fund, however, she attempted to win them over by asking them to dinner. Conflicts with other aid workers were more difficult to overcome. Her at times strained relationship with the American missionary Reverend J. F. Clarke most likely stemmed from his proselytising and zealous brand of Protestantism, although she did come to rely on his knowledge of needs in the area to help facilitate her projects. After she witnessed Clarke preach, Strangford remarked, 'I believe he is a Congregationalist whatever that is – he is very strict.'[36] A meeting with the Greek bishop revealed the tensions between the groups in the region when he criticised Strangford for not helping Greeks and accused her of not 'cultivating diplomacy'.[37]

Strangford, like Layard, took a paternalist view to both aid work and politics. 'The patients mostly say that I am both mother and father to them', she wrote to Layard as the conflict raged.[38] Her training and interest in nursing meant that she spent most of her time planning and establishing new hospitals with other aid workers like the Reverend Clarke and W. L. Stoney, an agent for the Central Relief Committee in Constantinople. Finding Bulgarian-run hospitals 'dirty' and badly arranged, Strangford built her hospitals on the English model. The scheme for the founding of a hospital first involved the outright purchase of the land and the buildings so that, as Strangford put it, they 'will not be taken from me'. Bulgarian officials objected to this scheme, wanting instead to have these properties deeded to them.[39] Calling these men 'selfish and shortsighted', Strangford defended her scheme by arguing that the Bulgarians had yet no ability to manage their own affairs. Comparing them to ignorant children, she claimed to have no 'illusions' about the Bulgarians. 'They have all the faults of an undeveloped young people', she reasoned, and thus needed to be given 'fair play' in order to develop on their own.[40] She summed up her feelings in a letter to Layard in May 1878: 'I wish the English Government understood their position better and could befriend them in the only wise way – which is by *leading* them.'[41]

Lady Strangford's commitment to the notion of imperial stewardship continued in another project which she started to assist wounded Turkish soldiers in 1877. E. A. Freeman, an admirer of the late Lord Strangford and vocal advocate for the Bulgarian cause, criticised Lady Strangford's relief work on behalf of those who perpetrated atrocities: 'I cannot think that we are at all called upon to organise means of relief for a gang of brutal murderers, robbers and rashers or ostentatiously put them on a level with the heroes who are fighting and suffering in the noblest cause in which man ever drew the sword.'[42] Lady Strangford responded by touting the importance of neutral aid. Continued criticism of her work of helping soldiers who might have committed mass atrocities against the Bulgarians in the now Russian-occupied city of Sofia made hospital work more complicated and eventually led her to abandon the project.

In the early 1880s Lady Strangford used her influence to embark on a less controversial cause: famine relief. A fund set up for victims in 'Kurdistan, Armenia, and Western Persia' relied more than ever on the goodwill of officials who agreed to administer the monies raised for relief work in their districts. Ambassador Layard, along with British consuls Captain William Everett, Major Emilius Clayton and Major Henry Trotter, all stationed in the eastern provinces of the Ottoman Empire, took an active role in administering the over £13,000 raised for famine victims that Strangford hoped would be administered without 'any distinction or preference to creed or race'.[43] This new scheme directly linked diplomatic and philanthropic networks. Layard put it this way to Consul Everett in Erzeroom when famine hit his district in 1880: 'if assistance came in this district from the English people it would greatly raise our prestige here which is waning fast. It is not pleasant either to be appealed to save life and to be unable to do anything.'[44]

British Consul William Everett (1844–1908) facilitated Strangford's humanitarian relief work in the Ottoman Empire in Eastern Anatolia. Appointed Vice Consul at Erzeroom starting in 1878, Everett was in charge of a mountainous town of about 40,000 people with a large Christian minority population on the Russo-Ottoman border. Here he lived with his wife, Maria Georgina Calogeras, formerly of Corfu, and two daughters until he resigned from the consular service in 1888. Like other agents in the civil and imperial service, he enjoyed a great deal of power in the region because of his post. When the famine hit, Everett recruited American missionaries to serve on the relief committee, as Layard had assured him that 'the Americans will help us' with the project. One American missionary, the Reverend Chambers, soon complained that missionaries 'had not been sufficiently recognized in the Bluebooks' for their work. He went as far as to accuse Everett of misappropriating funds, reportedly calling him a 'conscienceless scoundrel', which made him furious.[45]

After the Bulgarian Atrocities, relief work had become an accepted part of the unofficial duties of the British consul stationed in the Ottoman Empire. Mutual distrust and competition from other European and American agents in the region eager to increase their own influence over the local population meant that consuls stationed in the provinces like Everett often took on direct responsibility for relief projects in times of distress. By 1881, famine relief consumed many of his official duties, with Everett distributing aid himself. Everett's decision to throw himself into famine relief certainly had much to do with this semi-official policy that saw aid as the way to win the hearts and minds of the local population. It also had a good deal to do with his own belief about aid work among the orthodox Christian minorities whom he served and characterised as having 'a strong bearing to our church'.

Everett, Strangford and Layard all became central to this humanitarian relief network, extending British informal influence deep into the interior of the Ottoman Empire. When Lady Strangford set up her appeal in 1881 she distributed funds directly to consuls like Everett living in affected areas. He investigated claims of starvation in his district in late January and received immediate approval to draw money from the fund administered by Layard for relief work. By early February, Everett started investigating the prices of goods himself after receiving letters from his district that 'report a bad state of things'. His diary from this period recorded his constant worry that local officials would cheat him and he insisted always on seeing the grain before purchasing it himself. He also kept a regular record of expenditures made in each district, while listing the price of grain, livestock and household goods and the items he handed out. On 9 March 1882 he recorded: 'Gave distribution of flour to 4 poor families.'[46]

Imperial humanitarian patronage

This hands-on relief work opened up possibilities for Layard to influence a host of private and public projects in the urban and provincial centres of the Ottoman Empire during his tenure at Constantinople. The Stafford House Project, the National Aid Society, the Red Crescent Society, the Turkish Compassionate Fund, along with a handful of American-run missionary projects, all relied on the support of the Ambassador at one point or another. Lady Strangford's projects held particular appeal. They worked together on relief efforts, with Layard using his position to provide material support for the work of Lord Strangford's widow. 'I must say it is a great comfort in this terrible time to have you at Constantinople', wrote Lady Strangford to Layard in 1877 upon setting up her relief hospital in Adrianople.[47] Over the next three years she used Layard to secure funds from other aid organisations, ease her passage through hostile territory and intervene on behalf of those under her patronage. Layard also served as a go-between in the management of the large amounts of cash that her funds brought in, thanks to his connections with the Ottoman Bank and relationship with the various consuls operating in the region.

Competition between various relief funds and the questions raised by liberal critics like E. A. Freeman regarding Lady Strangford's motivations and choice of relief projects eventually led to trouble. 'You know that my subscriptions were going as well and steadily when they were suddenly suffocated and almost closed off', she wrote to Layard in October 1877, 'in alarm, I asked the Red Crescent Society to front me five hundred pounds'. When this money did not come she pleaded with Layard to ask the Sultan to intervene with the Red Crescent Society, the Ottoman branch of the Red Cross, on her behalf: 'What can I do but apply to you? Will you help me? ... The *Daily Telegraph* and *Sheffield* paper and some other quarters all promise me help but I want it now.'[48] Layard's intervention with the Sultan and the Red Cross in England eventually secured the grant but Lady Strangford was not through with him. 'I always give my ambassador as little trouble as possible', she declared after numerous subsequent requests that included the purchase of supplies and an escort for her and her large party out of Sofia just before the Russo-Turkish war started. Layard's status also legitimated her work when others questioned the logic of her helping both the victims and perpetrators of the Bulgarian massacres. She even had Layard insert her projects into his official dispatches, asking at one point for him to send a message regarding 'a lost refugee child' in Philippopolis whose parents 'want(ed) it sent to them' in Scutari.[49]

Layard similarly used Strangford to further his own influence. During the Russo-Turkish War he asked her to investigate alleged atrocities committed by Bulgarians on the Turkish population that he hoped to use to counter Gladstone's claims in the 'Bulgarian Horrors' pamphlet that violence was one sided. In June and July of 1878 Strangford attempted to find evidence of atrocities committed by Bulgarians against 'Moslems'. 'I have not a single word of any "terrible crimes" much less "revolting cruelties" such as you allude to.' At Layard's urging she sent out Dr Stephenson, the head of her hospitals, 'to go up country for me' to 'enquire into the reports of the Bulgarian atrocities both towards Muselmans [sic] and Protestants'. Frustrated with the results of her search, she requested that Layard give her 'a few memoranda of the places where such things have happened as reported'.[50] Layard received no satisfaction from this investigation, which eventually strained relations between the two. A few months later, before closing her hospitals and leaving the country for good, Strangford admonished Layard for not taking a more active interest in her work as of late: 'I am sorry you did not think it worthwhile to visit my hospital as it would have pleased the Turks very much.'[51]

Evidence suggests that despite a sometimes difficult relationship Layard understood his work with Lady Strangford's projects as important to his humanitarian diplomatic vision. The cause of famine relief united Layard and Strangford. 'I was very unwilling indeed to take up the miserable state of Kurdistan and Armenia and for a long time would not consent to work with it. But I found that no one else would work and that not a penny would be subscribed if I did not come forward,' she wrote to Layard from England in February 1880. Funds went through Layard's account at the Ottoman Bank that he then distributed to the British Consuls at Van, Aleppo and Erzeroom. 'You will not ... raise the hopes among the Consuls of any large fortune being at hand but yesterday I had the pleasure of telegraphing 400 pounds to you for the half of the northern districts and 300 pounds for the southern. The 400 was paid yesterday into the Imperial Ottoman Bank ... the 300 pounds will be probably arranged today.'

The fund eventually raised over £13,500 from subscribers in Britain, which Strangford gave to Layard to distribute, knowing that he shared her sensibility: 'it is best for you to decide really to whom it goes ... provided it is sent to the Kurdistan or Armenian country, and provided its [sic] bestowed without any distinction or preference to creed or race'.[52] When confusions inevitably arose, Strangford attempted to mollify Layard by appealing to his stature as a diplomat: 'Pray understand we had no intention of giving you any trouble at all individually ... But we thought we might send the money through your hands, partly as a convenience to ourselves partly in order to give it an official flavour in the eyes of the receivers.'[53]

By the early 1880s it had become clear that Layard's position as defender of both the Ottoman administration and its dispossessed minority Christian population was untenable. Even he began to doubt that personal influence would change the Sultan 's mind about protecting religious minorities against abuses. The mood back in Britain, too, had changed and few had patience for the wait-and-see stance that characterised Disraeli's Ottoman policy. 'Mr. Gladstone is warm, glowing, cordial and appreciative to everybody', wrote Strangford to Layard on the landslide election of 1880 that historians credit the Bulgarian Atrocities with helping to oust the Conservatives from power and bring Gladstone and the Liberals back into office.[54] Hoping that Gladstone would infuse new life into her relief projects, Strangford faced the reality that her own Conservative credentials put her on uncertain ground with the incoming government: 'I am in despair about our meeting on the 6th of May as Gladstone has given up coming, though that sacred case is nearest to his heart so he writes to the committee.'[55] Layard fared much worse. Gladstone had not forgotten that Layard had challenged him as a 'vulgar pamphleteer' and decided to dismiss him from his post in Constantinople. 'My case is one of extraordinary hardship and cruel injustice', he declared soon after his dismissal, believing that he had been fired for his politics.[56] It was the last official diplomatic position that Layard would ever hold.

One of the last acts that Layard performed at Constantinople was an attempt to get a 'Protestant Constitution' made part of the 1878 Treaty of Berlin that ended the Russo-Turkish War. This document, pushed by Great Britain and Germany, Layard claimed would grant this small religious minority 'those rights and privileges which were accorded to every other religious sect in his [the Sultan's] empire'. Layard tried unsuccessfully over several months to use his personal influence to get the Sultan to agree to these terms, along with appointing religious minorities to higher government positions.[57] Looking back on his career, Layard claimed of the fate of one such religious minority, 'Although it was not possible to obtain for the Armenians all that Lord Beaconsfield's Government desired to obtain for them, and which I was most anxious to secure, yet some progress was made towards granting to Armenia a better administration, in which the Armenians themselves might share.'[58]

In reality, Layard's interventions produced few results and satisfied no one. 'The Constitution to be conceded to the Protestants of Turkey, promised to me over and over again by the Sultan and his Ministers, is still unsettled,' Layard wrote to Foreign Secretary Lord Granville on the eve of the signing of the Berlin Treaty. 'The conduct of the Porte in this matter has been without excuse … The question has been in discussion with the Porte during the three years that I have been here.'[59] In this, one of his final acts as Ambassador, Layard realised the limits of humanitarian diplomacy as configured in the wake of the Bulgarian Atrocities. His tenure, however, did ultimately have a lasting effect by bringing the Ottoman Empire closer into the cultural British world by creating a web of political, economic and cultural networks that increased Britain's stake in the Ottoman Empire during the late nineteenth century. This promoted the idea in the minds of various constituencies at home and in the Ottoman Empire that Britain had an obligation to intervene in Ottoman internal affairs even if that involvement rarely produced the intended effect.

Conclusion

The Victorian diplomat embodied by men like Layard relied on a patronage network that helped to define a new brand of activist diplomacy. The founding of humanitarian aid institutions, raising money, and even securing these interests in the founding of financial institutions like the Ottoman Bank strengthened British ties with the Ottoman Empire. It also spread ideas and institutions in an uneven way that could undermine an already muddled foreign policy that attempted to join humanitarian and diplomatic concerns to determine which of the Great Powers would wield the most influence over a declining

Ottoman Empire. Commitments to protect Christian minorities in the Treaty of Berlin negotiated by Disraeli's government came in part out of fear that Bulgarian, Greek, Assyrian and Armenian Ottoman Christians would appeal to Russia for protection.

In the end, Britain's hands-on diplomacy failed in terms of both its geopolitical and humanitarian aims.[60] Reforms to the Ottoman administration did not come and Britain failed to fully limit the influence of its European rivals in the region. The pogroms against minority Christians in the mid-1890s, 1909 and later the Armenian Genocide of 1915 showed how little real influence this new diplomacy had over the Ottoman Empire, which ended up joining the First World War on the side of Germany. Though Britons like Layard and Strangford made their homes there and brought with them their institutions and ideals, the influence of officials, civil servants, missionaries and philanthropists over stopping the oppression of minority populations and furthering British diplomatic objectives was very small indeed.

Notes

1 Gladstone quoted in Gordon Waterfield, *Layard of Nineveh* (New York: Praeger, 1963), p. 358.

2 On Gladstone and the Bulgarian Atrocities controversy see: R. W. Seton Watson, *Disraeli, Gladstone, and the Eastern Question* (New York: Norton, 1972) (reprint); David Harris, *Britain and the Bulgarian Horrors of 1876* (Chicago: University of Chicago Press, 1939); Richard Shannon *Gladstone and the Bulgarian Agitation 1876* (London: Thomas Nelson and Sons, 1963); Richard Millman, *Britain and the Eastern Question, 1875–1878* (Oxford: Clarendon Press, 1979); and Ann Pottinger Saab, *Reluctant Icon: Gladstone, Bulgaria and the Working Classes, 1856–1878* (Cambridge, MA: Harvard University Press, 1991).

3 No official numbers exist, leaving a wide range of possible statistics. David Harris quotes numbers given by a Turkish tribunal, a British consular agent, American investigators, and Bulgarian historians ranging from 12,000 to over 100,000 dead. Harris, *Britain and the Bulgarian Horrors*, p. 22.

4 Michelle Tusan, '"Crimes against Humanity": Human Rights, the Armenian Genocide and the British Empire', *American History Review*, 119 (2014), 47–77.

5 G. C. Thompson, *Public Opinion and Lord Beaconsfield, 1875–1880*, vol. 1 (London: Macmillan, 1886), p. 184; Harris, *The Bulgarian Horrors*, pp. 44–5, 110–11.

6 W. E. Gladstone to Henry Layard, [19] April 1877. Huntington Library, Gladstone Papers, GLA 437.

7 Layard to Gladstone, 9 May 1877. Layard Papers, British Library, Add. MS 44454, fol. 113.

8 This was the largest number of consuls ever employed in the Near East since the British government had taken over administration of this system in the 1820s from the Levant Company, which had run the consular system as a loose commercial network starting in 1592. Reforms to the Levant Consular Service in 1877 raised standards for applicants and set out to make the service more 'English'. As Constantinople attaché Lord Strangford put it: 'We must have Englishmen in our public service in Turkey, if we do not send out Englishmen we must Anglicize our Levantines, and for my part I think we can afford to do both.' John Dickie, *The British Consul* (London: Hurst, 2007), pp. 61–3.

9 On late nineteenth-century missionary activity in the Near East see: Michelle

Tusan, 'Gleaners in the Holy Land: Women and the Missionary Press in Victorian Britain', *Nineteenth-Century Gender Studies*, 6:2 (Summer 2010), www.ncgsjournal.com/issue62/tusan.htm; on philanthropists see Dorothy Anderson, *The Balkan Volunteers* (London: Hutchinson, 1968).

10 Scholars interested in Britain's engagement with the Ottoman Empire primarily have relied on accounts written by travel writers to understand this world. Billie Melman, *Women's Orients* (Ann Arbor: University of Michigan, 1992); Gerald Maclean, *The Rise of Oriental Travel* (Basingstoke: Palgrave, 2004); Nancy Stockdale, *Colonial Encounters among English and Palestinian Women* (Gainesville: University of Florida Press, 2007). A notable exception is Priya Satia, *Spies in Arabia* (Oxford: Oxford University Press, 2008).

11 Dickie, *The British Consul*, pp. 17–19.

12 Henry Layard, *Discoveries in the Ruins of Nineveh and Babylon*, Part 2, (London: John Murray, 1853, Elibron reprint), p. 431.

13 Sir A. Henry Layard, *Autobiography and letters from his childhood until his appointment as HM Ambassador at Madrid*, vol. 1 (London: John Murray), 1903, pp. 157–60.

14 Layard, *Autobiography*, pp. 248–51.

15 Sir Arthur Otoway, quoted by Bruce in Layard, *Autobiography*, pp. 112, 267.

16 Layard to Granville, quoted in Gordon Waterfield, *Layard of Nineveh* (New York: Praeger, 1968), p. 236.

17 Layard to Lady Huntly, 25 April 1853, Layard Papers, British Library, Add. MS 38944, fol. 120.

18 Layard to Lady Huntly, 23 October 1857, Layard Papers, British Library, Add. MS 38944, fol. 164.

19 Layard to Morelli, 20 July 1876, Layard Papers, British Library, Add. MS 38966, fol. 198.

20 Layard to Lady Gregory, 30 November 1876, Layard Papers, 38966, fol. 198. Shannon, *Gladstone*, p. 109.

21 Shannon, *Gladstone*, p. 195.

22 Shannon, *Gladstone*, pp. 121–2.

23 'Our Relations with Turkey: Notes of a Conversation with Sir. H. Layard', *Contemporary Review*, May 1885, pp. 609–16, at p. 612.

24 Layard, *Nineveh*, p. 4.

25 Layard to Viscount Redcliffe, September 10, 1877. Layard Papers, British Library, Add. MS 39124, fol. 114.

26 This was spelled out in article 61 of the Berlin Treaty, which recognised Britain as the legitimate protector of Ottoman Christian minority interests.

27 Lord Strangford attended Oxford and served as a student attaché to Constantinople in 1845. He later served as Oriental Secretary during the Crimean War. Beaufort's own interest in the Ottoman Empire stemmed from a tour to Syria, Asia Minor and Egypt which provided the basis of a popular two-volume travel book, that went into multiple editions, based on her adventures in 1861 and called *Egyptian Sepulchres and Syrian Shrines including some stay in the Lebanon, at Palmyra, and in Western Turkey*. She met her future husband after he reviewed her book and they married soon after, in February 1862. Their mutual interest in the western lands of the Ottoman Empire resulted in her second book, *The Eastern Shores of the Adriatic*, published in 1864 after a tour they took to Albania, Montenegro, Dalmatia and Corfu. *Dictionary of National Biography*, 1882, and *Dictionary of National Biography* (hereafter: *DNB*), 2004, pp. 467–8.

28 Upon the death of her husband, Lady Strangford took charge of her own fortune, from which she had been drawing only a £200 allowance. Lord Strangford was worth £3,000 when he died, while her fortune was estimated at £27,885 when she died. Lady Strangford's will, Francis Beaufort (Sir) Papers (hereafter: Beaufort Papers), Huntington Library, San Marino, California, Box 35.

29 Dorothy Anderson, *The Balkan Volunteers*, pp. 14–5, 208.

30 Lady Strangford's Bulgaria Journal, Beaufort Papers, Huntington Library, Box 35; *DNB*, 2004, p. 457.

31 Lady Strangford's Bulgaria Journal, 11 February 1877.
32 Lady Strangford's Bulgaria Journal, 18 February 1877.
33 Eugene Schuyler to Lady S, Philippopolis, 1876 (Turkey), Beaufort Papers, Huntington Library, Box 35.
34 Lady Strangford's Bulgaria Journal, 14 October–11 November 1876.
35 Lady Strangford's Bulgaria Journal, 13 and 20 February.
36 Lady Strangford's Bulgaria Journal, 14 October 1876.
37 Lady Strangford's Bulgaria Journal, 11 November 1876.
38 Strangford to Layard, 8 September 1877, Layard Papers, British Library, Add. MS 39015, fol. 54.
39 Lady Strangford's Bulgaria Journal, 11 February 1877.
40 Lady Strangford's Bulgaria Journal, 11 November 1876.
41 Strangford to Layard, May 22, 1878. Layard Papers British Library, Add. MS 39020, fol. 134: emphasis in original.
42 Freeman quoted in Anderson, *Balkan Volunteers*, p. 16.
43 Strangford to Layard, 19 February 1880. Layard Papers, British Library, Add. MS 39031, fol. 243. More relief schemes followed, including the Victoria Hospital at Cairo for British. She died on the outbound voyage to Port Said, where she was on her way to set up a subscription hospital for British seamen.
44 Layard to Everett, 7 February 1880. Everett Collection, Middle East Centre Archives (MECA), St Antony's College, Oxford University, Box 2, File 4b.
45 Diary, 8 February 1882, Everett Collection, MECA, Box 2, File 2c.
46 Diary, 7, 8 February and 9 March 1882, Everett Collection.
47 Strangford to Layard, 2 September 1877, Layard Papers, British Library, Add. MS 39015, fol. 54.
48 Strangford to Layard, 24 October 1877, Layard Papers, British Library, Add. MS 39016, fols 86–8.
49 Strangford to Layard, 10 May 1878, Layard Papers, British Library, Add. MS 39020, fol. 71.
50 Strangford to Layard, 1 July 1878, Layard Papers, British Library, Add. MS 39021, fol. 1.
51 Strangford to Layard, 21 September 1878, Layard Papers, British Library, Add. MS 39022, fol. 82.
52 Strangford to Layard, 19 February 1880, Layard Papers, British Library, Add. MS 39031, fol. 243.
53 Strangford to Layard, 5 April 1880, Layard Papers, British Library, Add. MS 39032, fol. 240.
54 Shannon, *Gladstone*; Millman, *Britain and the Eastern Question, 1875–1878*; Saab, *Reluctant Icon*.
55 Strangford to Layard, 30 April 1880, Layard Papers, British Library, Add. MS 39033, fol. 95.
56 Personal writings, 11 March 1883, Layard Papers, British Library, Add. MS 39143, fol. 279.
57 Confidential Print Correspondence on 'Protestant Constitution' negotiations, April, May, June 1880, Layard Papers, British Library, Add. MS 39156.
58 'Conversation with Layard', *Contemporary Review*, 1885, p. 611.
59 Layard to Granville, 1 June 1880, Layard Papers, British Library, Add. MS 39156, fol. 145.
60 Michelle Tusan, *Smyrna's Ashes: Humanitarianism, Genocide and the Birth of the Middle East* (Berkeley: University of California Press, 2012); Donald Bloxham, *Great Game of Genocide* (Oxford: Oxford University Press, 2005); Akaby Nassibian, *Britain and the Armenian Question* (London: Croom Helm, 1984).

CHAPTER FIVE

A semi-exclusionary empire? The use of British colonial ideals in Trinidad and Bengal

Martin J. Wiener

The somewhat cryptic title of this chapter refers to an influential collection of essays edited by the distinguished US colonial historian Jack Greene, entitled *Exclusionary Empire.* That work was dedicated to 'all of those subordinated people who lost their lands, cultures, freedoms, and lives in the construction of Britain's "empire of liberty", which denied them civic space'.[1] Such an unusually polemical dedication to a work of scholarship is very much of our time, when the issue of historic injustices to indigenous peoples has moved high on the agenda of contemporary political causes. It is past time, many historians feel, to challenge self-satisfied accounts of 'the progress of Western civilization' and, within that, of Anglo-American 'liberty' by focusing on those who bore the costs of that progress, those who were excluded from that liberty.

This sort of 'challenging' has flourished in the recent historiography of the British Empire – as book titles like *Britain's Gulag,* on the Kenyan Mau Mau rebellion; *The Unmaking of the Middle East,* on Britain's takeover from the collapsing Ottoman Empire; or *Churchill's Secret War: The British Empire and the Ravaging of India* suggest. Such a righteous impulse, however, even in critique of an equal and opposite righteousness, holds dangers for the work of historians. It pushes us towards simplistic discourse, smoothing over complications and denying paradoxes. As Greene himself noted in 2002, 'the English people assigned an especially prominent, even determinative, role to the English system of laws and liberties'.[2] As Greene himself was then aware, this system had a tendency to escape the control of its creators, and even as many Englishmen abroad sought, often successfully, to exclude others from its benefits, many of those others laid claim to the benefits, and not necessarily in vain. The history of the very un-unitary British Empire is characterised by both exclusion and inclusion, and if the story of 'English liberty' has not been a simple 'whiggish' one of gradually and steadily expanding inclusion, neither has it been its opposite, a story of freedom and rights for 'Englishmen', to the on-going exclusion of all others. The long history of the empire is best grasped, I would propose, as 'semi-exclusionary', or 'semi-inclusionary' – at some times a 'white man's empire' and at other times an 'empire of infectious liberty'. All depended, in this various and even fragmented political entity, upon the play and balance of circumstance.

This essay will try to illustrate this claim by describing two conflicts that took place almost simultaneously, on opposite sides of the world – one conflict in which 'English rights' were called upon to rebuff a challenge to white rule, and one in which the extension of such rights to subaltern non-whites was successfully protected against an effort from on high to recall them. From 1891 to 1894 in Trinidad, white planters invoked traditional English rights like habeas corpus and freedom of the press to defeat the efforts of a reformist chief justice to extend the full spectrum of English justice to black and East Indian labourers. At the same time, in Bengal, a lieutenant-governor's determination to pull back a previous piecemeal extension of the right of trial by jury to many Indians was defeated by a subaltern appeal, supported by many 'European' lawyers and judges there, to what they called the 'sacred principles' of English justice.

Trinidad, a tropical island off the coast of Venezuela, had become by the later nineteenth century a backwater of empire, its continuing cultivation of sugar now of steadily diminishing profitability. First, emancipation had reduced the supply of ready labour for the gruelling work of raising this crop as many former slaves deserted plantations to work smallholdings, and then, in 1854, the end of preferential sugar tariffs had exposed planters to the full force of competition from slave-grown sugar in Cuba and Brazil. Desperate planters had persuaded the British authorities to allow the importing of indentured labourers from India. By 1880, 130,000 labourers had been brought over to the island, most choosing to remain when their five-year indentures expired, and in doing so transforming the social composition of the colony. In 1891 those of Indian descent numbered about 70,000 in a population of barely 200,000. Perhaps 20,000 of the rest were more or less 'white', and the remainder were descendants of former slaves.

An English medical man visiting from India in 1891 rather sanguinely noted: 'Of all the colonies in the West Indies, Trinidad is the favoured home of the coolie settler, where [in contrast to the land of his origins] he can easily and rapidly attain comfortable independence.'[3] On the other hand, Trinidad's white elite had originally been based on the ownership of slaves and, despite emancipation, its members expected to run their estates or businesses, and their workers, as they saw fit, not readily brooking 'interference' from imperial officials. 'In the colonial setting of Trinidad', the writer V. S. Naipaul was later to remark of his birthplace, 'where rights were limited, you could have done anything with these people [the indentured labourers].'[4]

Trinidad was a crown colony, ruled without elective representation by a governor appointed from Whitehall. However, the Governor had a nominated Legislative Council, a majority of whose members were not government officials. All of these 'unofficial' members were white, and substantial men of property, and most governors followed their lead. 'The theory of the constitution', it has been observed of Trinidad then, 'asserted autocracy. The practice of politics assumed an oligarchy.'[5] For a brief period during and following slave emancipation, the governors had truly ruled. But as many British sympathisers with abolitionism became disillusioned with the insufficiently 'productive' behaviour of the freed Afro-Caribbean population, the strength of the abolitionist lobby had waned, and with the loss of that prod, central government interest in the internal affairs of the West Indies colonies had similarly diminished. Planters had then been able to regain political leverage over governors.

During the later nineteenth century, colonial governors appointed to West Indies backwaters were more likely to cultivate than to confront their planter elites. As the well-known man of letters J. A. Froude noted in 1888 after a visit (just as our story opens), these islands had 'been made to serve as places where governors try their 'prentice hand and learn their business before promotion to more important situations. Whether a man has done well or done ill makes, it seems, very little difference unless he has offended prejudices or interests.'[6] As Philip Harling has described in Chapter Three of this volume, the growth of world competition and the loss of tariff protection placed the business of sugar cultivation under increasing pressure in the later nineteenth century, making those West Indian planters who had survived the blow of emancipation determined to resist any further inroads into their control of their business either from their workforce or from reformist officials. The rebellious examples of Haiti and Jamaica always in their minds, planters were especially wary of any signs of political mobilisation among their workers. These fears were heightened by a growing number of strikes, and came to a head in October 1884, when, at a moment when sugar prices were falling and consequently wages were being cut, an Indian festival seemed to be turning into a disorderly political protest and the Governor authorised police to shoot down a number of unarmed people.[7]

This shooting seems to have awakened the Colonial Office; some months later it appointed a new Governor, Sir William Robinson, and a new Chief Justice, Sir John Gorrie, both of whom proved more independent of the local oligarchy than their predecessors had been. Gorrie, who had in his youth worked for the Jamaica Committee (led by John Stuart Mill and other 'Radicals') to bring a criminal prosecution against that colony's Governor, Edward Eyre, for his brutal suppression of a small uprising, particularly raised local hackles. The officials in the Colonial Office knew that his reformist reputation would make his appointment unpopular with the white community but, as the Under-secretary remarked, 'in the West Indies it is generally a good thing to have a Chief Justice who does not care for popularity'.[8] However, he may have under-estimated just how unpopular Gorrie would become.

Gorrie took his appointment as a mandate for reform, and, overruling elite objections, he within a short time made Trinidad's sluggish and expensive legal system more available to the wider public by speeding up procedures and making legal aid available to those who convinced him they were in need. The number of lawsuits, particularly those in which fees were waived after a declaration of 'poverty', soared, and ordinary people began in large numbers to bring their grievances, particularly those against landlords and moneylenders, to court. Gorrie also restricted magistrates' highly discretionary use of the master and servant laws to help employers control their workers. In court he sharply criticised lawyers, medical men and even the chief of police for failing in their duties to the public, nor did he hesitate to pronounce from the bench his views on current political questions. In the space of a year, there were few members of the white elite he had not offended. Planters, merchants and professional men began to feel under siege, harassed in the midst of an economic depression by a chief justice seemingly determined to deprive them of any way of maintaining control of their increasingly restive labourers, their share-croppers or their debtors.

In little more than a year after Gorrie's arrival the Chamber of Commerce, the Trinidadian Bar and the Medical Board all produced petitions asking for an official enquiry into his behaviour. These moves called forth an even larger popular counter-petition in his support; he became a well-known public figure, cheered in the streets. As an 1887 street ballad's first stanza ran:

> All you who have ears to hear and brain to understand,
> Come listen to Judge Gorrie's praises the wisest in the land,
> He likes the poor to get their right, the rich he does not fear;
> He is the greatest blessing of this great Jubilee year.

Such signs of Gorrie's popularity only raised for his critics the spectre of race and class conflict.[9] Even Governor Robinson, no friend to the planters and a past critic of the state of justice in the colony, lost patience with Gorrie's outspokenness, complaining to the Colonial Secretary in London that '[he] resembles the metaphorical "Bull in a China Shop"'.[10] Whitehall officials privately agreed: Edward Wingfield, in charge of the West Indies desk, sadly concluded that Gorrie was 'a violent and reckless person'.[11] Still, the Colonial Office swallowed its irritation and, recognising the value of having a strong chief justice who could stand up to West Indian planters, refused an enquiry. But the situation continued to deteriorate, as Gorrie took no heed of criticism, continuing to rule against planters in cases before him, not hesitating to publicly chastise men of position when they failed, in his eyes, to behave appropriately. All this made him an even greater hero to the non-white populace. As a leading newspaper complained in 1889, 'the name of Sir John is commonly used by the working-classes to employers and planters as a threat to enforce their insolent and unreasonable demands'.[12]

Finally, in 1891, the stars aligned for Gorrie's opponents. As part of the Colonial Office's policy of frequently moving governors around, a new Governor, F. N. Broome, more sympathetic to the planters than his predecessor, arrived in Trinidad. At the same time, an undeniable judicial scandal emerged: one of the other two judges in the colony, Justice Cook, had turned out to be an alcoholic and had rendered verdicts while under the influence. This conjunction provided the right soil for a new effort to depose Gorrie.[13] A planter who had been jailed, and set very high bail, on dubious grounds for contempt of court by Justice Cook, a jailing upheld on appeal by Chief Justice Gorrie, instituted upon his release a suit against them both, and a Civil Rights Defence Fund was created to send him to England to pursue his action, which he did. He and his supporters described themselves there in a letter to the *Pall Mall Gazette* as 'individuals enjoying hitherto some remnants of the rights of free men and British subjects, and bent on defending and, if possible, preserving those rights'.[14] Back in Trinidad, with Governor Broome instructing the official members to abstain, the Legislative Council passed a resolution urging a formal enquiry into the conduct of the two judges. Gorrie's opponents made sure to bring some English opinion to their side, including not just the *European Mail*, the newspaper of the 'West India interest', but *Truth*, a London paper owned and edited by the Liberal politician Henry Labouchere, and even the *Pall Mall Gazette*, which had at first been sympathetic to Gorrie and his well-known 'love of justice', but which by the end of the controversy welcomed the appointment of a successor, observing how 'the confidence of investors' had been 'rudely shaken' by the unfortunate conflicts between the branches of government in the colony.[15]

A question was asked in the House of Commons, a West Indian Civil Rights Defence Committee was set up in an office near the Law Courts, and a cry was raised of colonial liberty and property under threat from judicial 'tyrants', a cry that could always rouse sympathy in the House and on Fleet Street.[16]

Finally the Colonial Office gave way, and a Commission consisting of two distinguished jurists, Sir William Markby, a Liberal, and Sir Frederick Pollock, a Conservative, was sent out in 1892 to take evidence and report on the administration of justice in Trinidad.[17] The Commissioners first investigated Justice Cook, and found that he should be removed from the Bench; he was eventually dismissed without pension. Gorrie's case was more difficult, and they ruled some of the charges against him to be without substance. However, the majority of charges, they concluded, were well founded. Although they made it clear that 'we see no reason to doubt that Sir John Gorrie was actuated by a desire to do justice', they found that he had on numerous occasions transgressed the limits set by a reasonable interpretation of judicial discretion and by the scope of his office: encouraging litigation, and appointing free legal representation without clear evidence of inability to pay, for example, were not, they noted, proper activities for judges. They crushingly concluded that in his desire to do substantial justice, Gorrie 'perversely disregarded the explicit provisions of the Ordinances and of well-established principles of law and procedure in dealing with the rights of parties, leading to arbitrary and unjust results, and tending to destroy confidence in the administration of justice'.[18] As one of the planters' English supporters observed in an article entitled 'Are Judges Above the Law?', 'the exaction of excessive bail by Justice Cook was contrary to the Bill of Rights, but Gorrie and Cook actually pleaded in their defence that "The Bill of Rights did not apply to the Islands of Trinidad or Tobago"'.[19] Technically, they were probably correct, but such a defence could only outrage the British public.

Governor Broome asked for the Chief Justice's resignation (as was within his powers), but Gorrie refused to provide it and instead applied for leave to go to England to put his case personally to the Privy Council, the highest legal authority for the empire. By this point, however, his health had seriously deteriorated, and soon after arriving back in England he took ill and died, bringing the issue to a close without requiring further rulings. Gorrie was, a leading Trinidad paper summed up in an obituary, 'an enemy-making man, especially as his lot was cast in those tropical Crown Colonies where white and coloured peoples are found together'.[20] In these mixed-race colonies, a judge determined to provide equal justice would inevitably make powerful enemies, and if he also had an imperious temper and lost the shield that a friendly governor could provide, it was hardly surprising that his career ended in humiliating dismissal.[21] In Trinidad, judicial 'tyranny' in the interests of the submerged coloured majority was crushed.

At the same time, on the other side of the world, another struggle over 'the rights of the subject' was going on, with quite different results. In Trinidad in the early 1890s, the Bill of Rights became a rallying-cry against a judge; in Bengal, the most populous province of British India, it was similarly invoked, this time against a lieutenant governor. However, if in Trinidad it was the wealthy white settlers who were successfully calling upon the Constitution, in Bengal it was native Indians.

By 1892 Bengal's Lieutenant Governor, Charles Elliott (who, despite his title, was the actual Governor of the province – because the capital of British India, Calcutta, was located in Bengal the province's chief administrator was technically subordinate there to the Viceroy, but in practice he exercised the powers of a provincial governor), had become steadily more unhappy about a long-declining rate of criminal convictions. In that year, consequently, he issued a Notification announcing his intention to remove the most serious offences, including riot and murder, from jury trial (unless the defendant was 'European').[22] To Elliott's mind, the existing legal system had come to follow English models unthinkingly, failing to appreciate the great differences between India and England.[23] In doing so, it threw up numerous 'obstacles' to effective prosecution – over-strict evidentiary rules, over-lenient rights of appeal and, most of all, trial by jury, which though it did not exist in most of India, had become entrenched in the major cities – Calcutta, Bombay and Madras – and had gradually been extended into rural areas around those cities. Hindu culture, Elliott argued, made Indian juries too lenient to persons of high caste or social standing, and in any event they were notoriously open to influence and outright bribery. Trial by jury was the obstacle that was most within his power to restrict, and he intended to do just that.

Elliott's Notification unleashed a storm of protest. Political Indians, who had been pressing for a further expansion of trial by jury, denounced the Notification as a major step towards despotism. They not only passed resolutions at large public meetings and submitted a petition to the India Office, but (as Trinidad planters were doing) also lobbied Members of Parliament and leading British papers. There they evoked more sympathy than Elliott had ever anticipated, for trial by jury was seen, virtually across the political spectrum, as one of the most fundamental principles of the English constitution.[24] Lord

Kimberley, Secretary of State for India, observed from his Whitehall office that he could 'hardly remember any [Indian] matter which has excited so much feeling here ... the unanimity with which the Press, quite independent of politics, has condemned the measure is very remarkable', he warned Lord Lansdowne, the Viceroy.[25]

Moreover, the opposition in India itself was not confined to natives. The High Court of Bengal, all but one of its members 'European', quite unusually criticised the Notification publicly, as did the presiding Judge of the Assam Valley District, home of most of India's tea plantations, where racial tensions were perhaps the highest in all India. As a result, the judges (despite the fact that many of them held low opinions of the trustworthiness of the Indians that came before them in court) became for a while popular heroes, lauded in the Indian press (not unlike Gorrie's situation in Trinidad).[26] Even many Anglo lawyers and newspaper editors criticised the Lieutenant Governor, worried that this change, even though it exempted 'European' defendants, would set a dangerous precedent.[27] Elliott privately confessed that 'I have been surprised to find how much the non-official Calcutta Englishman sympathises with the feeling [against his action]. The belief that the Executive Government is inclined to be despotic is ingrained in them.' Such prejudice against government's dangerous tendency to over-reach was a typically British political sentiment that at least momentarily united Indians and many Europeans in India in defence of juries and judges against the executive power.[28]

This behaviour of the High Court was not an isolated event; throughout the history of the Raj a fault-line had run between the executive and judicial branches of government, which frequently prevented its theoretically despotic authority from being realised in practice. Each branch could draw support from members of the European community, depending on the circumstances. This fault-line offered a potential wedge for Indians to cite 'sacred British political principles' in defence of their interests in this nominal autocracy, in a way not unlike the way that West Indian planters could defend their interests by appealing to 'constitutional principles'.[29]

The Viceroy was instructed by the India Office to lower the temperature by the familiar device of referring the issue to a Commission for further study. This Commission, headed by Justice Henry Prinsep of the Calcutta High Court, a bench that Elliott had previously criticised for acquitting law-breakers on technicalities, and whose members bore him little good will, reported in 1893 against change; the Lieutenant Governor had to give in and withdrew the Notification.[30] However, he then shifted his efforts to another front. Within the year the High Court sent a protest to the Viceroy to be forwarded to the Secretary of State complaining that the Lieutenant Governor was continuing to criticise the courts, and in particular was applying fresh pressure upon magistrates and police to obtain more convictions, which was causing police to fabricate evidence and torture suspects for confessions.[31] The Indian-run press rushed to support the judges: after all, one editor noted, 'in England the judiciary has always been independent of the executive, and every reader of history knows how much blood this independence cost England in the past'.[32] The embarrassed India Office forced a public cessation of this quarrel. The Viceroy was told to make it clear that Bengal officials were not to publish any criticisms of judges or juries, and for their part judges were to confine themselves strictly to the cases before them.[33] The Lieutenant Governor's 'law and order' campaign was over, and, embittered, he took leave to return to England. His temporary replacement, the more liberal A. P. MacDonnell, astutely deprecated him to Lansdowne as a man preferring to govern by 'Continental rather than English methods'.[34] None of Elliott's successors revived his effort to restrict jury trial; indeed, in the course of the twentieth century, with the growth of local and regional self-government, jury trials were extended to more areas of India. Ironically, however, jury trial met its end once India became independent: in 1960 the Government of India, claiming that juries were too susceptible to media influence and to corruption (both complaints that Elliott had made) abolished it. If the 'radical' Gorrie was vindicated by history, so too was the 'reactionary' Elliott. The shades of both may have been gratified.

What have we seen here? Two cases of defeated officials, both for supposed 'unconstitutional' behaviour that infringed upon 'English rights'; but one of them championed non-white 'subalterns' while the other tried to roll back their access to justice. Politically, one case underlined the exclusionary side of empire, in which the cry of 'English rights' served to protect a narrow elite and rebuff an effort to extend access to justice; the other case highlighted its inclusionary side, successfully defending the extension of new rights – very 'English' rights – to the colonised. The exclusionary drama could have been repeated in many plantation colonies; the inclusionary one, on the other hand, took place in the largest British possession by far, the 'jewel in the crown'. Which revealed the 'real' empire? Neither. There *was* no 'real' British Empire. Rather, the empire was a complex and often contradictory entity, a 'semi-exclusionary', or, if one prefers, a 'semi-inclusionary' empire, shaped at least as much through on-going political contention 'on the spot' as in the rooms of the Colonial Office. Throughout the history of the empire, and throughout its worldwide territories, these interests and pressures – for inclusion in the 'English' constitutional order on the one hand, for exclusion on the other – warred, with the outcome depending upon particular circumstances. In the long run, inclusion gained the upper hand almost everywhere – but only, tragically, when the empire itself was on the verge of dissolution. And, in a further historical irony, it was only after the empire's end that some aspects of attempted imperial 'exclusion' triumphed.

Notes

1 Jack Greene (ed.), *Exclusionary Empire: English Liberty Overseas, 1600–1900* (Cambridge: Cambridge University Press, 2009).

2 Jack Greene, '"By Their Laws Shall Ye Know Them": Law and Identity in Colonial British America', *Journal of Interdisciplinary History*, 33:2 (2002), 247–60, at 253–4.

3 Quoted in Walton Look Lai, *Indentured Labor, Caribbean Sugar: Chinese and Indian Migrants to the British West Indies, 1838–1918* (Baltimore: Johns Hopkins University Press, 1993), p. 141. Indentured labourers in Trinidad also benefited from the tradition established during the long tenure of Dr Henry Mitchell, Agent-General of Immigration from 1850 to 1883 (p. 81).

4 V. S. Naipaul, *A Way in the World* (New York: Knopf, 1994), p. 19.

5 F. R. Augier (1966), quoted in Bridget Brereton, *Race Relations in Colonial Trinidad* (Cambridge: Cambridge University Press, 2002), p. 25.

6 James Anthony Froude, *The English in the West Indies, or The Bow of Ulysses* (London: Longmans Green, 1888), p. 92.

7 J. J. Thomas, *Froudacity: West Indian Fables by J. A. Froude Explained* (London: T. Fisher Unwin, 1889), p. 70.

8 Minutes by Antrobus and Herbert, 2 November 1885, quoted in Brereton, *Trinidad*, p. 231.

9 J. J. Thomas, the foremost politically active black in the colony, praised him in 1888 as 'vigilant, fearless, and painstaking'; Thomas, *Froudacity*, p. 109. Two newspapers begun in the preceding few years claimed to represent middle-class black Creoles, and in the late 1880s agitated for an end to the indenture system and for black political representation on the Legislative Council.

10 Robinson to Holland, 17 September 1887, Colonial Office files, The National Archives (hereafter TNA, CO) 295/315. Robinson acknowledged, 'on the other hand there is no doubt that the work of the Supreme Court has hitherto been disgracefully scamped'.

11 TNA, CO 295/321, file 105, minutes of 15 April 1889. Wingfield, a product of Winchester and New College, Oxford, had been called to the Bar and had practised for several years before becoming an assistant under-secretary in 1878, and thus was familiar with appropriate legal procedure.

12 *Port of Spain Gazette*, 20 March 1889, p. 5.

13 For an example of Broome's attending to the interests of planters, see his acquiescence in 1894–95 to shifting the tax burden further away from them and onto the general populace; Brereton, *Race Relations*, pp. 30–1. 'That the course adopted by Sir. F. Broome', Wingfield sourly observed after this surrender, 'was the most convenient for himself there is no doubt', but it was hardly in the best interests of the Government. TNA CO 295/363, file 210, minute of 3 July 1895.

14 *Pall Mall Gazette*, 12 December 1890. On the course of this litigation, and its significance for English law, see Patrick Polden, 'Doctor in Trouble: *Anderson v Gorrie* and the Extension of Judicial Immunity from Suit in the 1890s', *Legal History*, 22 (2001), 37–68. The suit ended only in 1895, after Gorrie's death, when the House of Lords dismissed it in a leading ruling that buttressed judicial immunity from suit. Ironically, a clash that exposed the weak political position of colonial judges

as compared to their home colleagues, and which had led to the removal of one and threatened the imminent removal of another, had the result of strengthening judicial immunity in England. Viewing the situation from England, Polden does not fully appreciate the difficult situation that faced colonial judges, who may have been immune from suit, but not at all from removal.

15 *Pall Mall Gazette*, 22 September 1890; 2 December 1892 (the new Chief Justice, it happily noted, was apparently possessed of 'common sense'.)

16 See, for example, *Truth*, 4 August 1892, and Hugh H. L. Bellot, 'A Judicial Scandal: Are Judges Above the Law?' *Westminster Review*, 145 (January–June 1896), 237–46, 388–406.

17 Markby had served for some years on the Calcutta High Court and was a reader in Indian Law at Oxford; Pollock was also at Oxford as a professor of Jurisprudence, and was a very highly regarded barrister.

18 From a telegram summarising their findings, TNA, CO 295/338, file 170 (15 June 1892).

19 Bellot, 'A Judicial Scandal', 401.

20 *European Mail*, 13 August 1892.

21 With Gorrie gone, the Governor could comfortably rebuff Inspector of Immigration Gibbins's request of February of that year to be allowed to provide legal assistance to immigrant labourers charged with criminal offences, since magistrates frequently would not. In May, Broome told him that would be impossible, since he was not legally qualified; the question would have to remain at the discretion of the magistrates. TNA, CO 295/338, file 160.

22 In Bengal, conviction rates for property crime had not changed significantly, but for crimes of violence they had (and it was this category from which Elliott sought to remove jury trial): with the total number of cases changing little, a conviction rate that had been 53.4 per cent in 1879 had fallen to 38.6 per cent by 1892; Annual Returns of Bengal Criminal Statistics, Oriental and India Office Collection, British Library (hereafter OIOC), V/24/2201 and 2202. It is unlikely, however, that jury trial had much to do with this, as criminal conviction rates had fallen even further in other parts of India where jury trial was rare: in the United Provinces, the percentage of convictions in all criminal cases had decreased even more, from 74.8 per cent in 1875 to 43.6 per cent in 1892; David Campion, 'Watchmen of the Raj: The United Provinces Police, 1870–1931 and the Dilemmas of Colonial Policing in British India', Ph.D. dissertation, University of Virginia, 2002, p. 155.

23 David Washbrook has noted Elliott's fall from favour over a number of issues with the large, Western-educated Indian population of Calcutta, 'who had developed a lively public opinion and a press often critical of British rule. Having served "up-country" most of his life, Elliott was not used to being subject to public comment and reacted strongly'; David Washbrook, 'Elliott, Sir Charles Alfred (1835–1911)', *Oxford Dictionary of National Biography*, Oxford University Press, 2004; online edn, January 2012, www.oxforddnb.com/view/article/33004 (accessed 26 January 2015).

24 Just a few years earlier, the *Times* had observed, after an argument conducted in its pages about its deficiencies, particularly in civil litigation, that 'trial by jury is still in possession' of English public opinion. Until that changed, 'any attempt to limit a man's right to a jury will surely excite vehement resistance in the name of liberty'. *Times*, 4 September 1890, p. 9.

25 Kimberley to Lansdowne, 5 January 1893, OIOC LP C.558/6/1. Writing to Gladstone a year later, Kimberley called the appointment of Lansdowne as Viceroy his 'one great blunder'. Letter, 21 January 1894, in *Liberal by Principle*, p. 214, OIOC LP C.558/6/1.

26 Henry Prinsep, unpublished memoirs (1912), p. 438, OIOC. The barrister members of the High Court had already demonstrated their resistance to tampering with trial by jury by refusing to make use of a provision in Stephen's Code of Criminal Procedure that allowed the High Court to overturn a jury verdict it found clearly in error; Prinsep, unpublished memoirs, p. 407.

27 Elliott to Lansdowne, 24 November 1892, OIOC M/3/103 (Lansdowne Papers). Not that this influenced him: 'I cannot admit', he continued to the Viceroy, 'that a single argument has been adduced against my action; it has been pure interpolation.'

28 In both British India and British West Africa, local native lawyers were instrumental in pushing these issues forward, professional self-interest and the wider interests of their compatriots coming together (as of course had been true in colonial America).

29 For more on this fault-line and its consequences, see Martin J. Wiener, *An Empire on Trial: Race, Murder and Justice under British Rule, 1870–1935* (Cambridge: Cambridge University Press, 2009), chs 5 and 6.

30 OIOC L/P&J/6/342, file 570: telegram from Viceroy to India Office, 25 March 1893, summarising the Juries Commission report.

31 OIOC L/P&J/6/351, file 1241: 6 June 1893.

32 *Hitavadi*, 31 August 1893, OIOC L/R/5/19.

33 OIOC L/P&J/6/338, file 217: Kimberley to Lansdowne, 1 June 1893.

34 OIOC Mss. Eur. D 558/25, Macdonnell to Lansdowne, 13 July 1893.

CHAPTER SIX

The curious case of the *chabutra-wallahs*: Britons and Irish imperial culture in nineteenth-century India

Barry Crosbie

Less than two years after the financially troubled Dublin Industrial Exhibition of 1853 closed its doors to the public, the editors of the influential London magazine, *The Art Journal*, poured scorn on the very notion that mid-Victorian Ireland could somehow be dragged from its existing state of distress and poverty to host a grand imperial exhibition on the same scale as London or Paris. 'As a means of encouraging and developing Irish industry', the *Journal* noted, 'it [the Industrial Exhibition of 1853] was simply absurd.' 'The Dublin experiment was to Hibernian industry what a dress coat and white kid gloves would be to the shirtless, shoeless, and bare-headed gossoon.'[1] A joint venture hosted by the Royal Society of Arts in England, and its sister organisation in Ireland, the Royal Dublin Society, the Dublin Exhibition of 1853 was originally conceived as an 'Irish Crystal Palace', an Empire exhibition of the arts and manufactures designed to strengthen 'the economic bonds between Britain and her colonies' by stimulating industrial development and growth in post-famine Ireland.[2] At the centre of the Dublin Exhibition was the East India Company's prized 'Eastern Collection' of Indian and Oriental art and objects, loaned for display in Dublin by the Royal Society with the express purpose of 'making the arts and manufactures of India better known in Europe'.[3] With public interest in Indian affairs at a high point following the renewal of the Company's Charter in 1853, and Lord Dalhousie's ambitious programme of scientific and technological reform as Governor-General in full swing, Indian industry was being held up as an important model within the emerging dependent empire of British imperial 'development' and 'progress'. By bringing 'together the best and most illustrative specimens of the arts and manufactures of the East, especially articles which exhibit the habits and customs of eastern nations', the Royal Society of Arts hoped that such a display could not fail to 'exert a beneficial influence on the arts of design to this country [Ireland]'.[4]

That Irish and Indian culture should intersect so precisely in the context of the flow of mid-nineteenth-century colonial knowledge and material culture is not all that surprising, given the long association and connection between both countries. Despite the misgivings expressed by the editors of *The Art Journal* over Ireland's ability to harness the empire's vast economic potential, such attitudes obfuscate the major Irish contribution to the spread of British imperialism overseas during the same period. From the mid-eighteenth until the late nineteenth century, Ireland and India were joined together by an intricate series of networks of military recruitment, intellectual exchange and political interdependence. These networks were imperial in nature and were born out of direct Irish involvement in British territorial expansion into South Asia during the Seven Years' War (1756–63).[5] Here, Irish men and women (both Catholic and Protestant) served as soldiers, missionaries, educators, doctors, scientists and administrators within the various colonial services of the Raj, where they played an important part in the formation of the colonial state and in defining its expanding roles and responsibilities in its Indian environment.

Although not officially a 'colony' of the British Empire, Ireland was nevertheless subjected to extensive Tudor colonisation during the sixteenth and seventeenth centuries, and was joined legislatively to Great Britain under the Act of Union between 1801 and 1922. Owing to the existence of various constitutional anomalies lying at the heart of the Union, however, Ireland developed its own unique political status within the empire replete with its own quasi-colonial administration and police force.[6] Yet, unlike the combined forces of Protestantism and war that worked to secure Scotland's integration into the United Kingdom as well as the emergence of a common 'British' identity among the English and Scots after 1707, the vast majority of Ireland's Catholic population – long subjected to penal legislation that prevented them from sitting in Parliament, owning land or obtaining commissions in the British army or entering the professions – were never fully integrated into the sinews of metropolitan power.[7] While classified as 'Britons' under the Union, Irish people (including many other marginalised non-Anglican Protestant groups such as Irish Presbyterians and Methodists) were never quite comfortable with a 'British' designation, and did not necessarily see themselves as such. In this sense, late eighteenth- and nineteenth-century Ireland was never an homogenous economic, political or religious entity whose historic relationship with Britain was straightforward or uniform. Instead, Ireland comprised a multiplicity of communities, each with their own distinctive traditions and cultural values, and each with their own particular relationship with the empire. For William Hoey, a Belfast-born Irish Presbyterian magistrate based in Lucknow in the 1880s, there was a clear distinction between Irish and English people in India which could not be easily reconciled. According to Hoey, 'the Irish Protestant stood outside that English Mutual Admiration Society for which he calls the Union or the Empire. The Irish Protestant simply seized on English power; used it for his own purposes ... with freedom from the scruples of world politics. The business was Irish business, not English; and he was Irish.'[8] For Richardson Evans, a Cork-born Wesleyan Methodist stationed as an Assistant Magistrate and Collector in Mirzapur in the 1860s, an Irish Protestant identity was compatible with contemporary understandings of Britishness. Once recalling how he had been mistaken for a British 'Chabutra-Wallah with an unusual accent' rather than a 'proud Irishman from Cork', his response was that he was filled 'half with pride at being one and half with pride that [he had] been mistaken for an Englishman'.[9] For Patrick Heffernan, a Tipperary-born Catholic employed in the Indian Medical Service in the 1890s, imperial service did not necessarily confirm the nationalist view of them as typical 'Shawneens' or 'West-Britons'; in his memoir he recalled how he and his colleagues deeply 'believed in the British Empire' and how as 'Irish Europeans, cosmopolitans and citizens of the world' the empire enabled them to 'live satisfying lives ... perhaps contributing a share, great or small, to human progress and human civilisation'.[10] For Heffernan, his and his colleagues' long association with Britain and the empire did not diminish their sense of Irishness; careers in India, and more broadly within the British imperial administration itself, did not mean 'that we did not consider ourselves good Irishmen, we did'.[11]

Clearly, Irish people (of various religious denominations) in the service of empire viewed themselves as being both part of, yet separate from, the British imperial system. This is evidenced in the certain measure of discomfort and defensiveness in the articulation of identities by individuals such as William Hoey, Richardson Evans and Patrick Heffernan. While the contradiction of being both colonised 'other' and coloniser of indigenous peoples in the same historical moment contributed further to the inherent tensions that existed between nineteenth-century Irish, British and imperial identities, there is little doubt that different conceptions of race, ethnicity (and, quite possibly, of class) among the different categories of Irish lie at the heart of such tensions. Although evidence suggests that the Irish were as enthusiastic as any other Britons about the opportunities that the empire afforded them, there were, nevertheless, subtle differences in how the Irish viewed the empire, the degree to which they embraced their 'imperialness', as well as the extent to which they were imbued with an awareness of empire and the imperial ideal. These fundamental differences were often reflected in the diverse nature of Irish interactions with India, with intent ranging from self-interest to full imperial participation, and suggest that the Irish should not be cached under any single descriptor. While their presence may have served imperial purposes, archival evidence suggests that their motivations were different from those who fully embraced and contributed to imperial interests, and were important factors in differentiating the Irish from other Britons both at home and abroad during the nineteenth century.

This is significant because in recent years an increasing number of scholars have begun to consider more fully the distinct experiences of separate Irish, English, Scottish and Welsh relationships with the British Empire.[12] For over two decades, proponents of the 'New British History' have attempted to view the domestic history of Britain and Ireland in the context of the experiences of the four primary ethnic groups that constituted these lands, namely, Irish, English, Scottish and Welsh.[13] Yet, the history of the British Empire – integral to the unfolding of the history in each of these locations – has until the past fifteen years been treated separately. Traditional accounts of metropolitan-focused imperial history, for example, have tended to view the history of the British Empire almost exclusively from the perspective of London. By focusing upon the binary interactions between 'metropole' and 'periphery' such accounts have helped to consign the history of Irish, Scottish and Welsh involvement to the margins of imperial history, while simultaneously obscuring the crucial role of indigenous peoples and the colonies themselves in the imperial process.

As an integral component of the larger British world in the nineteenth century, the Irish were central in the economic, political and cultural construction of that system; during that time most Irish people thought of themselves in distinct ethnic and racial terms and saw their contributions to British imperialism and culture as being wholly separate from their English, Scottish and Welsh counterparts. Indeed, one of the key objectives of this chapter is to problematise the idea of 'Britishness' by looking at some of the ways in which one specific component of nineteenth-century Britain (Ireland) impacted directly upon the empire and vice versa. Although the idea of the Irish as agents of empire is not new, the extent to which distinct Irish, Welsh and, particularly, Scottish personal, commercial and professional associations spun linkages and ethnically based networks of their own, foregrounding 'British' imperialism and culture, is only beginning to be uncovered. Building on the work of scholars such as John MacKenzie, Tom Devine and Keith Jeffery, this chapter examines how cultures of religious, scientific and political thought drew from Irish institutions, methods and personnel, and how an awareness of these processes can be used to inform our understanding of the extent to which 'Britishness' was influenced by 'Irishness', and how British imperial culture was suffused with distinctly 'Irish' elements.[14] Moreover, the examples in this chapter serve to demonstrate how nineteenth-century Ireland functioned as an important site from which knowledge, expertise and personnel all moved with great fluidity back and forth across the British world. This supports one of the book's central concerns, namely the decentring of imperial culture by challenging traditional metro-centric views of the conduits and directionality of cultural flows radiating from London outward. Rather than ideas, personnel and knowledge flowing from an imperial centre to a colonial periphery, this chapter argues that they travelled in multiple directions, sometimes bypassing metropolitan Britain altogether. In doing so, this chapter aims to advance an understanding of the British Empire as a system foregrounded by a plethora of imperial cultures; a system held together by more than the material factors of demography, economics and military power.

Following Catholic emancipation in the late 1820s, many of Ireland's newly founded seminaries and religious institutions began to play an important role in influencing the growth and development of Catholicism in India, particularly in terms of supplying vicars apostolic and clergy to attend to the spiritual requirements of the empire's ever-expanding Irish soldiering communities. In this fashion, several Irish religious networks came to dominate numerous Indian Catholic communities and British military cantonments throughout the nineteenth century and played a prominent role in shaping Catholic practices in an Indian environment as well as informing official attitudes to it. This period, in particular, witnessed the beginning of a gradual integration and later steady flow of Irish-born and Irish-educated Catholics (religious figures and university-trained professionals) to complement the large number of Irish Protestants already active within Britain's wider imperial system in the East. With the renewed confidence that was provided by the psychological boon of emancipation, many early nineteenth-century Irish Catholic clergy on the subcontinent worked to promote the interests of a particular Gaelic Irish dimension within Anglo-Indian society. They ministered to the East India Company's many Gaelic-speaking Irish soldiers; set about introducing a reconstructed parochial system in India which was, in part, modelled along post-emancipation Irish lines, through the building of churches and other ecclesiastical infrastructure; and promoted the education of (high and low caste) Indian and Eurasian children. Indeed, the varying levels of Irish involvement on issues relating to caste, educational provision and church administration demonstrate the myriad ways in which Irish Catholic religious networks became gradually embedded not only in Indian society from the 1830s onward but more broadly in the work of empire building.

In an attempt to cater to the spiritual requirements of the growing number of Irish Catholics overseas as well at home, six major new seminaries, including institutions in Carlow and Maynooth, were founded in Ireland between 1782 and 1837. In addition to these new seminaries and training colleges, an additional special 'foreign missionary seminary', All Hallows College, was established in Dublin in 1842. With over 120 candidates for the priesthood enrolled within the first four years of its inauguration, it was originally anticipated that All Hallows would provide much-needed spiritual support for the growing number of emigrant Irish Catholic communities in North America and Australia in the post-Famine years. However, conscious of the growing number of Irish Catholics recruited into the ranks of the imperial armed forces in India at the time, the founder of All Hallows, Father John Hand, was convinced that Ireland, as one of the principal Catholic countries within the empire, should be the natural centre from which Catholicism should reach out to the non-settler colonies in the East.

One such example of numerous Irish Catholic religious networks that were forged in India in the first half of the nineteenth century and that linked the Company's Catholic rank and file to the activities of both the Irish clergy and local Indian Catholic communities was that established by Father Daniel O'Connor, a former Provincial of the Augustinians in Ireland, who was appointed Vicar Apostolic of the Vicariate of Madras by Propaganda Fide in 1834. Following the appointment of O'Connor, the Vicariate of Madras became something of an Irish Catholic stronghold over the next seventy-five years. In total, there were five successive Irish Catholic bishops appointed to Madras in the nineteenth century; Daniel O'Connor (1834–40), Patrick Carew (1838–40), John Fennelly (1841–68), Stephen Fennelly (1868–80) and Joseph Colgan (1882–1911).[15] Despite initial support from the colonial authorities for their activities in Madras in the 1830s, however, it is interesting to note that the particular religious culture that O'Connor and his Irish priests introduced to Madras in the 1830s was subjected to much criticism from sections of the Indian Catholic community. Many of O'Connor's Indian detractors, for example, asserted that while Portuguese priests were lacking in knowledge of Indian languages, they could at least speak Portuguese, which was understood by three-quarters of the congregation of the Capuchin church over which O'Connor presided. Irish priests, they complained, knew neither Tamil nor Portuguese and could officiate only in either English or Latin.[16] Moreover, many of O'Connor's Indian parishioners objected to the particular type of Catholicism that the Irish introduced into Madras.

It was alleged among a group who described themselves as 'poor Indians', for example, that O'Connor and his Irish priests paid little heed to proper liturgical practices.[17] The 'native part of the community' were said to be extremely 'displeased and discontented' because of O'Connor's failure to provide High Mass during the week as well as on Sundays. Furthermore, they alleged that O'Connor's Irish priests in Madras did not provide novenas for the lay confraternities, nor did they arrange processions or provide a cross for the pulpit. Other Indian Catholics criticised the Irish clergy's dress code, complaining that the Irish in Madras dressed too informally, and that they resembled their Protestant counterparts more than Roman Catholic priests. O'Connor countered such criticism by some of his Indian congregation by stating that he and his fellow Irish priests always wore the soutane whilst saying Mass, and that only when he went abroad like other 'British and Europeans' did he wear 'the same ... dress worn by Priests and Bishops in England, Ireland and Scotland'. Furthermore, O'Connor maintained that by adopting an informal mode of dress, he and his Irish priests were far better placed to gain access to difficult geographical areas outside of Madras city. Although they were guilty of breaching traditional Catholic ecclesiastical protocol, O'Connor insisted that the adoption of informal dress by his Irish priests would enable the missionaries to serve the needs of India's neglected class and would thus 'produce the greatest advantage to the religion' of India's poor and distressed.[18]

Interpreting O'Connor's official explanations as an affront to high-caste Indian Catholic sensibilities, many high-caste Indian Catholics belonging to the influential Parava caste grew restive. They complained to the Vicar General that the Irish missionary priests in Madras did not speak Tamil and devoted much of their time to the Irish Roman Catholic soldiers in nearby British military cantonments. The Irish, they protested, were trying to treat Indian Catholics as if they were Irish and not Indian. They did not adhere to Indian Catholic customs such as the separation of the sexes during Mass, nor did they take their shoes off before entering the church. For many of O'Connor's Indian detractors, the final straw came when O'Connor decided to re-arrange the seating in his new cathedral church in Madras into two distinct sections, an arrangement which some Indian parishioners interpreted as being motivated by caste bias.[19] In the first section, O'Connor assigned seats for Europeans and Indians in European dress only, while in the second those wearing Indian dress were put together. As a result of

O'Connor's actions, many high-caste Tamils who resented being mixed together with low-caste pariahs threatened to raise money of their own to build a separate Catholic church in Madras if something were not done to alleviate the problem. What alarmed Indian Catholics most was that it seemed to them as if O'Connor and his Irish priests were somehow trying to blur the lines between high- and low-caste Indian Catholics in Madras. O'Connor, however, was resolute and insisted that his seating arrangement in the cathedral church dissatisfied only a few high-caste Indians. Despite attempts by O'Connor's Vicar General, another Irishman, Reverend Moriarty, to subdivide the Indian section of the church into separate high- and low-caste areas, over eighty high-caste families stopped attending O'Connor's services and withdrew to churches under the direct control of the more conservative *padroado*.[20]

However, despite the criticism pointed at O'Connor and his Irish missionaries in Madras in the 1830s, the substantial missionary work (particularly their concentration on infrastructural issues) did not go unnoticed. In 1838 the Madras Vicar General, Reverend Moriarty, travelled to Rome in an attempt to defend O'Connor's actions in front of Propaganda Fide. Moriarty argued that the Madras mission had already been seriously undermined by the internal feuding and controversy caused by O'Connor's predecessors, the French and Italian Capuchins. The mission in Madras, Moriarty claimed, contained many different and opposing factions, each trying to secure its own particular interest in south India. In addition, Moriarty argued that before the Irish had arrived in Madras, many Indian Catholics had been paying too much attention to religious pomp and ceremony. Not enough attention, he maintained, had been paid to the practical requirements of the mission itself, such as providing education and welfare for India's poor, or the ministering of the sacraments.[21] Though not specifically an Irish phenomenon, these were all important initiatives undertaken in the years following emancipation by a reorganised Catholic Church in Ireland whose members largely identified with the marginalised and poorer sections of societies that they were ministering to overseas. In fact, many well-respected and established figures within the Indian Catholic Church, such as the Pondicherry-based Abbé Luquet, praised O'Connor and his Irish priests for their approach to missionary work and interaction with Indian society in general. Luquet asserted that, in contrast to the social conservatism of the French Jesuits in India, the Irish paid little deference to high-caste Indians, and applauded their neutral disposition when it came to the issue of caste in general. In Luquet's opinion, the French Jesuits had made a serious error in judgement in their preferential treatment of high-caste Indian Catholics. He maintained that as O'Connor's guest in Madras in 1835 he had observed schools and churches established by the Irish missionaries open to all castes, and that Brahman, Pariahs and the Sudras children mixed freely without any complications.[22]

In addition to the strong Irish military and religious presence, a greater number of Irish university-trained professionals began entering the various imperial services in India from the late 1840s onwards. This was due, in part, to the introduction of open-competitive examination in place of the old system of patronage, which provided more equal opportunities for educated Irishmen interested in securing colonial appointments, but was also due to the desire of Irish universities and colleges at the time to compete with their English, Scottish and Welsh counterparts on an international footing. This influx ultimately served to balance the number of Irish Protestants who had passed through to India via Trinity College, Dublin, the Royal Belfast Academical Institution and the universities of Edinburgh and Glasgow in various capacities during the eighteenth century. Indeed, the large number of successful Irish Catholic candidates who obtained employment in India at this time was aided considerably by Irish universities and colleges (including the non-denominational Queen's College in Belfast, Cork and Galway established in 1845) who were quick to seize the opportunities afforded by Ireland's growing imperial connection and subsequently tailored their curriculum to the specific requirements of the entrance examinations for the colonial services.[23]

The formation and impact of key Irish professional networks in the context of colonial science in mid-nineteenth-century India, for instance, was particularly visible in the case of Thomas Oldham and his work on the Geological Survey of India (GSI). Head-hunted by the East India Company in 1851, Oldham and his coterie of Irish geologists (mostly Trinity College Dublin graduates) were responsible for reorganising and restructuring the GSI into a thoroughly modernised scientific institution and inaugurating the first systematic and sustained approach to the investigation of India's stratigraphy and mineralogy. Under Oldham's directorship, the field of geology shed its amateur status and became an integral branch of the new colonial administration in the 1860s and 1870s. Until his retirement in 1876, Oldham completely transformed the institution, meeting international standards in geological collecting and producing research that was best reflected in its publications, *Memoirs of the GSI*, *Records of the GSI* and the regular *Annual Reports*. As superintendent of the GSI for over twenty-five years, Oldham was responsible for cultivating a scientific network based upon ethnic affiliation. Within these networks specimens, samples, theories, ideas and agendas (scientific and other) were transmitted across the empire from Calcutta to London, and also directly between the colonies themselves. Devoid of cultural dependence upon the metropole, Irish scientific networks were notable in their efforts to promote the education of Indians and were prominent in forging alliances with comparable networks in other parts of the empire, eager to promote the autonomy of science in the colonies.

The first of a large personnel network of Irish geologists to join Oldham on the GSI was Joseph Medlicott, son of a Church of Ireland rector from Loughrea, Co. Galway.[24] Indeed, from 1851 to 1920, twenty Irish geologists joined the GSI, while during the same time there was only a sixteen-year period when an Irish geologist did not act as the Indian Survey's Director.[25] Most of these men were graduates of Trinity College Dublin, and had previous experience working with one another at various levels on the Ordinance Survey of Ireland (OSI). In 1854, for example, Joseph Medlicott was joined on the Great Trigonometrical Survey of India (GTS) by his brother, Henry Medlicott, after spells on both the Irish and English surveys, while another prominent Indian geologist, Valentine Ball, was a friend and coeval of the Medlicott brothers from their time together in Dublin. William King, the son of a professor of geology at the Queen's College Galway, joined Oldham's staff shortly afterwards, while Oldham, himself, secured several appointments for his family members, most notably for his brother Charles and son, Richard Dixon Oldham, who later carried out important early work on the study of seismology and earthquakes in India.[26] From the outset, geological explorations undertaken by Oldham and his colleagues assumed a direct economic bearing.[27] With the development of steam travel in the 1830s, the economic and military value of geological investigations meant that the search for workable coalmines, in particular, became a priority for Company officials obsessed with balancing the books and keeping costs at a minimum.[28] The pursuit of scientific enquiry for solely economic purposes in India, however, quite frequently resulted in increased levels of conflict and tension between Company authorities and sections of its employees during the mid-nineteenth century. This can be clearly seen through the experience of Oldham, who embroiled himself in several disputes with Company and Crown officials throughout his Indian career, largely because of perceived metropolitan interference in and condescension towards colonial initiatives, but also partly because of his particular intellectual background and earlier experiences in Ireland. As a middle-class Anglican Protestant, Oldham had a particular mind-set that was informed by the intellectual milieu long associated with Trinity College Dublin.[29] Having spent his formative professional years on the OSI in the late 1830s and 1840s, Oldham's work on the GSI reflected a strong tradition of Irish antiquarian and historical research that was at times at odds with the utilitarian ethos and evangelical spirit of the East India Company.[30]

During the first half of the nineteenth century, scholarly interest in Irish antiquarian and historical research melded with contemporary investigations by socio-scientific societies into the political and social condition of the Irish people. During the 1820s and 1830s the OSI came to exert a significant degree of influence upon the organisation and technical structure of the GTS, particularly in terms of the application of anthropological and ethnographic work being carried out by the Irish survey's superintendents, Thomas Colby and Thomas Larcom. In Ireland, Colby and Larcom had begun collecting information for the Survey's parish memoirs, intended to provide knowledge about the origins and nature of Ireland's social problems, as well as information necessary to address and resolve them. Having witnessed at first hand the conditions in pre-Famine Ireland while undertaking fieldwork, Colby and Larcom were deeply disturbed by the poor state of the Irish peasantry and quickly became involved in Irish political affairs. After studying the literature and participating in debates about possible causes and remedies, they concluded that Ireland's poverty, unemployment and popular discontent were due to the nature of its underdeveloped economy, agriculture and infrastructure, and subsequently accused elites and policy makers of negligence, ignorance and mismanagement. Colby, in particular, rejected claims that Ireland was responsible for its own problems, that its natural resources were inadequate and that its population was incapable of improvement. He argued on the contrary, that Ireland's assets were neglected, its potential ignored and its ability thwarted by a combination of bad government and ineffective legislation under the Union.[31]

In part, such views also reflected the beginning of an important shift in outlook within sections of the wider intellectual community in Ireland, towards the second half of the nineteenth century, that began moving away from Anglocentric models of socio-economic development of putatively universal applicability.[32] In the aftermath of the Great Famine in the 1840s, there was a stark realisation within Britain that the prescriptions of early nineteenth-century classical political economists had failed to transform Ireland into a diminutive England of improving landlords and prosperous farmers. Throughout the 1850s, the once unwavering belief in the efficacy and applicability of Anglocentric theories that held British structures of land tenure as a 'superior model' for the rest of the civilised and civilising world began to be scrutinised and questioned. Around this time, a whole range of scholars, most notably sociologists and anthropologists, began adopting new models of enquiry that challenged the normative assumptions of the utilitarians and classical political economists. This scholarship ultimately gave a new theoretical respectability to a set of popular contemporary ideas that sought to preserve and fortify local custom and agrarian structures rather than impose the imprint of British-based concepts, laws and practices onto overseas possessions.[33] In turn, this had an important impact upon the way the Irish middle class (many of whom came from declining landowning backgrounds and had sought employment in the Indian colonial services from the late 1840s) viewed tenurial relations in India, where they were responsible for influencing a measure of pro-tenant legislation in the second half of the nineteenth century.[34]

Alternate views and understandings of history, land and famine impacted upon the careers of Irish administrative and scientific personnel in India in equally significant ways. Oldham's work of compiling individual soil-maps for counties in the south-east and north-west of Ireland on the OSI in the late 1840s, for example, coincided with some of the worst instances of famine and pestilence in Irish history. Before departing for Calcutta in 1851, Oldham's correspondence with Sir Andrew Ramsay (the English survey's director) was laden with several references to the poor working conditions for geological undertakings on the Irish survey, as well as the on-going plight of the Irish peasantry during the Great Famine.[35] A deep interest in recording and noting down the socio-economic condition of the Indian peasantry was also something that characterised much of Oldham's early writings on geological explorations in Bengal. In the year before the publication of the first volume of the GSI's *Memoirs* in 1859, Oldham was instructed to investigate the economic potential of the iron mines of Cuttack and Talcher in the province of Orissa in Bengal, with a view to opening them out 'to the steady march of industry'.[36] In his findings Oldham reported to the government that while there were no beds of 'workable coal' to be found in the district, the level of poverty he encountered in many of the iron-manufacturing villages greatly concerned him. He stated that the mining of iron ore was a task that seemed to be 'pursued only by a particular caste of the [Talcher] people, who always appear to be among the poorest and the most wretched of the inhabitants'. Oldham maintained that the labour of the poor was being crudely exploited by wealthy Bengali *mahajans* who, by a system of advances and payments, became the proprietors of the iron-smelting furnaces and fuel. What Oldham referred to as the 'truck system' in operation in Talcher reduced 'the poor workmen to slavery', to the point where they find it almost 'impossible to obtain even a starvation allowance of food of the poorest kind without the aid of the *mahajans*'.[37] Certainly

Oldham was not convinced that the government's approach to geological investigations in India was thoroughly appropriate, and he was critical of the state's handling of the Indian peasantry in general.[38]

Issues of famine, poverty and the welfare of an impoverished tenantry in both Ireland and India not only provided shared affinities in relation to popular scientific thought, but were also important concerns in the daily duties and activities of hundreds of Irish administrators employed by the Indian Civil Service (ICS) during the same time. During the second half of the nineteenth century, following the introduction of open competitive examination for positions in the ICS, Irish universities supplied a disproportionate number of recruits for employment in India's colonial bureaucracy. In 1857, for example, Irish universities supplied no less than 33 per cent of the total number of recruits selected for the ICS during that year, a yearly intake that waned little throughout the course of the century.[39] Serving variously as provincial administrators, revenue collectors, legal officers or judges, many Irish Catholic ICS officials – including Anthony MacDonnell and Charles J. O'Donnell – were strong advocates of tenancy legislation who understood colonial India in a particular Irish context.[40] Son of a small Catholic landowner from rural Connaught, MacDonnell, for example, became a leading authority on famine relief and tenure policy at a time when official thinking in India favoured men from backgrounds that gave them an acute awareness of the peasant problem. By the time he retired, MacDonnell had served as the administrative chief of four provinces of India including Burma, the Central Provinces, Bengal and the United Provinces.[41]

Frequently drawing upon analogies of the land system in Ireland, both MacDonnell and O'Donnell carried out their work under the conviction that North Indian Muslims were not dissimilar from Irish Protestants in that they had effectively enjoyed a long monopoly over government office and landownership.[42] Born in Co. Donegal in 1849, Charles O'Donnell secured an appointment in the Indian Civil Service in 1872 after completing his education at Queen's College Galway, where he studied English literature, history and political economy.[43] As a junior officer in the Sarun district of Bihar, O'Donnell was officially censured and temporarily demoted by the Government of India for publicly criticising his own provincial administration for its ineffective tenure policies and its mismanagement of famine relief.[44] A few years before the Bengal tenancy bill was introduced, O'Donnell had ordered a police investigation of the estates of the Maharaja of Hutwa, a leading Bihar landowner and one of Britain's more reliable client-*zamindars* (landlords), whom he described as a 'grievous rack-renter and ... a vindictive oppressor of his tenantry'.[45] MacDonnell, too, was also known for the extreme benevolence he displayed towards Indian *raiyats* (peasants).[46] Indeed, it has been alleged that throughout his Indian career MacDonnell was 'haunted' by the 'bitter memories of the terrible condition' of the Irish tenantry as he confronted the 'wretched condition of the Indian peasantry'.[47] As Lieutenant Governor of the United Provinces in 1900, MacDonnell identified with the North Indian Hindus, who he believed resembled the Catholic peasantry in Ireland. According to MacDonnell, both sets of people urgently required land reform as well as a recognition of their religious and cultural differences.[48] Towards this end, MacDonnell was responsible for allowing the Hindi language in the Devanagari script to be put on an equal footing with Urdu written in the Persian script during the day-to-day transactions within British courts of law in India.[49]

Alongside other Irish colleagues in Bihar, such as Michael Finucane, Peter O'Kinealy, Patrick Nolan and Dennis Fitzpatrick, MacDonnell and O'Donnell formed part of a closely knit Irish administrative network in Bengal who advocated that aspects of Irish land legislation should be applied in modified form to India. Pro-*raiyat* Irish ICS administrators were often bound by social and professional ties, thereby enabling them to form informal alliances between one another. MacDonnell and Finucane, for instance, had collaborated with one another from their early days as freshly recruited greenhorn 'competition-wallahs' in Darbhanga. In 1880, Nolan, MacDonnell and Finucane jointly suggested a plan to curb illegal rent enhancements in Bihar.[50] In providing the initial impetus for the Act, these Irishmen played a critical role in transforming a landlord-enabling bill, the Bengal Tenancy Act of 1885, into a measure conferring tenant protection. In their official reports to the Government of India these Bihar officials pointed to the rapacious nature of leaseholders, the persistence of produce rents, the lack of agricultural improvement and the crushing poverty of local *raiyats*. Such persistent features, they alleged, would continue to weaken the Indian economy and would lead to the eventual political alienation of the rural masses.[51]

Indeed, many Irish civilians, such as O'Donnell, who had published work on the impoverished state of Indian and Irish tenants, landless peasants and rack-renting landlords in Bihar, had acquired a reputation among some British and Indian officials as pro-*raiyat* sympathisers.[52] The Maharaja of Darbhanga, for instance, a member of the Select Committee whose estates comprised over 2,460 square miles throughout Bihar, once intoned that 'Mr O'Donnell was an Irishman, and Irishmen were generally against landlords.'[53] Similarly, the conservative Bengal newspaper, *The Englishman*, alarmingly declared in 1880 that: 'It is remarkable how many Irish civilians have, during the last few years, been located in different parts of Bihar. An Irishman was collector at Darbangah [*sic*] during the "agitation" in that district in 1877.... It was an Irish civilian who first wrote those memorable letters in *The Pioneer* on the evils of the indigo planters and planting, and another Irishman (Patrick Nolan) first reports an "atrocity" committed by a planter in Shahabad.'[54] Others, including Charles McMinn, a Collector in Tripura and one-time supporter of Anthony MacDonnell's work with the Indian Famine Commission, later admitted that his 'strong sympathy with the people of India ... did not find favour with authority'. Writing on the origin, history and etiology of the Indian Famine in 1902, McMinn regretted that because of his unwavering political views on the various abuses being carried out by the *zamindars* (Indian landlords) he had been 'punished in various ways, deprived of allowances, refused officiating appointments' and even placed under the authority of his juniors.[55]

Although the intellectual and moral concerns articulated through the writings and official correspondence of Irish civil servants such as O'Donnell and McMinn at once stimulated and inspired Indian nationalism, it is perhaps one of the greatest ironies of Irish involvement in the administration of the empire in South Asia that their very presence working to maintain British colonial rule in India helped to prevent and deny it. Nevertheless, Irish interventions in the debates over land and famine in India in the 1870s, 1880s and 1890s enabled Irish parliamentarians to effectively develop and clarify an increasing anti-imperial strand in Irish nationalism and, more importantly, to redefine their roles in contemporary global politics. Here the main channel of discussion and dissemination between Irish and Indian reformers and nationalists was through the Irish and Indian press, both English language and vernacular, though close personal contacts were also sporadically forged through burgeoning nationalist societies, student movements and extra-parliamentary bodies and associations that took root in Dublin, Calcutta and London around the same time. Irish nationalist newspapers such as Patrick Ford's the *Irish World* and A. M. Sullivan's the *Nation* provided content that was endorsed and echoed in several Indian newspapers such as Kristodas Pal's the *Hindoo Patriot* and Subramania Aiyar's the *Hindu* and vice versa. These reports demonstrated that the importance of the connections between Irish and Indian nationalists was not lost on contemporaries and that by acknowledging each other's difficulties under British rule they were allowing one another to recognise the potential for political independence. Moreover, as C. A. Bayly has demonstrated in Chapter Two of this volume, the expressed political views of individuals such as O'Donnell and McMinn appeared all the more controversial because they were made public at a time when a developing nationalist critique of Britain's responsibility to its imperial subjects was being formulated by radical liberals and nationalist groups throughout the empire. Significantly, these individuals' passage into the ICS coincided with the era that brought the Irish Home Rule party into the House of Commons and marked the beginning of the period in the late nineteenth century when Irish nationalists mounted the most direct and vociferous attack on British imperial authority.

As the majority of networks under investigation in this chapter concentrated primarily on connections fashioned by Irish people or institutions, and less so by Indians, they were, by their very nature, undergirded and supported by the superior military, political and legal structures of British authority that effectively privileged Irish networks over their Indian counterparts. Similarly, not all Indo-Irish networks and their participants enjoyed equal positions of power and status within the imperial paradigm. Irish networks involving military personnel from poor, disadvantaged backgrounds are a case in point. To be sure, quantifying the Irishness of these connections means also being alive to the degree to which these networks shifted and changed over periods of time; meaning that at certain historical moments other ethnic elements were incorporated within these networks, while at others the Irish element was absorbed within more dominant metropolitan networks operating alongside them. While it is impossible to deny these obvious shortcomings in relation to tracing narratives of linkage and reciprocity between Ireland and India directly, networks as a heuristic device, nevertheless, provide a particularly useful method in understanding how sets of Irish people or institutions were historically interdependent within the wider British world, often tied together by family connections, business interests, educational backgrounds, shared localities or sets of common values and interests. In recalling C. A. Bayly's cautionary remark that any attempt to decentre the empire must not be made at the expense of downplaying the empire's dominant economic and political machinery in London, it is important to be mindful of not over-emphasising the global diffusion and impact of what were evidently less dominant forms of imperial culture emanating from subordinate centres throughout the British world.[56] Clearly, though, the Irish were at the forefront of aiding the spread of British imperialism overseas, and Irish institutions had the ability to directly supply the empire with many of its fundamental needs, supplementing the primary supply from the metropole when required. Looking at Irish contributions to imperial culture in this manner at once complicates and destabilises how Ireland can be viewed within the empire and its relationship with other Britons and centres of metropolitan power. At the same time, tracing such connections forces us to re-evaluate the active circuits of imperialism within both the union state and the wider British world, while challenging us to rethink some of the traditional orthodoxies of British, Irish and imperial historiography.

Notes

1 'Copies of documents, papers and correspondence relating to the history of the India Museum, collected by Raymond George Coulter Desmond, Deputy Librarian at the India Office Library and Records 1973–85, for his book 'The India Museum 1801–1879' (London): India Office Records MSS/EUR/195/74, British Library, London (hereafter IOR), BL, London.
2 For a short contemporary account, see, John Sproule (ed.), *The Irish Industrial Exhibition of 1853: A Detailed Catalogue of its Contents* (Dublin: James McGlashan, 1854); T. D. Jones, *Record of the Great Industrial Exhibition* (Dublin: John Falconer, 1853). See also A. C. Davies, 'The First Irish National Industrial Exhibition: Cork, 1852', in *Irish Economic and Social History*, 2 (1975), 46–59.
3 IOR, MSS/EUR/195/74, British Library, London.
4 Sproule, *The Irish Industrial Exhibition*, pp. 112–18, 474–5.
5 Barry Crosbie, *Irish Imperial Networks: Migration, Social Communication and Exchange in Nineteenth-Century India* (Cambridge: Cambridge University Press, 2012).
6 David Fitzpatrick, 'Ireland and Empire', in *The Oxford History of the British Empire: The Nineteenth Century* (Oxford: Oxford University Press, 1999), pp. 494–521.
7 Alvin Jackson, 'Ireland, the Union, and the Empire, 1800–1960', in Kevin Kenny (ed.), *Ireland and the British Empire. Oxford History of the British Empire Companion Series* (Oxford: Oxford University Press, 2004), pp. 123–52.
8 William Hoey, *A Monograph on Trade and Manufactures in Northern India* (Lucknow: American Methodist Mission Press, 1880), pp. 47–200.
9 R. Evans Papers, Ms. E 404, Box 1, fol. 354, OIOC, BL.
10 Major P. Heffernan, *An Irish Doctor's Memories* (Dublin: Clonmore & Reynolds, 1958), p. 28.
11 Heffernan, *An Irish Doctor's Memories*, pp. 1–3.
12 See J. M. MacKenzie, 'Irish, Scottish, Welsh and English Worlds? A Four-Nation Approach to the History of the British Empire', *History Compass*, 6 (2008), 1244–63.
13 H. Kearney, *The British Isles: A History of Four Nations* (Cambridge: Cambridge University Press, 1989).
14 See, for example, John M. MacKenzie, *The Scots in South Africa: Ethnicity, Identity, Gender and Race, 1772–1914* (Manchester: Manchester University Press, 2012); T. M. Devine, *Scotland's Empire: The Origins of the Global Diaspora* (London: Penguin, 2012); Keith Jeffery (ed.), *'An Irish Empire'?: Aspects of Ireland and the British Empire* (Manchester: Manchester University Press, 1996).
15 Edmund M. Hogan, *The Irish Missionary Movement: A Historical Survey, 1830–1980* (Dublin: Gill and Macmillan, 1990), pp. 26–7.
16 See Kenneth Ballhatchet, 'The East India Company and Roman Catholic Missionaries', *The Journal of Ecclesiastical History*, 44 (April, 1993), 273–88.
17 'Memorandum of the Funds and Other Particulars of the Capuchin Church, etc.', in The Archives of the Sacred Congregation De Propaganda Fide, Rome, Collectanea Sacrae Congregationis (SC) India Orientalis (Ind. Or.), 605–6v.
18 Memorandum, SC Ind. Or. 5, 605–6v.
19 See Foreign Missionary Correspondence (India) of Dr Russell, President of Maynooth

College (1857–80). Russell Papers 13/43 (Box 13 – Folder 43), St Patrick's College, Russell Library, Maynooth, Co. Kildare.

20 G. M. Sinnappa Pillai to Fr Michel d'Onnion, 25 November 1838, SC Ind. Or. 7, 99–100.

21 Moriarty to Propaganda Fide, 8 September 1838, SC Ind. Or. 6, 527–30.

22 Luquet to Propaganda Fide, 9 April 1845, The Archives of the Sacred Congregation De Propaganda Fide, Rome, AP, Acta 208, 130ff; Carlo Merces de Melo, *The Recruitment and Formation of the Native Clergy in India (16th–19th Century): An Historical-Canonical Study* (Lisbon: Thesis–Pontificia Università gregoriana, 1955), 257ff.

23 Samuel Haughton, *University Education in Ireland* (London: Williams and Norgate, 1868); Anonymous, 'Spirit of the Universities, TCD', *The University Magazine*, 5 (1880), 14–25; and Annual Reports of Her Majesty's Civil Service Commissioners: *Parliamentary Papers*: 1863, vol. 20, pp. 392–3.

24 Thomas Oldham, *Annual Report of the Superintendent of the Geological Survey on India and the Museum of Geology* (Calcutta: Geological Survey on India, 1860), p. 5.

25 L. L. Fermor, *First Twenty-Five Years of the Geological Survey of India* (Calcutta: Geological Survey of India, 1976), p. 2.

26 R. D. Oldham, *A Bibliography of Indian Geology: Being a List of Books and Papers, Relating to the Geology of British India and Adjoining Countries* (Calcutta: Geological Survey of India, 1888).

27 Deepak Kumar, *Science and the Raj, 1857–1905* (Delhi: Oxford University Press, 1997), pp. 44–5.

28 C. S. Fox, 'The Geological Survey of India', *Nature*, 160 (1947), 889–91.

29 Tony Ballantyne, 'The Sinews of Empire: Ireland, India and the Construction of British Colonial Knowledge', in Terrence McDonough (ed.), *Was Ireland a Colony? Economics, Politics, Ideology and Culture in Nineteenth-Century Ireland* (Dublin: Irish Academic Press, 2005), pp. 145–65, at pp. 151–4.

30 Oldham's interest in the Irish antiquarian and historical tradition followed him to India, where he published an important piece on the origins of encaustic and ornamental tiles used as pavements for Irish ecclesiastical buildings. See T. Oldham, *Ancient Irish Pavement Tiles* (Dublin: J. Robertson, 1865).

31 Colby to Larcom, 26 December 1842, Larcom papers, National Library of Ireland, MS 7553.

32 C. Dewey, 'Images of the Village Community: A Study in Anglo-Indian Ideology', *Modern Asian Studies*, 6 (1972), 291–328, at 306.

33 C. Dewey, 'Celtic Agrarian Legislation and the Celtic Revival: Historicist Implications of Gladstone's Irish and Scottish Land Acts 1870–1886', *Past and Present*, 64 (1974), pp. 30–70.

34 S. B. Cook, *Imperial Affinities: Nineteenth-Century Analogies and Exchanges Between India and Ireland* (New Delhi: Sage Publications, 1993), p. 85.

35 Oldham to Ramsay, Gorey, Co. Wexford 26 April 1847. Letters to Sir Andrew Ramsay (1846–48), KGA/RAMSAY/8/610/18, Imperial College Archives, London.

36 T. Oldham, 'Preliminary Notice on the Coal and Iron of Talcheer in the Tributary Mehals of Cuttack', in *Memoirs of the Geological Survey of India*, vol. 1 (Calcutta: Geological Survey of India, 1859), pp. 1–31, at p. 10.

37 T. Oldham, 'Preliminary Notice', p. 12.

38 *Annual Report of the Superintendent of the Geological Survey of India and the Museum of Economic Geology* (London, 1858–59).

39 Papers Regarding the Selection and Training of Candidates for the Indian Civil Service: *Parliamentary Papers*: 1876, vol. 55, p. 31. Critics resented the limited and decreasing representation of suitable candidates from Oxford and Cambridge, whose entry numbers into the ICS fell dramatically from 62 per cent of the overall number of recruits selected in 1858 to a lowly 8.2 per cent by 1874. J. M. Compton, 'Open Competition and the Indian Civil Service, 1854–1876', in *The English Historical Review*, LXXXIII (1968), 265–84, at 270–1.

40 S. B. Cook, *Imperial Affinities*, pp. 88–94, 103–5.

41 Curzon to MacDonnell, 5 November 1901, Curzon Collection, Eur F111/204, fols 74–5, OIOC, BL. See also, George Wyndham to MacDonnell, 24 February 1903, MacDonnell Papers, Mss. Eng. Hist. e.215, Bodleian Library, Oxford (hereafter, Bod. Lib., Oxford).

42 See letter book containing copies of letters from MacDonnell as acting Lieutenant-Governor of Bengal, 14 June–20 November 1893, Mss. Eng. hist. d.235, Bod. Lib., Oxford.

43 Biographical detail for late nineteenth-century Indian Civil Service recruits is contained in both the 'Annual Reports of Her Majesty's Civil Service Commissioners' (ARCSC): *Parliamentary Papers*: 1859–83 and in the annual lists for civilians contained in L/P&J/6 series, 1881–1914, India Office Records, OIOC, BL.

44 C. J. O'Donnell, *The Ruin of an Indian Province: An Indian Famine Explained* (London: Kegan Paul & Co, 1880); and 'C. J. O'Donnell's protest and censure', L/P&J/3/79 (1349), OIOC, BL.

45 O'Donnell to Reynolds, 15 March 1880, L/P&J/3/70, no. 67 (1389), OIOC, BL.

46 MacDonnell's speech outside the Hotel Metropole, 15 October 1898, MacDonnell Papers, Mss. Eng. Hist. c.395, Bod. Lib., Oxford.

47 Anne MacDonnell, notes, MacDonnell Papers, Mss. Eng. hist. c.415, Bod. Lib., Oxford; John L. Hill, 'A. P. MacDonnell and the Changing Nature of British Rule in India, 1885–1901', in Robert I. Crane and N. Gerald Barrier (eds), *British Imperial Policy in India and Sri Lanka, 1858–1912* (Columbia, MO: South Asia Books, 1981), pp. 58–74, at p. 59.

48 Minute by MacDonnell, October 1901, MacDonnell Papers, Mss. Eng. hist. 350–70, Bod. Lib, Oxford.

49 See Francis Robinson, *Separatism among Indian Muslims. The Politics of the United Provinces' Muslims 1860–1923* (Cambridge: Cambridge University Press, 1975), pp. 42–3.

50 See Patrick Nolan, 8 November 1880, 'Report of the Government of Bengal on the Proposed Amendment to the Law of ... Landlord ... and Tenant' (hereafter RGBPA), V/27/312/13, OIOC, BL.

51 See the opinions of Nolan, MacDonnell and Finucane in RGBPA.

52 *Hindoo Patriot*, 28 July 1879, 23 and 30 January 1882; and C. J. O'Donnell, 'The Wants of Behar', *Calcutta Review*, LXIX, 1879, 146–66.

53 *A Full Report of the Public Meeting of the Landholders of Bengal and Behar regarding the Bengal Tenancy Bill, held, 29 December 1883* (Calcutta: Indian Daily News Press, 1884).

54 *The Englishman*, 16 September 1880, OIOC, BL, Reel SM 49.

55 Charles W. McMinn, *Famine Truths, Half Truths, Untruths* (Calcutta: University of California Libraries, 1902), p. 48.

56 C. A. Bayly, 'The British and Indigenous Peoples, 1760–1860: Power, Perception and Identity', in Martin Daunton and Rick Halpern (eds), *Empire and Others: British Encounters with Indigenous Peoples, 1600–1850* (Philadelphia: University of Pennsylvania Press, 1999), pp. 19–42, at p. 21.

CHAPTER SEVEN

Sorting out China: British accounts from pre-Opium War Canton

John M. Carroll

In both Chinese history and British imperial history, the Canton System, which from the mid-1750s to 1842 confined China's trade with the West to a tiny section of Canton (Guangzhou), has generally been seen as an example of the fundamental incompatibility of East and West. This view has been challenged by several studies showing how the system worked remarkably well. Paul Van Dyke has argued that over the long term the Canton System's 'strengths overshadowed its weaknesses'. Far from being an anachronism, the Canton trade was 'one of the most important contributors to the rise of modern "global" economies'.[1] Nor was the Canton System necessarily a cultural clash waiting to erupt. In his study of British naturalists in Qing China, Fa-ti Fan describes Canton as a 'contact zone', showing how these naturalists relied on an extensive network of Chinese helpers and how, through the China trade, Canton 'developed a culture that was at once local and international'.[2] Li Chen has demonstrated that the *Lady Hughes* case of 1784, when a British gunner was executed by Qing authorities for accidentally killing two Chinese boatmen, was not an example of the arbitrary and barbarous nature of Chinese law. Despite the outrage provoked in England, a defendant charged with such a crime would have been just as likely to be found guilty there as in China.[3]

Accounts by Britons who visited or resided in Canton reveal that the city could be as much a site of encounter and affinity as of conflict and difference. Even though Britons and other foreigners often complained about the Canton System, the magnitude of the trade – perhaps unparalleled anywhere else in the world at any time – was enough for them to return season after season. By 1800 more than 8,000 foreigners visited Canton each year, and by the late 1830s almost one hundred foreign firms were trading along the South China coast. To be sure, exposure to China and its people often reinforced

British attitudes of superiority. There is little evidence to suggest that their time in Canton caused Britons to question their own culture, identities or ideologies. Until the mid-1830s, however, and especially before the abolition of the East India Company's monopoly in 1833, Britons, like other Western visitors and residents, often wrote favourably about the Canton System and the Chinese people who kept it running.[4] In Canton they found much that was familiar, while that which seemed strange could often be explained by way of comparison and contrast, either with the British past or with other societies and cultures. We often forget that what happened in Canton was part of the larger and longer process of British encounters with 'indigenous' peoples discussed by Philippa Levine in the opening chapter of this book.[5] Furthermore, as Ulrike Hillemann has argued, British knowledge of China was shaped partly by British experiences and networks in South and South East Asia.[6]

This is not to suggest that Britons in China showed the kind of interest that some did in India, as described by David Kopf some forty years ago in his book on British Orientalism, or by Maya Jasanoff more recently in her study of imperial collecting.[7] Nor did Britons in Canton evince the same sort of curiosity, awe and wonder as Chinese travellers to the West did several decades later.[8] Still, as many of the chapters in this volume show, the 'cultural British world' extended well beyond the borders of formal or even informal empire: these writers commented on almost everything they saw in China, and speculated about much of what they did or could not see. The conventional emphasis on politics and diplomacy when studying early Sino-British relations has obscured some of the cultural and social aspects of this encounter, preventing us from seeing Canton as a place and a process: a place from where China could be observed and interpreted; and a process for doing this observing and interpreting. For these Britons, Canton was both physical and epistemological.

The sources

Who were these men and why were they in China? (Western women were not allowed to live or travel in China until after the Treaty of Nanking in 1842, though a few managed to slip into Canton briefly from Macao.) The sources analysed here are by Britons who spent time in Canton from the late 1700s through the 1830s. William Hickey (who also features in Chapter Ten of this book) had been despatched to India in 1769 to reform himself after embezzling £500 from his father, a prominent solicitor. From India he quickly escaped to Canton, and later wrote about his few months there in his memoirs. Aeneas Anderson and John Barrow accompanied Lord Macartney on his embassy to Peking in 1792–93, Anderson as his valet and Barrow as his private secretary. Clarke Abel, Basil Hall and John Davis were part of Lord Amherst's embassy in 1816–17. Abel was the chief medical officer and naturalist. Naval officer, traveller and author Hall became separated from the embassy and waited for some time in Canton for it to arrive from the North. Davis had been in Canton for twenty years as a writer for the East India Company. C. Toogood Downing was a surgeon who wrote three volumes, more than one thousand pages in all, based on his two years in Canton. The first Protestant missionary to China, Robert Morrison, had arrived in Canton in 1807. There he also worked for the East India Company as a writer and interpreter. He died in Canton in August 1834, shortly after being commissioned as interpreter to Lord Napier's ill-fated mission. Walter Henry Medhurst, another pioneer in the Protestant missionary movement, first came to Canton in 1816. To evade the restrictions on missionary activity he chose to work instead among the overseas Chinese communities in South East Asia, though he later made several expeditions up the Chinese coast to investigate the possibilities for missionary work there.

Several common themes emerge from these accounts, which together constituted a British network of information about China that was often circulated and recirculated: the lack of morality among Chinese people, their hostility and contempt for foreigners, China's backward technology and despotic government, foot binding and infanticide, and superstition and idolatry. Yet not everything in these accounts was so condemnatory or disparaging. And they often asked important and thoughtful questions. What was the true size of China's massive population? How did it explain Chinese values? What did it mean for Christian evangelisation? Which sources could be trusted? How had China's history affected its present? The general conclusion was that China's history had not developed much since reaching its zenith many centuries earlier, whereas Britain's had changed dramatically in less than one century. How could one explain China's impressive law and order? The usual answer was that it was possible only because of Chinese despotism and, however admirable, would never work in a nation as enlightened and free as Britain. What was 'true' about China and what was not? How was it to be understood? Although Canton did not provide the level of intellectual exchange discussed in Chapter Two in Christopher Bayly's chapter on British radicals in India, it nonetheless offered the kind of encounter unavailable to foreigners elsewhere in China.

These men's curiosity rarely started or ended with China. Indeed, scholars have rarely asked what knowledge of the fabled Middle

Kingdom foreigners took with them to China, or how it changed along the way and once they arrived, especially since no one went directly from England to China but via many other places, including South America, Africa, India and the East Indies. China thus existed along a spectrum of foreign locales, and no one who came to Canton did so without making comparisons with other places. Clarke Abel, for example, recorded detailed observations on an almost unlimited range of topics, both on the voyage to and from Canton and on the unsuccessful mission to Peking: in Brazil, a musical instrument popular among black slaves; in Java, a circumcision ceremony, the local people's dexterity in climbing coconut trees and a snake swallowing a goat; in Spanish Manila, methods of execution; in Sumatra, the orang-utan, of which he became the first Western scientist to observe; and in St Helena, a visit with the exiled Napoleon Bonaparte.

None of these authors suggested that sorting out China was a straightforward process. Aware of the contemporary interest in Europe in 'the religious and superstitious opinions and practices' of the Chinese, surgeon Toogood Downing explained that in an empire of 'such vast extent, and the three hundred millions of inhabitants composed of so many nations, Chinese, Tartars, Monguls, Indian Lolos, and savage Miaos from the mountains, it cannot be supposed that they should all have the same ideas on these subjects'.[9] No one professed to be the only reliable source of information on China. They realised that understanding China meant confirming, refining, correcting or even refuting previous knowledge of China and the many ideas about China circulating in Europe, some influenced by the pronouncements of the Jesuit missionaries, some in direct opposition to them and some derived from Chinese or Chinese-like porcelain and paintings. 'People in Europe', opined John Davis, 'have been strangely misled, in their notions of Chinese physiognomy and appearance, by the figures represented on those specimens of manufacture which proceed from Canton, and which are commonly in a style of broad caricature.' As a consequence, 'a character of silly levity and farce has been associated, in the minds of many persons, with the most steady, considerate, and matter-of-fact people in the world, who in grave matters of business are often a match for the best of Europeans'.[10]

Even though it meant being confined to a small section of the city, with few opportunities to explore the surrounding countryside, Canton became a place for developing a deeper, first-hand understanding of China. Downing recalled how, although foreigners were 'carefully debarred' from entering the city, they could still examine 'the town at a distance, and thus satisfy their curiosity'. The view was particularly good from the top of the Thirteen Factories, the only section of Canton where foreign trade was allowed, affording an 'extensive view of the interior'. From here, the first place British residents took their visitors, one could behold 'a highly fertile country, laid out in patches of luxuriant vegetation, interspersed with hills and mountains of every tint, and watered by a thousand silvery streams alive with human beings'. According to Downing, the members of the Amherst embassy, who had travelled for more than one thousand miles in China, 'declared that in a few days they had seen in Canton not only everything they had met with before, but could observe it to better purpose than during the journey'.[11]

Canton: the place and the system

By the late 1700s, Canton was the second-largest city in China and one of the most important ports in the world. Situated on the north shore of the Pearl River and housing a population of more than 750,000, the city had been an international port for more than a thousand years. Canton owed its prosperity as much to its favourable geographical location and political setting (it was the administrative capital of Guangdong province) as it did to China's Manchu rulers, who in 1759 declared it the only legal Chinese port for trade with the West. But access to this valuable trading port did not come easy. All foreign trading ships were required to report at the Portuguese territory of Macao, where they had to hire a local pilot to guide them past Bocca Tigris (Humen, or Tiger's Mouth). Ships that passed Bocca Tigris anchored at Whampoa (Huangpu), a small island thirteen miles downriver from Canton. All Chinese agents, boatmen and pilots working for foreigners had to be licensed. With so many duties and trans-shipping costs, Canton's port fees may have been the highest in the world. But this never stopped foreign traders from coming: the familiarity of Western traders with the region can be seen in the nicknames for the various riverine islands, passages and reaches near Canton: French Island, Dane's Island, Elliot Pass and Cambridge Reach.[12]

Under the Canton System, international trade was conducted through a group of Chinese hongs, merchant houses specially authorised and licensed by the Qing government. These hongs monopolised trade with foreign merchants, collected customs dues and taxes for the Qing government and acted as security merchants for the foreign merchants. According to the so-called 'Eight Regulations', foreigners were allowed to trade in Canton only from October to March, confined to the factories and without their women and children. Gideon Nye, an American trader and later Vice Consul at Canton, recalled how the situation of foreigners in Canton had once been 'aptly likened to the condition of the Animals in the Zoological Gardens of London'. The inmates were 'free to play what pranks they pleased, so that they made no uproar, nor escaped from confinement'.[13] The list of restrictions could seem endless: sedan chairs or boats were not to be used for pleasure, and there were to be no excursions into the city itself, except for three visits per month to the public gardens on Honam (Henan) Island. Toogood Downing observed how 'not even the slightest outhouse' could be built without permission from the Canton authorities.[14]

Over time, many of these rules were broken. And even though British residents and visitors frequently grumbled about the restrictions, Canton amazed them with its diversity and sheer human energy. The image was often formed before reaching the city itself, often even before making it to Whampoa. This initial impression was usually a positive one, mainly because of the balance between strange and familiar. William Hickey described the view of Canton as 'strikingly grand, and at the same time picturesque. The magnitude and novelty of the architecture must always surprise strangers. The scene upon the water is as busy as the Thames below London Bridge, with this difference, that instead of our square-rigged vessels of different dimensions, you there have junks.'[15] Aeneas Anderson, Lord Macartney's valet, noted how the river, 'as it approaches the city, is equal in breadth to the Thames, in its widest part'. Anderson marvelled at the approach to Canton from Whampoa: 'it is impossible to describe the magnificence of its navigation; for we saw, without exaggeration, several thousands of trading junks; nor were the vessels which were crowded with people to see us pass inferior in number; while the banks on either side were covered with houses, built very much in the style of European architecture'.[16] 'Nothing', exclaimed Toogood Downing, 'strikes the stranger with more astonishment on his first visit to China, than the almost endless variety of craft which is seen upon the river.' This ingenuity was proof that the Chinese, 'as a nation, are endowed with great originality and with a very considerable proportion of the noblest faculties of man'.[17]

The interior of the city, at least the part the foreigners enjoyed access to, was equally intriguing. Canton teemed with attractions, especially its shops and markets. Aeneas Anderson, who as a valet took an especially keen interest in dress, paid great attention to the fur shops, impressed by how even in warmer Canton people of all classes could afford to wear furs.[18] Toogood Downing found 'such a peculiarity, such a neatness and ingenuity about every thing made by the Chinese, that a European feels in the situation of a child, taken, for the first time in his life, into a large toy-shop containing what he considers a world of wonders'. Downing recalled how his first journey to Canton 'made such an impression on me, that I think it never could be erased if I were to live for a thousand long years to come. You feel perfectly awed and overcome, and, although habit may somewhat abate the astonishment after frequent visits, a person would be excused, if upon his first progress up to Canton he should really believe that he was at the entrance of Pandemonium.'[19]

Observing and scrutinising China

If these Britons were impressed by the sight of Canton, they did not always agree on the size of its population. Aeneas Anderson felt that the usual estimate of one million in the city, not including the half million in its 'large and extensive suburbs', could not possibly include the large population that lived on the river.[20] John Davis, citing the lack of any 'authentic information', felt the figure of one million exaggerated. Given the small size of the city and the low height of its buildings, he found it 'difficult to imagine how such a monstrous number as a million can be stuffed within its precincts'.[21] Based on the 'mass of moving human beings in the square before the factories', with 'the crowd every moment replaced by herds of others, who seem to have no occupation', Toogood Downing suggested that the city's population must be even larger than one million.[22]

Why did the size of Canton's population matter? Because it was part of the larger problem of assessing China's gigantic population, which was in turn part of understanding China and the difficulties inherent in doing so. Most of these Britons agreed that the Chinese government deliberately made it hard for foreigners to understand China. For the missionary Walter Henry Medhurst, who had a much better opinion of the Chinese than some Britons did and even argued that the Qing authorities had good reason to worry about foreigners in Canton, given the rise of British power in India and the expansion of the opium trade, their secretiveness nevertheless verged on paranoia:

> They are afraid of every petty horde on their borders, and suspect every foreign nation of having designs on their country. They anticipate nothing but disaster from the reciprocation of kind offices, between their own countrymen and strangers.... In short, any statistical, political, commercial, or general information, relative to the interior, falling into the hands of foreigners, would be regretted by them, as leading others to covet and overthrow their country: they have, therefore, resolved to keep to themselves as much as possible.[23]

To Medhurst, the Manchus' restrictive policy led them 'to exclude all foreigners from the interior of the empire, to order off all vessels from any other than the authorised port, to disapprove of strangers landing elsewhere than in Canton, to prevent their proceeding far in land, to require them to depart as soon as possible, and to provide that shipwrecked mariners be forwarded, by the most expeditious means, to Canton, without being allowed to loiter in the districts where they may be cast on shore'. Although the Manchus had once retained a 'few foreign literati' (by whom he meant Catholic missionaries) in Peking for their skills in astronomy and mathematics, they had since stopped employing foreigners 'in order that they may keep native information from leaking out, and foreign opinions from creeping in'.[24]

No one was naïve enough to assume that China could be understood entirely through Canton. Basil Hall, who arrived with the Amherst embassy but became separated and had to remain in Canton, explained how 'most of the information which we possess in Europe on the subject of China, consists of what we hear from day to day respecting the state of society at the great sea-port of Canton'. It would be 'obviously as unfair to judge of the Chinese by such data, as it would be to estimate the character of the English' from their own ports and dockyards.[25] As chief physician and naturalist to the Amherst embassy, Clarke Abel was particularly interested in Chinese medicine and botany. From the coast to and from Peking, he paid especially close attention to a variety of related topics, including plants and insects, illness and disease, and druggists' shops. His stay in Canton, however, provided the opportunity for much deeper and sustained contact. Here he was able to visit pharmacies, learning how Chinese medicine was sold and administered. With an East India Company physician as his interpreter, Abel met 'one of the most respectable native practitioners of Canton', though he found him 'entirely destitute of anatomical knowledge'.[26] In Canton, Abel, like other visitors, was able to observe the medical efforts of the East India Company. Chief surgeon Alexander Pearson had introduced the smallpox vaccine one decade earlier, and Chinese vaccinators trained by Pearson had begun inoculating the Chinese lower classes. In a temple near the British factory, Abel witnessed them inoculating hundreds of children.[27]

Similarly, Toogood Downing enjoyed access to hospitals in Canton, and 'frequently into the most private recesses of the natives'. As a physician, he explained, 'you are able through its means to ascertain many things which would otherwise be buried in obscurity', such as the 'real state of medicine and surgery in the country' and 'the nature of the diseases and accidents to which the Chinese are subject'. He also tried to learn about Chinese medicine, frequently visiting a drug shop to chat with 'my professional brother', who appeared equally keen to learn about Western medicine. Downing learned how most Chinese medicine was derived from plants and minerals, the importance of *yin* and *yang*, the popularity and medical properties of ginseng, and how many Chinese had begun to rely on both Chinese and Western medicine, especially surgery and treatment for eye diseases. Although he found the Chinese physicians 'very deficient' in anatomy, he was intrigued by how well they understood the skeletal structure – a result, perhaps, of the practice of disinterring corpses and reburying them in 'more sanctified places'. And 'however ridiculous' some Chinese medical theories might be, they were 'not more absurd than many of those which a few years since prevailed in the most civilized nations of the west'.[28]

Canton was also a place for scrutinising Chinese religious practices. Clarke Abel recalled how the Amherst embassy's time there provided the only opportunity for witnessing Buddhist rites on 'a great scale'. The embassy was housed in parts of a large Buddhist temple, 'ornamented exteriorly with all the tawdriness that perverted taste could suggest', with 'intricate and mysterious' passages.[29] John Davis described a Buddhist temple in a suburb beyond the city walls, with one hundred priests and 'several spacious halls' – one of them built recently by a son of the wealthy hong merchant Howqua – and another 'very large' temple and monastery across the river from the European factories.[30] Toogood Downing regretted how 'the present limited state of our intercourse' prevented 'the transient visitor to Canton' from learning much about Chinese religious beliefs and practices. Still, he explained how, although a visitor to Canton had little chance to become 'personally acquainted with Confucianism', he had ample opportunity to observe the 'ceremonies of other sects' and 'idolatrous practices' – not to mention *feng-shui* ('the pains which are taken to appease the spirits of the wind and waters by the native sailors'). Downing recalled how he and a friend once watched a 'native' religious festival, where the 'clang of gongs' reminded them of an English country fair.[31]

In Canton these Britons could also see how opium was consumed, as well as the effects of what they called 'this pernicious drug' or 'this pernicious narcotic'. Opium smokers, explained Clark Abel, had 'a very peculiar, sottish, and sleepy physiognomy, in consequence of the whole visage being turgid with blood'. He also described the process of smoking opium:

> Having lighted their pipes, they draw into their lungs as large a volume of smoke as possible, and having held their breath for a few seconds, throw it gradually forth through their nose, mouth, and ears, so as strongly to impress these organs of sense. They then fall into a sort of torpor and continue in it for several minutes, and much longer when they can command time for its indulgence.[32]

Whereas John Barrow in 1804 explained that opium was 'too expensive to be used by the common people', and Abel in 1818 wrote that 'no opium is exposed for sale in the shops, probably because it is a contraband article', those who were in Canton in the 1830s saw a very different situation.[33] John Davis observed how the consumption of opium had 'pervaded all classes' and had spread with 'astonishing rapidity through the country'. The 'engrossing taste of all ranks and degrees' meant that the importation of opium had in recent years 'exceeded the aggregate value of every other English import combined'.[34] Toogood Downing described how opium was smoked mainly by men, 'chiefly between the ages of twenty and fifty-five, and of all ranks in society'.[35] Walter Henry Medhurst explained how, despite government prohibitions, 'opium shops are as plentiful in some towns of China, as gin shops are in England.... Into these shops, all classes of persons continually flock, from the pampered official to the abject menial.'[36]

Here they were also able to witness the conniving and corruption associated with the opium trade. John Barrow noted how customs officers, who were 'not beyond a bribe', often actually purchased and resold 'the prohibited article'.[37] Medhurst wrote that 'no one makes a secret of the business or the practice, and though the officers of government are loud in denouncing the indulgence in public, they privately wink at what is patronised by their own example, or subservient to their own interests'.[38] Even higher-ranking officials, claimed Downing, not only participated in the illicit trade but even consumed opium themselves, while smoking opium left soldiers 'weak and decrepit'.[39]

'Very erroneous opinions'

Canton was also a place for correcting existing images of China. Toogood Downing explained how Canton was entirely different from the painted Chinese porcelain he had seen in England, which 'would make you imagine that the whole country was laid out as a parterre, with gravel walks and grottos; that you could not move one step without danger of running against a crockery-ware pagoda, or into a canal, filled with gold and silver fish'. He warned against the 'very erroneous opinions' that 'have prevailed in Europe with regard to the character of the Chinese, and the degree of civilisation to which they have arrived'. Even in England, Downing argued, a 'great proportion of the more unenlightened classes' looked upon 'the sons of Han as a peculiar and odd kind of savages or barbarians, and are almost unwilling to believe that such outlandish people possess any useful or praiseworthy institutions'.[40]

Almost everyone made some reference to the Jesuits, a testament to how influential their pronouncements on China had been. 'It is universally allowed', wrote Downing, 'that for the greater part of our knowledge of the manners and customs of the Chinese, we are indebted to the indefatigable exertions of those Romish missionaries, who some time back were well received in China, and even held high offices in the imperial cabinet'.[41] Early into his book, John Barrow explained that the Jesuits' and the philosophes' positive impressions of China were the ones that the Macartney embassy had taken along, only to be disappointed. Barrow believed that the Jesuits had exaggerated the level of China's civilisation. No one could doubt that China had been 'civilized to a certain degree before most of the nations of Europe, not even Greece excepted'. But whether it had 'continued to improve, so as still to vie with many of the present European states, as the missionaries would have it supposed', Barrow felt was 'not by any means so clear'.[42]

Barrow also believed that the Jesuits had denied the prevalence of gambling, which he found 'so universal' that in 'almost every bye-corner' groups could be found 'playing at cards or throwing dice'. Chinese men might even stake their wives and children 'on the hazard of a die'. How could the missionaries have failed to realise that two of the favourite and 'unmanly' amusements in China were cock fighting and quail fighting? The Chinese had even 'extended their enquiries after fighting animals into the insect tribe' – to the point where 'the custom of making them devour each other is so common that, during the summer months, scarcely a boy is seen without his cage and his grasshoppers'. The Jesuits had also downplayed the severity of flogging with the bamboo. Whereas they had considered it 'a gentle correction, exercised by men in power over their inferiors, just as a father would chastise his son, but not as a punishment to which disgrace is attached', Barrow insisted that this 'humiliating chastisement, to which all are liable from the prime minister to the peasant', was 'too often inflicted in the anger and by the caprice of a man in office, and frequently with circumstances of unwarrantable cruelty and injustice'. Most egregiously, the Jesuits had failed to condemn infanticide, a practice which Barrow's five weeks in Peking had convinced him was 'not to be unsurpassed among the most savage nations'.[43]

For John Davis, neither the Jesuits nor the new traders who had replaced them as the supposed experts on China had produced objective accounts. Whereas the Jesuits, 'however much they may have extolled the wealth, civilization, and resources of China', had usually 'viewed the moral and religious character of the people in a somewhat prejudiced light', the 'commercial adventurers from Europe, confined in their communications with the people to the neighbourhoods of seaports, unable commonly to gain correct information from books, and treated by the government as barbarous intruders', were 'predisposed to give way to unfavourable impressions'. Unlike Barrow, Davis believed that the incidence of female infanticide had been blown out of proportion, and that in the West it had 'been brought as an argument against the prevalence of parental feeling in China'. Infanticide indeed existed, but 'only in the chief cities, and the most crowded population, where the difficulty of subsistence takes away all hope from the poorest persons of being able to rear their offspring'.[44]

The Cantonese

If Canton was a place for understanding China, it also led to unsettling realisations. One was that however important the trade at Canton was to foreigners and the Chinese merchants, shopkeepers and servants involved, it was trifling compared to China's inland trade. John Barrow explained how the British needed the Chinese much more than vice versa, especially given that in Britain tea, only 'a century ago a luxury', had become 'one of the first necessities of life'.[45] Toogood Downing wrote that although 'a vast number' of Chinese depended 'entirely' on the trade at Canton and would be 'ruined and driven to desperation' if it were ended, the Qing emperor could afford to be 'careless as to whether the foreigners bring their trade to Canton'.[46]

Then there were the Cantonese. As they would be later in colonial Hong Kong (where in 1844 John Davis became the second Governor), the British in Canton were often convinced that the Cantonese disdained foreigners more than other Chinese did and were possessed of a lower moral character. 'Barbarians and savages we may be thought by the ignorant in other parts of the empire', wrote Downing, 'but in the vicinity of the commercial city, a portion of hatred and fear is mixed up with the general feeling.'[47] Barrow described how the contempt for foreigners became worse, the closer the Macartney embassy got to Canton:

> Hitherto the Embassy had met with the greatest respect and civility from all classes of the natives, but now even the peasantry ran out of their houses, as we passed, and bawled after us *Queitze-fan-quei*, which, in their language, are opprobrious and contemptuous expressions, signifying *foreign devils, imps*; epithets that are bestowed by the enlightened Chinese on all foreigners.[48]

Barrow believed that this 'haughty and insolent manner' in which Europeans in Canton were treated prevailed not only among the 'upper ranks, or men in office', but even among the servants in Canton, who although eager to work for Europeans nevertheless despised them. He recounted how he had once caught his servant 'busily employed' in drying tea leaves that had already been used that day for breakfast, which he now intended to mix with fresh tea leaves and sell. 'And is that the way', asked Barrow, 'in which you cheat your own countrymen?' 'No', replied the servant, 'my own countrymen are too wise to be so easily cheated, but yours are stupid enough to let us serve you such like tricks.' The servant did, however, insist that he had only meant to sell the tea to the 'second sort of Englishmen': the Americans.[49]

The most common way to explain the poor character of the Cantonese was to blame it on the Qing authorities, who, as John Davis put it, accused foreigners of 'the most horrible practices' and regularly exhorted local people to have as little contact with them as possible. Davis described the Cantonese as 'the very worst specimens of their countrymen', encouraged by local authorities to treat foreigners 'as if they were really a degraded order of beings'. The rulers of China, he insisted, 'consider foreigners fair game: they have no sympathy with them, and what is more, they diligently and systematically labour to destroy all sympathy on the part of their subjects, by representing the strangers to them in every light that is the most contemptible and odious'. The result was that Chinese in Canton behaved very differently towards foreigners than to their own people. To Davis, it was 'a matter of astonishment that the Chinese people at Canton should be no worse than we find them', given how they were ruled by a government which 'openly professes to "rule barbarians by misrule, like beasts and not like native subjects"'.[50] Basil Hall noted how, by contrast, 'in places remote from Canton, where it is the policy of the local authorities to discourage all inquiry, there is not naturally any jealousy or apprehension of strangers'.[51]

Toogood Downing reasoned that there were 'doubtless many reasons' for the 'ill feelings' towards foreigners, including their own conduct. But he blamed the government for encouraging 'these unfriendly notions among the common people, in order to prevent any traitorous coalition being established between them and the foreigners'. This was why 'the most abusive pamphlets are issued at the commencement of every season of business; placards are stuck up against the walls of Canton, and the proclamations are always written in the most contemptuous language'. Although, Downing explained, 'throughout the whole of the Celestial Empire, foreigners are considered *barbarians*, and are usually designated as such in the imperial edicts', in Canton they 'are disliked the most by the Chinese'. Here they were 'looked upon as little better than pirates, as those Europeans who first visited these parts actually were, and it has been the interest of different parties since that time to keep up the feeling against the rest'. Explaining why shopkeepers in Canton sometimes treated their

European customers so rudely, Downing argued that it was because they 'have to deal besides with a people whom they are taught to despise, and, therefore, cannot consider themselves bound by any ties of honour to behave with justice and propriety'.[52]

Try as they might to blame this behaviour towards foreigners on the Qing government, these Britons could rarely avoid an unsettling conclusion: the alleged depravity of the Cantonese appeared to be caused partly by their contact with foreigners! Aeneas Anderson lamented that the inhabitants of Canton were 'very different in point of honesty, from the people of every other part of China, where we had been; at least, as far as my means of observation would enable me to judge'. He attributed this local character – 'knavish in the extreme' – to the fact that they lived in 'the only place where there is any communication with the natives of other countries'.[53] Toogood Downing believed that 'the language, as well as every thing else, is much depreciated in the neighbourhood of Canton, on account of the great intercourse with foreigners'. Indeed, 'the morals of the people suffer very much from this cause, so that the national character is by no means seen there to advantage'.[54]

The brink

Despite their declarations about the low moral character of the inhabitants of Canton, these Britons often warned against making assumptions about China based on Canton. By encouraging a better understanding of China, their accounts can be read also as efforts to decrease the likelihood of conflict with China. John Davis, who became disgusted by how British traders would return over and over again, even while complaining about how badly they were treated there, insisted that the Chinese had been 'under-estimated' or 'despised' on 'the score of their moral attributes'. This, he cautioned, made as much sense as trying to 'form an estimate of our national character in England' from 'some commercial sea-port'. If the British were to judge the Chinese on their experience in Canton, 'we in fact become as illiberal as themselves'.[55] Toogood Downing aimed in his three volumes to reveal 'the absurdity of prejudice' that Chinese and Europeans in Canton had for each other. 'The foreigners there regard the natives with dislike and contempt, as if they were of an inferior nature. The Chinese, in their turn, call the strangers barbarians and Fan-quis, and seem to loathe them as real demons and infernal spirits. They have no kind of sympathy or fellow-feeling with the inhabitants of other nations.' And even if the Chinese appeared in their 'very worst phase' in Canton, Downing could not help 'thinking highly' of them.[56]

It thus became possible to lament the poor character of the Cantonese yet stress the high level of China's civilisation. Dividing the peoples of the world into savage and civilised, Walter Henry Medhurst placed the Chinese in the latter category: instead of a 'savage and untutored people' they were a 'quiet, orderly, well-behaved nation, exhibiting many traces of civilization, and displaying them at a period when the rest of mankind were for the most part sunk in barbarism'. This civilisation could be seen 'in a more substantial form', in the Chinese discovery of paper, gunpowder and the compass, long before they had 'given an extraordinary impulse to the progress of civilization in Europe'.[57] Toogood Downing doubted that 'the dark races of mankind' were 'naturally inferior to the light-coloured in intelligence and moral feeling'. Even if they were, he reasoned, they 'deserve to rank at the head of those, so-called, inferior human beings'. Downing conceded that China's 'very high degree of civilization' had 'probably continued stationary for thousands of years', but he attributed this more to 'the peculiarity of their national customs and opinions' than to 'any deficiency of mental endowments'. An 'extremely learned' nation, China had produced as 'great statesmen, legislators, and moralists' as 'most other countries', and even had 'a great number of institutions which in some measure rival those of Europe'. Despite the 'very unfavourable specimen' found in Canton, 'the state of morality, according to their notions, is tolerably high throughout the empire'.[58]

No one suggested that China could equal Europe in terms of its civilisation. Walter Henry Medhurst explained that China lacked the 'high degree of improvement' and 'those well-defined civil rights, which are in a great measure the effects of Christianity'. It had not witnessed the advances in science and the arts that distinguished Europe. 'Railways, tunnels, machinery, and all the ramifications and operations of gas and steam, are not to be looked for in China.'[59] Rather, the usual explanation was that China's great civilisation had reached its zenith several centuries earlier and had since ceased to evolve. Medhurst could thus declare that China possessed 'as much civilization as Turkey now, or England a few centuries ago'.[60] Nor was China's relative backwardness necessarily to be regretted. In an overview of Chinese geography, history and customs published by the East India Company in Macau, the missionary Robert Morrison admitted that there were 'certainly not many things in which the Chinese are worthy of imitation'. There was, however, 'one benevolent cause' that they 'would never think of opposing' but that was encountering 'much unreasonable opposition' in Europe: making education as 'general as possible', preferring 'Moral Science' over 'Physical Science' and honouring virtue more than talent.[61]

Perhaps because of their failure to make any significant progress in Canton – Morrison appears to have converted no more than ten Chinese in some twenty-five years in China, and Medhurst chose to work mainly in South East Asia – it was the missionaries who most emphasised the need to Christianise China yet also pointed out the strengths of its civilisation.[62] Morrison explained how, although in China there was 'much to blame', there was also 'perhaps something from which to learn'. True, the Chinese were 'vastly prone to prevaricate, to deceive, to lie', and 'like the rest of mankind ... inclined to be satisfied with external observances, instead of Religious and Moral Rectitude'. But they also preferred reason to violence. A Chinese, declared Morrison, 'would stand and reason with a man, when an Englishman would knock him down, or an Italian stab him. It is needless to say which is the more rational mode of proceeding.' Insistent as he was that in morals the British were far superior to the Chinese, Morrison reminded his readers how 'nations denominated Christian, may yet learn from Heathens. As Confucius taught, our dislike of a man's vices should never be carried to such a height, as to make us blind to what is really good about him.'[63] In October 1807, shortly after he arrived in China, Morrison described how in Canton 'the grossest idolatry prevails'.[64] In early 1834, Morrison confided to his son John Robert, who had become the chief interpreter for the British in Canton, that he found his studies in the Chinese 'and other' scriptures 'very interesting and edifying'. Morrison advised his son to read the Four Books and Five Classics, which 'though pagan, are exhibitions of the highest morality of the human mind in pagan China' and which, unlike the Greek and Roman classics, would neither lower nor lead to the loss of 'the moral sense'.[65]

Given how they believed the Cantonese to be worse than other Chinese, it comes as no small surprise that these Britons could sometimes write so favourably of them. But it should surprise us only because our understanding of this encounter between Britain and China has been shaped by the teleology of the Opium War (1839–42), which has made the Canton period primarily one of tension and conflict. Especially after the end of the East India Company's monopoly, British merchants increasingly demanded a more aggressive policy toward China. Particularly vocal were the powerful traders William Jardine and Alexander Matheson, who through pamphlets and publications such as the *Canton Register* helped to push British opinion in Canton and London toward a more aggressive course of action and ultimately to persuade the British government to go to war with China. As Song-chuan Chen has argued, this 'British maritime public sphere' eventually helped to break down the Canton System.[66]

These jingoists' successful use of the pen to bring the sword to China should not, however, obscure how other Britons – even those who later welcomed the use of force to open China – wrote about it with different intentions and would continue doing so for more than a century. Citing the Chinese proverb about the frog at the bottom of the well – a person who judges others without forming a 'thorough acquaintance with them' – Walter Medhurst argued that 'the Chinese have been at the bottom of the well, with regard to foreigners, and that we are not unfrequently [sic] at the bottom of the well, with regard to them'. He hoped to 'bring each party to the brink, and exhibit them to each other'.[67] The two parties would indeed come to the brink. The result would be Britain's first war with China and China's first war with a Western nation. It would end with the Treaty of Nanking, which abolished the Canton System and opened Canton and four more ports to Western trade and residence, becoming known in China as the first of the 'unequal treaties' and the beginning of China's 'century of shame'. It did not, however, end British attempts to sort out China.

Notes

1 Paul A. Van Dyke, *The Canton Trade: Life and Enterprise on the China Coast, 1700–1845* (Hong Kong: Hong Kong University Press, 2005), pp. 161, 165.
2 Fa-ti Fan, *British Naturalists in Qing China* (Cambridge, MA: Harvard University Press, 2004), p. 17.
3 Li Chen, 'Law, Empire, and Historiography of Modern Sino-Western Relations: A Case Study of the Lady Hughes Controversy in 1784', *Law and History Review*, 27 (2009), 1–53.
4 John M. Carroll, 'The Canton System: Conflict and Accommodation in the Contact Zone', *Journal of the Hong Kong Branch of the Royal Asiatic Society*, 50 (2010), 51–66.
5 See also, for example, Martin Daunton and Rick Halpern (eds), *Empire and Others: British Encounters with Indigenous Peoples, 1600–1850* (London: UCL Press, 1999), pp. 42–78.
6 Ulrike Hillemann, *Asian Empire and British Knowledge: China and the Networks of British Imperial Expansion* (New York: Palgrave Macmillan, 2009).
7 David Kopf, *British Orientalism and the Bengal Renaissance: The Dynamics of Indian Modernization, 1773–1835* (Berkeley: University of California Press, 1969); Maya Jasanoff, *Edge of Empire: Lives, Culture, and Conquest in the East, 1750–1850* (New York: Knopf, 2005).
8 R. David Arkush and Leo O. Lee (eds), *Land without Ghosts: Chinese Impressions of America from the Mid-Nineteenth Century to the Present* (Berkeley: University of California Press, 1989).
9 C. Toogood Downing, *The Fan Qui in China in 1836–1837* (London: Henry Colburn, 1838), vol. 2, p. 287.
10 Sir John Francis Davis, *The Chinese: A General Description of that Empire and Its Inhabitants* (London: Charles Knight & Co., 1836), vol. 1, pp. 250–1.
11 Downing, *Fan Qui*, vol. 1, p. 66, vol. 3, pp. 73–4.
12 For an introduction to old Canton, see Valerie M. Garrett, *Heaven is High, the Emperor Far Away: Merchants and Mandarins in Old Canton* (New York: Oxford University Press, 2002).

13 Gideon Nye, Jr, *Morning of My Life in China: Comprising an Outline of the History of Foreign Intercourse from the Last Year of the Regime of the Honorable East India Company, 1833, to the Imprisonment of the Foreign Community in 1839* (Canton: n.p., 1873), p. 15.
14 Downing, *Fan Qui*, vol. 1, p. 298.
15 William Hickey, *Memoirs of William Hickey*, ed. Peter Quennell (London: Hutchison, 1960), p. 135.
16 Aeneas Anderson, *A Narrative of the British Embassy to China in the Years 1792, 1793, and 1794; Containing the Various Circumstances of Embassy the Accounts of Customs and Manners of the Chinese, and a Description of the Country, Towns, Cities, &c. &c.* (London: J. Debrett, 1795), p. 254.
17 Downing, *Fan Qui*, vol. 1, p. 103.
18 Anderson, *Narrative*, pp. 256–7.
19 Downing, *Fan Qui*, vol. 1, p. 216; vol. 2, p. 49.
20 Anderson, *Narrative*, p. 257.
21 Davis, *Chinese*, vol. 2, p. 26.
22 Downing, *Fan Qui*, vol. 2, pp. 1–2.
23 Walter Henry Medhurst, *China: Its State And Prospects, with Special Reference to the Spread of the Gospel; Containing Allusions to the Antiquity, Extent, Population, Civilization, Literature, and Religion of the Chinese* (London: J. Snow, 1838), pp. 498–9.
24 Medhurst, *China*, p. 499.
25 Basil Hall, *Voyage to Loo-Choo, and Other Places in the Eastern Seas, in the Year 1816: Including an Account of Captain Maxwell's Attack on the Batteries at Canton; and Notes of an Interview with Buonaparte at St. Helena, in August 1817* (Edinburgh: A. Constable & Co., 1826), pp. 40–1.
26 Clarke Abel, *Narrative of a Journey in the Interior of China, and of a Voyage to and from that Country, in the Year 1816 and 1817: Containing an Account of the Most Interesting Transactions of Lord Amherst's Embassy to the Court of Pekin, and Observations on the Countries which It Visited* (London: Orme and Brown, 1818), p. 216.
27 Abel, *Narrative*, pp. 218–19.
28 Downing, *Fan Qui*, vol. 1, vii, vol. 2, pp. 133–46, 157, 162–3, 179.
29 Abel, *Narrative*, pp. 226–7.
30 Davis, *Chinese*, vol. 2, p. 20.
31 Downing, *Fan Qui*, vol. 2, pp. 120, 288–9, vol. 3, p. 18.
32 Abel, *Narrative*, p. 215.
33 John Barrow, *Travels in China, Containing Descriptions, Observations, and Comparisons, Made and Collected in the Course of a Short Residence at the Imperial Palace of Yuen-Min-Yuen, and on a Subsequent Journey through the Country from Pekin to Canton. In Which It is Attempted to Appreciate the Rank that the Extraordinary Empire May be Considered to Hold in the Scale of Civilized Nations* (London: Cadell and Davies, 1804), p. 152; Abel, *Narrative*, p. 214.
34 Davis, *Chinese*, vol. 2, pp. 432, 436.
35 Downing, *Fan Qui*, vol. 3, p. 182.
36 Medhurst, *China*, p. 87.
37 Barrow, *Travels*, p. 152.
38 Medhurst, *China*, p. 87.
39 Downing, *Fan Qui*, vol. 3, p. 182.
40 Downing, *Fan Qui*, vol. 1, pp. 66–7.
41 Downing, *Fan Qui*, vol. 2, p. 285.
42 Barrow, *Travels*, pp. 28–9.
43 Barrow, *Travels*, pp. 159, 161, 171.
44 Davis, *Chinese*, vol. 1, p. 246, vol. 2, p. 73.
45 Barrow, *Travels*, p. 400.
46 Downing, *Fan Qui*, vol. 1, p. 235.
47 Downing, *Fan Qui*, vol. 3, p. 94.

48 Barrow, *Travels*, p. 591 (italics in original).
49 Barrow, *Travels*, pp. 591–3.
50 Davis, *Chinese*, vol. 1, pp. 195, 237–8.
51 Hall, *Voyage*, p. 54.
52 Downing, *Fan Qui*, vol. 2, pp. 31, 34, vol. 3, pp. 86, 93–5.
53 Anderson, *Narrative*, p. 260.
54 Downing, *Fan Qui*, vol. 2, pp. 99–100.
55 Davis, *Chinese*, vol. 1, pp. 237–8.
56 Downing, *Fan Qui*, vol. 3, pp. 316–17, 326.
57 Medhurst, *China*, pp. 97, 101.
58 Downing, *Fan Qui*, vol. 3, pp. 323–4.
59 Medhurst, *China*, p. 98.
60 Medhurst, *China*, pp. 97–8.
61 Robert Morrison, *A View of China, for Philological Purposes: Containing a Sketch of Chinese Chronology, Geography, Government, Religion & Customs. Designed for the Use of Persons Who Study the Chinese Language* (London: Black, Parbury, and Allen; Macao: Printed at the Honourable East India Company's Press by P. P. Thoms, 1817), p. 124.
62 For similar missionary experiences elsewhere, see, for example, Richard Price, *Making Empire: Colonial Encounters and the Creation of Imperial Rule in Nineteenth-Century Africa* (Cambridge: Cambridge University Press, 2008), chs 1–5.
63 Morrison, *View of China*, pp. 122, 124.
64 Letter to Thomas Wilson, Esq., Canton, 9 October 1806, in *Memoirs of the Life and Labours of Robert Morrison, Compiled by His Widow, with Critical Notices of His Chinese Works, by Samuel Kidd*, ed. Eliza Morrison (London: Longman, Orme, Brown, Green and Longmans, 1839), vol. 1, p. 172.
65 Robert Morrison to John Robert Morrison, 18 February 1834, MS5829 (Letters from His Father, the Revd Robert Morrison), Wellcome Library, London.
66 Song-Chuan Chen, 'The British Maritime Public Sphere in Canton, 1827–1839', PhD dissertation, University of Cambridge, 2008.
67 Medhurst, *China*, p. 99.

CHAPTER EIGHT

John Stuart Mill's other island: the discourse of unbridled capitalism in post-war Hong Kong

Mark Hampton

Post-war Hong Kong is well known for its official commitment to free trade and *laissez-faire*, even if in practice its government has been more than willing to intervene in the economy in case of market failure, most famously in the development of its public housing programme from the early 1950s onward. This benign neglect has been widely credited with producing Hong Kong's 'economic miracle', which entailed an average annual GDP growth of 7.5 per cent between 1961 and the end of British rule in 1997.[1] By the 1970s, free market scholars and think-tanks in both the UK and the USA had begun regularly touting Hong Kong as the world's most free economy (though occasionally it fell to second behind Singapore), so much so, in fact, that even the colony's return to Chinese sovereignty after 1997 failed to dampen the enthusiasm of British and American advocates of low taxation and deregulation.[2]

Not surprisingly, this *laissez-faire* or, in local parlance, 'positive non-interventionism', has often been cited in the context of praising the British achievement in building modern Hong Kong from a nineteenth-century 'barren island'. Less well remarked is that the generally (but not exclusively) celebratory post-war discourse concerning Hong Kong's unbridled capitalism was part of a broader cultural connection between empire and metropole. During an era primarily associated with decolonisation and Britain's retreat from world power, including a renunciation of a role 'east of Suez' following the late 1960s, Hong Kong remained not merely an anachronistic Crown possession but the locus of an alternative version of Britishness – one that kept alive nineteenth-century economic values during an era of welfare-state consensus politics in the metropole and maintained a foil with which the latter could be criticised during the breakdown of this consensus during the 1970s.

During the first few post-war decades, Hong Kong was often portrayed as a territory free of the rules that constrained economic choices elsewhere – a site of unbridled capitalism. Although this motif contained its share of myth, it contributed to the idea of Hong Kong as a place in which British qualities and liberties that were stifled in the metropole could be given free rein. Moreover, in the context of the Thatcherite attack on the welfare state from the mid-1970s onward, Hong Kong was frequently cited as a salutary model. My concern in the present chapter is not to settle the question of the nature of the colonial state. This chapter will treat colonial non-interventionism neither as a quality to be measured nor, strictly speaking, as a political ideology, as, for example, in the assertion by Ngo Tak-wing that *laissez-faire* was a legitimating tool for British rule.[3] Rather, it approaches *laissez-faire* as one way (and not always the best way) in which commentators on Hong Kong articulated a particular vision of Britishness that championed the individual against the state and the man of action against mass mediocrity. This discussion illustrates two of the book's central themes, namely the manner in which the empire was central in the construction of both metropolitan and colonial identities as well as how a plethora of imperial cultures were constituted in the movement of many of the ideas, practices and beliefs that permeated the British world-system.

More British than Britain: Hong Kong's Victorian economy

Most of the writers or observers cited in this chapter celebrated Hong Kong's economic freedom. Following the creation of the post-1945 British welfare state, embattled capitalists could look to Hong Kong as a sort of colonial 'world we have lost', in which taxes were low, profits were high, labour was quiescent and the state's reach was limited.[4] As Harold Ingrams wrote in 1952, 'It is not only in the material things of life – the many surviving *large* rooms, the *fat* newspaper with porridge, *two* eggs and bacon and *very* fragrant coffee for breakfast – and all the rest – that Hong Kong offers to those who can afford it, an escape to the past, but in much of its atmosphere.'[5] The 'atmosphere' was one that encouraged, even demanded, true British virtues. While the climate in post-war Britain itself was, according to the economist Joseph Schumpeter, actively hostile to entrepreneurship or any sort of income earning not directly tied to labour, Hong Kong remained a site in which the industrialists, merchants and entrepreneurs could flourish – or fail.[6] Although the setting was very different, Hong Kong thus joined the settler colonies in post-war Africa as a place in which the 'best elements in "the British culture"' could continue to flourish, in contrast to idle and effeminate Britain, which was 'no longer fully British'.[7]

This paradoxical idea that Hong Kong was more British than Britain contributed to ambivalent feelings toward the metropole on the part of Britons in Hong Kong, often veering toward *schadenfreude*. A member of Britain's Department of Health and Social Security, S. M. Davies, reporting on a 1970 trip to Hong Kong to promote Britain's lagging medical-supplies industry, noted that 'Expatriate Britons are notorious for their masochistic delight in denigrating their home country.'[8] Similarly, John le Carré's fictional 1977 depiction of the Hong Kong Club portrayed *Telegraph* readers grousing about Britain's ubiquitous strikes and the decline of the pound.[9] More than a matter of declinism, it was frequently observed that Britons in Hong Kong were increasingly alienated from post-war British life. In 1970, for example, the British Council's Hong Kong Representative claimed that 'citizens of Great Britain living in Hong Kong tend to think, with a curious dichotomy of mind, of Britain as a foreign country (which, by comparison, it is)'.[10] This reversal forms an interesting counterpoint to the eighteenth-century nabobs described by Tillman Nechtman in Chapter Ten; where they defensively demanded their colony's conceptual inclusion as 'British', those Britons in post-war Hong Kong rhetorically excluded the metropole itself.

Paradoxically, it was Hong Kong that was the more classically British, while Britain itself had changed. In the title of one 1960s pamphlet published by a pro-free market think-tank, the Institute of Economic Affairs, Hong Kong was 'John Stuart Mill's Other Island', and the only question was whether or not it was an appropriate model for other developing economies.[11] The peripatetic British political scientist Peter Harris, who founded the University of Hong Kong's Political Science Department after stints in Rhodesia and London (and degrees from Wales, London and Natal), described in 1978, in more dispassionate terms, the prevailing view of an administrative state in which the Financial Secretary could enforce a *laissez-faire* line by his ability to say 'no'; he quoted the American scholar Alvin Rabushka, shortly to be known for his championing of a 'flat tax' for the United States, as referring to Hong Kong's 'official line' as 'Gladstone reincarnated'. By the late 1970s, following a 'crisis of legitimacy' after serious rioting between 1966 and 1968, Harris could note that this picture of Hong Kong's government had grown somewhat outdated. Nonetheless, even with recent changes and assorted caveats, Financial Secretary C. P. Haddon-Cave could still credibly claim that the Government 'consciously refrain from substituting a bureaucratic decision-making process for the process of market determination'.[12]

Evocations of Hong Kong's continuing adherence to nineteenth-century economic values took their place within a wider range of claims concerning Hong Kong's superior British credentials to those of a home country in which they had disappeared. This can be seen, for example, on the invitation to a 1977 Christmas party that, according to *Hong Kong Tatler*, attracted 500 guests. The invitation's first page included a quotation from Sir Winston Churchill stating that the hosts 'Invite you to insure that: "It is right that the British Empire in it's [sic] collective united aspect should put itself solidly on the map."' The second page revealed the evening's programme, which included the 'Royal Fanfare' and the National Anthem, as well as separate toasts to The Queen and The Empire; it also announced a dress code of 'hunting or tweeds' for the gentlemen, and 'scarves, twin sets and pearls' for the ladies. Yet the hosts' self-conscious articulation of their superior Britishness came most clearly in a ten-line poem that contrasts Britain's diminishing power, the pound sterling's collapse and Urdu signs on British streets, on the one hand, with the remaining 'British Bulldogs', on the other hand, who, far from 'dead', live in Hong Kong, where they 'stand for what is British, what is noble, just and right'.[13] In the context of a caricaturistic display of Hong Kong Britishness, the dig at Britain's currency crisis reaffirmed the wisdom of Hong Kong's rejection of the welfare state of Britain itself.

Even those who spoke about Hong Kong with a critical voice generally affirmed its identification with pre-Attlee economic and social policies. This point is illustrated, for example, by a 1974 pamphlet *Hong Kong: A Case to Answer*, anonymously written by Jon Halliday and published by a radical London-based organisation called the Hong Kong Research Project that was founded by former Hong Kong policeman Walter Easey. This pamphlet essentially saw Hong Kong as a repressive colonial police state whose chief function was to transform a thorough exploitation of Chinese workers into 'high levels of capital accumulation, and high profits'.[14] Similarly, John Gordon Davis's 1979 novel *Typhoon* includes a scene in which senior police inspector Bernard Champion lectures an American journalist that Hong Kong 'exists for one reason only. Money!' He elaborates that corruption, Triad criminality and philanthropy were all intertwined and embodied in the same social elites, while British hypocrisy recognised such figures with knighthoods and honours – specifically in the case of the novel's villain, Sir Herman Choi. John le Carré's *The Honourable Schoolboy* (1977) includes a similar, though less cartoonish, character in Drake Ko, O.B.E., described by one character as 'to all outward purposes ... something of a Hong Kong prototype: Steward of the Jockey Club, supports the charities, pillar of the integrated society, successful, benevolent, has the wealth of Croesus and the commercial mentality of the whorehouse'.[15]

Indeed, for many of Hong Kong's critics, such instances of unbridled capitalism were linked to the lack of a (modern) British-style social welfare system and more equitable distribution of income, as evidenced in its lack of popular representation. For example, in April 1969, during the House of Commons Oral Answers concerning the conferring of the title 'Royal' upon the Hong Kong Police following its heroic performance in containing the 1967 riots, one Labour member, the 79-year-old John Rankin, objected that Hong Kong 'as a State stands for everything that we in this country reject' and noted that this un-British system was 'loyally backed up by the Hong Kong Police Force'.[16] According to Duncan Campbell, writing in the *New Statesman* in 1980, this wealth-serving police state was further supported by a thorough surveillance network that, in the words of his article's title, contributed to a 'secret plan for dictatorship' in case the normal measures of repression failed.[17] Yet it was not only critics who linked a lack of democracy with Hong Kong's economic success. Peter Bauer, in the *Spectator* in an admiring review of the American political scientist Alvin Rabushka's *Hong Kong: A Study in Economic Freedom*, linked Hong Kong's success to its minimal government and low taxes, and cited the 'absence of election promises' as one of the key factors in discouraging political activism aimed at interventionist economics.[18]

James Clavell's Hong Kong

The idea of Hong Kong as a site for unrestrained wealth building was something that was ultimately built into the colony's founding mythologies. In his 1985 book *Hard Graft in Hong Kong*, a sympathetic scholarly account of the creation of the Independent Commission against Corruption, the Hong Kong-based sociologist Henry J. Lethbridge, for example, described nineteenth-century Hong Kong's European society as a 'distorting mirror of mid-Victorian England – outwardly respectable, conservative, snobbish, and Sabbatarian'. Yet beneath this 'lacquer', he wrote, life entailed a 'frantic scramble for wealth, with the intruding reminder that life was short on the China coast'. According to Lethbridge, early Hong Kong was a virtually lawless society or, more precisely, one in which merchants were 'prepared to cut corners, to sail close to the law'.[19]

Nowhere was the identification of Hong Kong – both in the nineteenth and twentieth centuries – with quick money, earned in a virtually lawless environment, more evocatively rendered than in two novels by Australian-born writer James Clavell. *Tai-Pan*, published in 1966, mythologises the nineteenth-century founding of British Hong

Kong and its leading company engaged in the China trade, Jardine Matheson, while *Noble House*, published in 1981, provides a vivid portrayal of Hong Kong capitalism in 1963. Born in 1924 in Australia, Clavell served in the British military in the Asian theatre during the Second World War. Enlisting in the Royal Artillery at age 16, by the end of the war he had been wounded by gunfire and imprisoned in Japanese prisoner-of-war camps in Java and Singapore. According to literary critic Gina MacDonald, his experiences in Singapore's Changi prison, in which 'unholy realities of a Japanese prison camp' tested the idealistic British military values he had been taught by his patriotic father, underlie his lifelong commitment to the value of individual freedom and private enterprise.[20] Clavell's championing of the heroic side of British imperial history may well have reflected an attempt to escape from what he considered Britain's loss of its way; as he told an interviewer in 1966, he felt that after the war 'the country had lost its morality and sense of obligation'.[21]

Despite being an opium trader, the hero of *Tai-Pan*, Dirk Struan, embodies the best of Britishness: rule of law, the anti-slavery movement, fair play and support for free trade and peace. At the same time, he willingly borrows from the best of Chinese civilisation – drinking tea instead of water, hygienic practices, medicines such as quinine – and regards China and Britain as partners in advancing human civilisation. In Clavell's typically didactic manner, we learn Struan's thoughts:

> Stop it, he said to himself. You're acting like a madman. Aye, and they'd all think you mad if you told them that your secret purpose was not just to get rich on trade and to leave. But to use riches and power to open up China to the world and particularly to British culture and British law so that each could learn from the other and grow to the benefit of both. Aye. It's a dream of a madman.
>
> But he was certain that China had something special to offer the world. What it was, he did not know. One day perhaps he would find out.[22]

Clavell's narrative does not shy away from the sordid aspects of British imperialism – the drug trade, the exploitative side of the profit motive, the brutality. Clavell appears to endorse the school of imperial thought that making omelets requires breaking a few eggs.[23] As one pre-publication review noted, 'Some of the merchants' actions verge on piracy, some of their cargo is opium, but they are brave and resourceful in facing their trade risks, their precarious position on the verge of a vast empire which hates them, and the personal danger to themselves and their families.'[24] The end result is that Hong Kong – that barren rock – is established as a beneficent site of British and Chinese cooperation. Again, we see Struan's thoughts upon the founding of Hong Kong:

> The treaty would stand because it was fair. Then, over the years, the Chinese would gradually open their ports willingly – seeing that the British had much to offer: law, justice, the sanctity of property, freedom.
>
> For the ordinary Chinese want what we want, he thought, and there's nae difference between us. We can work together for the benefit of all. Perhaps we'll help the Chinese to throw out the barbaric Manchus. That's what will happen so long as there's a reasonable treaty now, and we're patient, and we play the Chinese game with Chinese rules, in Chinese time. Time measured not in a day or year, but in generations. And so long as we can trade while we're waiting. Without trade the world will become what it was once – a hell where only the strongest arm and the heaviest lash was law. The meek will never inherit the earth. Aye, but at least they can be protected by law to live out their lives as they wish.[25]

Where *Tai-Pan* argues the significance of Hong Kong's creation, *Noble House* shows its flourishing just over a century later. It tells the story of an American businessman, Linc Bartlett, arriving in Hong Kong in 1963 (with his assistant Casey Tcholok), ostensibly to arrange a deal with Ian Dunross, a descendant of Dirk Struan and taipan of the firm Noble House. In fact, Bartlett schemes with Dunross's rival, Quillian Gornt, to take over Noble House – a plot that comes dangerously close to success before Dunross secures mainland Chinese backing. Throughout the novel, the association of Hong Kong with money and, in particular, quick money, is clear, even heavy handed. This association appears in the Americans' motivation for coming to Hong Kong: Casey is trying to score a quick US \$2 million of 'drop dead' or 'screw you' money, and though she is unsure how to get it, she thinks 'somehow I know this is the place'.[26] Clavell assures us that she is right to think this way: upon the Americans' arrival by plane, Bartlett 'caught a strangeness on the wind, neither pleasant nor unpleasant, neither odor nor perfume – just strange and curiously exciting' – a smell noticed as well by Casey. Asking what the smell was, he was informed by the Superintendent, 'That's Hong Kong's very own, Mr. Bartlett. It's money.'[27] (Fragrant harbour, indeed!)

Nor is Casey wrong to hope for quick riches. As Dunross's sister, Kathren, explains to her, Hong Kong is a vengeful place, a 'piratical society with very few curbs'. It is a 'place of transit – no one ever comes here to stay, even Chinese, just to make money and leave'. Hong Kong's vengeful quality and air of quick money derive, in part, from foreboding: 'we live on the edge of catastrophe all the time: fire, flood, plague, landslide, riots'. In part they derive from Hong Kong's temporary status: 'China can swallow us any moment. So you live for today and to hell with everything, grab what you can because tomorrow, who knows?'[28]

Yet concerns over a future communist Chinese takeover were not the only perceived threats to the popular 'get rich quickly' mentality among Hong Kong's expatriate community. Clavell, for instance, contrasted his hero, Ian Dunross, with the periodic meddling of London politicians. In a typically didactic passage, Dunross, asked what his politics are, explains to an interlocutor that Hong Kong is apolitical, ruled on behalf of the Crown by a governor whose despotism is not so much benevolent as benignly neglectful: 'Wisely he leaves things alone. He listens to the business community, makes social changes very cautiously and leaves everyone to make money or not make money, to build, expand, go broke, to go or to come, to dream or to stay awake, to live or die as best you can.' He goes on to boast of the low tax rate – applied only to money earned in Hong Kong – and asserts 'I'm royalist, I'm for freedom, for freebooting and free trade. I'm a Scotsman, I'm for Struan's, I'm for laissez-faire in Hong Kong and freedom throughout the world.'[29]

Yet despite Dunross's pronouncements, Hong Kong was not entirely free from London's periodic intrusion, as seen in Clavell's explication of Dunross's thoughts as the latter talks with Robin Grey, a visiting Labour MP. Dunross chose his words 'carefully', knowing that the 'anti-Hong Kong lobby in Parliament was strong'. Yet this latest threat to Hong Kong's status merely joined the list of surmountable obstacles Hong Kong had always faced: 'Never mind, he thought. Since 1841 we've survived hostile Parliaments, fire, typhoon, pestilence, plague, embargo, depression, occupation and the periodic convulsions that China goes through, and somehow we always will.'[30] During the course of the novel parliamentary interference does not materialise and Clavell, writing much of this book against the backdrop of the 1979 election that brought Margaret Thatcher to power, clearly endorses this benign neglect.

Parliamentary interference did not, of course, exist only in Clavell's imagination. Although by the 1960s the Hong Kong Government was increasingly autonomous – and increasingly self-financing – questions of working conditions and corrupt oligopolistic dominance periodically attracted enquiry from London. This could result from a Labour MP's ideological opposition to the very nature of Hong Kong's economy, or from pressure from British manufacturing interests concerned to protect their markets from the 'dumping' of Hong Kong's wares.[31]

Where Clavell celebrated even the more sordid aspects of Hong Kong's commercial mentality, other writers were less enthusiastic about the colony's devotion to mammon. For some, Hong Kong's economy was too 'short-term' focused, concentrating on quick profit at the expense of sustainable, long-term investment. Others were wary of the debilitating effects of official corruption. In 1975, during a series of high-profile police corruption trials, Robert Elegant, for example, noted in *The Australian* that the Royal Hong Kong Police Force was the 'best police force money can buy in Asia' – both because it was certainly one of Asia's top three police forces and because 'many policemen, from constables to senior officers, are for sale to lawbreakers'.[32] The radical Urban Councillor Elsie Elliott often similarly focused her anti-corruption rhetoric on the idea that legal justice and bureaucratic administration were, in effect, commercialised. More germane to the present discussion, she noted the extent to which even civil servants imbibed the commercial mentality. In her 1981 autobiography, she noted that on one occasion she applied to the Education Department for permission to erect some army huts, which she had acquired at a bargain, to use as a new building for the charitable school she operated. The bureaucrat was less than sympathetic: 'The official who interviewed me (I remember his name but will not shame him by repeating it here) said, "Why don't you copy Mr. So-and-so? He runs private schools, and now runs around in a big American car." He was not joking either.'[33] According to Marjorie Topley, writing in 1963, such commercial considerations predominated in Hong Kong. She quoted the prevalent Chinese observation that 'Most things are decided in Hong Kong on the basis of whether or not the abacus makes a satisfying click', and went so far as to claim that few religious goods existed 'that would not be sold if the price offered were sufficiently attractive'.[34]

Laissez-faire *and the Chinese character*

Much more common, again, was the emphasis on Hong Kong as a site for financial gain. In part, so went the conventional wisdom, Hong Kong's character was not only attributable to the genius of British limited government, which stayed out of the way of economic incentives, but it also was frequently linked to the character of either the Chinese or, more specifically, the Cantonese. For example, while F. D. Ommanney attributed Hong Kong's 'exaggeratedly commercial outlook' to sheer economic necessity for its population, at the same time he viewed the Cantonese work ethic as a 'natural' characteristic:

> Another characteristic of the Cantonese which strikes one on arrival in Hong Kong is their industry, which is astonishing. It is like that of the ant-heap, directed towards the same end: survival. Work is for them a natural bodily function, like breathing or the heart-beat. It is automatic and without it life stops.

For this reason, although he did not directly criticise Western attempts to reduce Hong Kong people's working hours, he nonetheless concluded that 'If shorter hours are forced upon them by Welfare State legislation they fill the extra hours of enforced leisure with some other work.'[35] James Pope-Hennessy, writing in 1969, referred to such an attitude as one of the 'stock official answers' to any query he made 'about, say, restaurant working hours': not only did the Chinese 'like overworking', but even if legislation were passed that reduced working hours, it would be unenforceable, since employers would have no difficulty finding workers who were willing to 'work the old excessive hours without lodging any complaints'. He concluded that, 'in fact, the tenets of the mill-owners of Victorian England still prevail'.[36] Jan Morris, in the 1997 edition of her popular history of Hong Kong, generalised that the Hong Kong Chinese 'are tireless workers'.[37] A government-sponsored report on the 1967 riots, *Colony in Conflict*, claimed that 'To a race, which is so hard working by nature, long hours do not become a main source of discontent.'[38] Former Governor Alexander Grantham, in a 1968 interview, blamed the Chinese work ethic for the difficulty of finding a non-Hong Kong home for early 1950s refugees from the People's Republic of China: 'None of the countries in South-East Asia would have them because the Chinese are not popular there, they work too hard.'[39] A Cambodia-based journalist in John le Carré's *The Honourable Schoolboy* similarly evoked the Chinese work ethic, but put a more favourable spin on it, arguing that hard-working Chinese had 'fixed our [Cambodia's] money market, our transport monopoly, our rate of inflation, our siege economy'. As a result, Chinese controlled 80 per cent of Cambodian commerce, while 'lazy' Cambodians remained 'content to take [their] profit out of American aid'.[40] Such a British view of Chinese labourers, contrasting so sharply with images of lazy West Indian workers described by Philip Harling in Chapter Three, has a long history, and one not limited to Hong Kong; early nineteenth-century proposals to replace Trinidad's slave labour with Chinese workers on long-term contracts hinged on visions of Chinese natural industriousness, as did working-class resistance to importing Chinese labour to South Africa at the turn of the twentieth century.[41] It is striking, though, that these images continued late into the twentieth century to circulate in otherwise responsible accounts of Hong Kong.

Edward Szczepanik, a Polish-born economist (and later Prime Minister of the final Soviet-era Polish government-in-exile), who made an academic career in Britain and Hong Kong, in 1958 published what he called the first economic history of Hong Kong. For Szczepanik, the work ethic in Hong Kong went beyond any inherent Chinese qualities (though he also credited these); this would not explain Hong Kong's recent economic growth and advantage over the rival ports of Singapore and Macau. Rather, Hong Kong's Chinese population had a distinct 'historical structure'. Unlike Singapore and Macau, where the Chinese were 'descendants of settlers who gradually trickled away from their native villages as farmers, fishermen, craftsmen, or merchants', the Chinese in Hong Kong were, in the 1950s, disproportionately new arrivals fleeing the Mainland. Szczepanik, whose own country had only recently begun a tentative de-Stalinisation in the mid-1950s, said of these recent migrants: 'They came in bulk, frightened by Communism and prepared to work hard rather than live under terror again.'[42] Similarly, Marjorie Topley, writing in 1963, noted that observers often contrasted the materialism of Hong Kong Chinese with the more 'cultivated' northerners; she argued, however, that these observers unwittingly contrasted the northern upper classes with Hong Kong people of 'more humble origin'.[43] This type of specificity was, however, rare; most commentators, though they certainly would have understood that the Communist takeover in China was the reason for the flood of refugees, attributed their hard work ethic to their Chineseness more generally, not to their social class or their fear of Communism.

Evocations of the Chinese work ethic coexisted nicely with what Lau Siu-kai has called the distinctive Hong Kong trope of utilitarianistic familism, as both justified inaction by the state in the face of widespread poverty.[44] Hong Kong people, the thinking went, looked to their own efforts to pull themselves up by their bootstraps, and where they needed help, they looked to their extended families. British observers, particularly before the late 1960s, also emphasised the quiescent nature of Hong Kong's Chinese: however difficult their circumstances might appear to Western sensibilities, the Chinese were content.[45]

One could, of course, distinguish between a refugee's incessant working, born out of low wages and desperate poverty, and a racial or cultural tendency to 'like overworking'. John Walker, writing in the early 1970s, argued that the long hours of the Chinese working classes came 'not out of some pernicious Chinese penchant for hard work, but for the more understandable human motive that they need the money ... people have to work very long hours merely to be able to continue to exist'.[46] As Robin Porter argued in a 1975 pamphlet published by the Bertrand Russell Peace Foundation, 'low wages and inadequate social security', rather than Chinese culture, explained the tendency toward overworking, including child labour.[47] Anthony Shang, writing in 1985, agreed: 'Hard work is a necessity. People need all they can earn to feed large families and save for the future; Hong Kong has no state pensions or unemployment benefits. People are expected to look after themselves in times of trouble and to provide for their elderly parents.'[48] Not every account emphasised the desperate side of the Chinese work ethic; others pointed to the carrot of wealth as much as the stick of poverty.[49] Regardless of its source, this Chinese penchant for overwork justified a lack of economic regulation and welfare provision.

The Government's declining to regulate working hours was not the only example of positive non-interventionism justified by the supposed Chinese character. In addition to their penchant for working, Hong Kong's Chinese displayed a love of gambling. This point is illustrated by Leo Goodstadt, who notes that in refusing to countenance government insurance of bank deposits, officials not only made the familiar 'moral hazard' argument, but frequently argued, in addition, that the Chinese had something of a gambler's mentality, and willingly entrusted their cash to the bank that would pay the highest interest rate, in full expectation of losing their entire capital from time to time.[50] This meme was conveyed at great length in John Gordon Davis's 1974 novel *The Years of the Hungry Tiger*, in lengthy observations made by British banker Derek to Jake McAdam, fast-track police officer and first-person narrator. Derek's world-weary observations, set in the early 1960s, coherently tied together several themes: British Hong Kong's precarious existence, which Mao could end instantly 'with a telephone call'; Hong Kong's taste for luxury – in this case property; and the Chinese penchant for speculation and quick profits. In Derek's view, the luxury property market was in a decided bubble: properties flipped repeatedly at ever-higher prices, before they had even been conveyed. The problem was not only the speculative fever of the Chinese buyers, but that of the banks that lent, without adequate reserves, on the assumption the prices would keep rising, despite Hong Kong's precarious status; and also of depositors who sought out the banks with the highest interest rates without attention to the banks' soundness. Derek is quick to point out, of course, that his own bank, the Hong Kong Shanghai Bank, would not touch such loans, 'nor [would] any of the big established banks with economic know-how, we're not encouraging this madness: no, it's the goddam Chinese banks. The one-eyed pisspot family banks.'[51] McAdam's own musings, from his chair in the Hong Kong Club, highlight the downside of British non-intervention: prudent reserve requirements would prevent the bubble from developing, as would a willingness to prosecute the newspapers that, in pursuing circulation-grabbing headlines over responsible journalism, published unfounded rumours of bank insolvency and provoked ruinous bank runs. With its commitment to *laissez-faire*, of course, the Hong Kong Government chooses neglect over prudence.[52]

In *Typhoon*, published five years later and set a decade later, in Governor Murray MacLehose's reformist mid-1970s, Davis once again emphasises the speculative side of the Chinese pursuit of money, in this case through the stock market. As with housing and high-interest lending in the 1960s, the smart money either stays on the side-lines or gets out early, sometimes on the basis of insider information but often simply out of prudence, while the unconnected and impecunious working classes blindly and irrationally chase unsustainable returns. For Jake McAdam – by now retired from the police force and living as an investor and philanthropic environmentalist – a quick 40 per cent based on an insider tip and a slight delay of releasing unfavourable news to the press was simply prudent (though hollow), but his moral code forces him to draw the line at issuing a public offering of his own business in order to cash in on the sort of unsophisticated Chinese investors who would lose everything when the stock market eventually crashed. In his thoughts, McAdam likened such investors to those who bet on horses: 'All he understood was that you buy, then sell at a profit; it was like betting on a winner at the races at Happy Valley except that at the stock exchanges all the shares were winners.'[53]

Horse racing was, of course, the perfect combination of ostentatious display and gambling fever. A common expression, cited by several writers of both fiction and non-fiction, was that Hong Kong was governed by the Hong Kong and Shanghai Bank, the Royal Jockey Club, Jardines and the Governor; the order varied, but always with the Governor coming last. The Royal Jockey Club was an opportunity for social power, in which the wealthy and connected competed for positions as stewards, raced the horses they owned and could be seen by the masses. It was a site of what Law Wing Sang calls 'collaborative colonial power' and John Carroll (speaking of an earlier period) refers to as 'patterns of collaboration and accommodation' between Chinese elites and British colonials.[54] It was also, though, for the masses, a regulated and legal form of gambling. John le Carré's *The Honourable Schoolboy* describes Happy Valley as offering the 'gambler's dream of instantaneous salvation' from 'grey skyscraper slums crammed so tight they seemed to lean on each other in the heat'.[55] The gambler's mentality was similarly noted in a 1978 *New Statesman* article that pointed out that nearby Macau attracted two million Hong Kong visitors per year to its casinos.[56]

Victorian values and their discontents

As mentioned above, Hong Kong's labour conditions attracted the periodic attention of social reformers and manufacturing interests in Britain. In the mid-1960s, Elsie Elliott's campaigns included visits to London to encourage parliamentary intervention.[57] David Clayton has shown that British governmental pressure was crucial in pushing the adoption of the eight-hour day for female workers in the late 1960s, and London bureaucrats and social reformers took the Hong Kong Government's weakening of the new law as evidence of Hong Kong's retrograde (Victorian) social character.[58] A mid-1970s pamphlet published by the Bertrand Russell Peace Foundation, already cited above, referred to Hong Kong as an exemplar of a modern industrial economy that had failed to shed its pre-industrial acceptance of child labour. Instead, author Robin Porter wrote, 'traditional employment of children has been carried over into modern times with the excuse that it is the local cultural norm'. In Porter's view, Hong Kong was marked by a 'hybrid Nineteenth Century laissez-faire economy' in which desperate parents sent their children to work because they needed their wages in order to survive, and were able to do so because of inadequate workplace inspections that did not enforce even Hong Kong's minimal labour laws.[59] Yet for Keith Joseph, founder of the anti-Keynesian think-tank Centre for Policy Studies and Margaret Thatcher's key supporter, Hong Kong offered a clear model for Britain itself, one in which Victorian economic arrangements facilitated dynamism and economic growth.[60] Hong Kong was one of three Asian territories (the others were South Korea and Singapore) that he cited in a January 1979 interview with *Forbes* magazine as favourable contrasts with the 'failure of the collectivist idea'; in Joseph's words, 'You'd think the contrast between what's happening there and elsewhere would have some effect.'[61] Speaking to the Hong Kong General Chamber of Commerce in 1981, Joseph congratulated Hong Kong on its achievements, which had, in certain key areas such as life expectancy and infant mortality, surpassed Britain's own, and which resulted from the operation of a 'market economy within the rule of law'. Reminding his audience that 'it was in the United Kingdom, in Scotland to be precise', that the benefits of these structures had first been articulated, he argued that 'we forgot the truths which we had been, through Adam Smith, the first to perceive'. Only with the coming of the Thatcher government in 1979 had the British begun returning to their original wisdom which, as he implied, the people of Hong Kong had never forgotten.[62]

Richard West made similar points in an article in the *Spectator* that same year. Responding to London politician Ken Livingstone's recent favourable contrast of Communist China with Hong Kong's 'rat race', West in turn contrasted Hong Kong's prosperity with British stagnation. Not only did the continuing importance of the extended family mean that Hong Kong did not have the same need for Western-style state-provided social welfare, but Hong Kong's privatised transport was more efficient and its losses did not have to be covered by taxpayers. As a result,

> Low tax means that shops and businesses thrive, and provide employment even to most of the hundreds of thousands of refugees who have come to the colony in the last ten years. Because of the profitability of manufacture and retail business, these have attracted investment and capital which, in England, would go to property speculation.

Even the image of '"sweated labor" – conjuring up a picture of stick-limbed, opium-crazed coolies, women and children at work in steamy rat-infested cellars beside the port', if it had ever been true, was now outdated. Instead, since 'British industry, backed by the British trade unions' had lost its ability to suppress competition, Hong Kong wages were 'high and increasing'. Accordingly, Ken Livingstone's referring to Hong Kong as a 'rat race' meant only that 'the Hong Kong Chinese work more than the English, and are getting paid for it'.[63]

Yet not all British commentary celebrated Hong Kong's 'Victorian values'. First, as already mentioned, as Hong Kong factories began competing for British textile markets in the 1950s, the Lancashire textile lobby became vocal critics.[64] This aggressive pursuit of the British market followed the US-imposed trade embargo during the Korean War, a move that severely curtailed Hong Kong's position as an entrepôt and prompted the expansion of its industrial economy. In this context, accusations of dumping put Hong Kong manufacturers on the defensive, leading them in the late 1950s voluntarily to 'temporarily restrict exports' to the UK as an act of good will, in order to mollify Lancashire complaints.[65] As late as 1983, a Government Information Services booklet, *An Introduction to Hong Kong*, noted 'taunts and accusations' by Western industrialists, 'who resented this new source of competition', that the cheapness of Hong Kong products derived from low wages produced by '"slave labour"'; it dismissed them, though, as having become 'increasingly meaningless' as Hong Kong's manufacturing, like Japan's, became more sophisticated and attained higher levels of quality.[66]

Second, other commentators, often, but not uniformly, speaking from leftist perspectives, pointed to the precarious livelihoods and poor working conditions of the Hong Kong Chinese in this supposedly 'prosperous' colony. In 1957, George Edinger wrote in the *Spectator* that refugees in Hong Kong believed that it was 'amazing to feel free. And British justice too was admirable, if you could afford it. But you cannot eat freedom and, unhappily, a social conscience is one blessing you do not always find in Hong Kong.'[67] In a subsequent reply to readers' letters, Edinger elaborated on the causes of the 1956 Kowloon riot, citing the recently published Hong Kong *Annual Report*: 'Three hundred and fifty thousand homeless in warrens of shanty towns, some on the roofs of buildings! A quarter of a million more settled in slum conditions! And yet the luxury sky-scrapers go shooting up to wreck the beauty and open spaces on the Peak.'[68]

In the aftermath of the 1966–68 riots, critics became more vocal in not only pointing out poverty, but demanding that the Government address it. One member of the Urban Council, A. de O. Sales, blaming the widening wealth gap for the 1967–68 'disturbances', insisted that it was 'not enough' for the Government to 'set up and maintain the framework to foster the prosperity of Hong Kong'. Rather, ensuring that working people enjoyed their 'rightful share of such prosperity' was the Government's 'fundamental obligation'.[69] Faced with this perceived crisis of political legitimacy, and buttressed by continuing torrid economic growth, the Government became more willing to countenance a rudimentary safety net. Yet the identification of Hong Kong with a more pristine, Victorian version of British capitalism endured well beyond this era of reform.

Post-war Hong Kong was, then, a contested site of nineteenth-century British economic values, one in which the champions of unrestrained capitalism had a perpetual advantage over advocates of social reform. For its critics, Hong Kong was an unconscionable 'rat race' in which Chinese workers were exploited on behalf of capital and British workers were threatened with cheap Chinese competition, and an affront to British moral sensibilities. For its advocates, Hong Kong was an arena in which British rule ensured economic freedom in which entrepreneurs, both British and Chinese, could flourish in a way that they could not in post-1945 Britain, and in which workers were driven both by the hope of riches and the fear of penury. By the early 1970s, Hong Kong was increasingly a cudgel for those, such as Keith Joseph, who wished to roll back the British welfare state. Beyond its specific qualities, the discourse of Hong Kong's unbridled capitalism during this period points to the lingering interplay of metropolitan and colonial cultures, even during an era most notable for imperial retreat. Jordanna Bailkin has argued that the post-colonial and post-war were every bit as intertwined as the colonial and the metropolitan during the nineteenth and early twentieth centuries, so that, for example, the making of the welfare state can be understood only in the context of decolonisation.[70] Perhaps, then, it should not surprise us that the most important site of persisting colonialism was equally implicated in the resistance to, and counter-attack on, the welfare state.

Acknowledgement

I am grateful to David Clayton and Barry Crosbie for comments on an earlier draft of this chapter. An expanded version of this chapter appears in Mark Hampton, *Hong Kong and British Culture, 1945–97* (Manchester: Manchester University Press, 2016), ch. 2.

Notes

1 Leo Goodstadt, *Poverty in the Midst of Affluence: How Hong Kong Mismanaged its Prosperity* (Hong Kong: Hong Kong University Press, 2013), p. 10.
2 See, for example, Benjamin K. P. Leung, *Perspectives on Hong Kong Society* (Hong Kong: Oxford University Press, 1996), p. 115; James A. Dorn, 'Hong Kong: World's Freest Economy', Cato Institute, 28 July 2004, www.cato.org/publications/commentary/hong-kong-worlds-freest-economy (accessed 11 June 2014); Heritage Foundation, '2014 Index of Economic Freedom', www.heritage.org/index/ranking (accessed 11 June 2014); Stuart Lau, 'Hong Kong's status as world's freest economy threatened by Singapore, says Heritage Foundation', *South China Morning Post*, 14 January 2014, www.scmp.com/business/economy/article/1405318/hong-kongs-status-worlds-freest-economy-threatened-singapore-says?page=all (accessed 11 June 2014).
3 Ngo Tak-wing, 'Industrial History and the Artifice of Laissez-faire Colonialism', in David Faure (ed.), *Hong Kong: A Reader in Social History* (Hong Kong: Oxford University Press, 2003), pp. 543–71, at p. 566.
4 For conservatives of a more pastoral bent, Africa might be a more compelling model. 'Between 1945 and 1955, the white populations of Northern and Southern Rhodesia increased from 5000 and 80,000 to over 60,000 and 200,000 respectively.' Dominic Sandbrook, *Never Had it So Good: A History of Britain from Suez to the Beatles* (London: Abacus, 2006), p. 309. As in Hong Kong, the European population were more prosperous than their counterparts 'back home'. Bill Schwarz notes that in post-war Salisbury, Rhodesia, 'Nearly every white family owned a car, long before car ownership in Britain was widespread. From the beginning of the 1960s swimming pools, particularly, became symbols of the new wealth, with a greater concentration of pools amongst white families in Salisbury than amongst the inhabitants of Beverly Hills.' Schwarz, *The White Man's World* (Oxford: Oxford University Press), p. 408.
5 Harold Ingrams, *Hong Kong* (London: HMSO, 1952), p. 242 (emphasis in original). Among other things, Ingram's idea of 'atmosphere' included antipathy to the Labour government; see p. 241.
6 According to Schumpeter, writing in 1949, Britain's nationalisation policy was 'coupled with an attitude toward private enterprise in general that amounts to sabotage'. Joseph Schumpeter, 'English Economists and the State-Managed Economy', in Schumpeter, *Essays: On Entrepreneurs, Innovations, Business Cycles, and the Evolution of Capitalism* (Brunswick, NJ: Transaction Publishers, 1989), pp. 306–21 (quotation at p. 309).
7 Stephen Howe, 'When (if ever) did Empire End? "Internal Decolonisation" in British Culture since the 1950s', in Martin Lynn (ed.), *The British Empire in the 1950s: Retreat or Revival?* (Basingstoke: Palgrave Macmillan, 2006), pp. 214–37, at p. 219. See also Schwarz, *The White Man's World*, p. 212.
8 S. M. Davies, 'Visit to Hong Kong, 11–18 September 1970', 2. BN 76/29, The National Archives (hereafter, TNA).
9 John le Carré, *The Honourable Schoolboy* (New York: Scribner, 2002), p. 123.

10 The British Council, Hong Kong, Representative's Annual Report 1969/70, p. 3. BW 94/11. TNA.

11 Henry Smith, *John Stuart Mill's Other Island: A Study of the Development of Hong Kong* (London: The Institute for Economic Affairs, 1966). For a critical review, see L. F. Goodstadt, 'John Stuart Mill's Other Island', *Far Eastern Economic Review* (27 October 1966), 237–8.

12 Peter Harris, *Hong Kong: A Study in Bureaucratic Politics* (Hong Kong: Heinemann Asia, 1978), pp. 130–1 (quotation at p. 131).

13 'A Perfectly British Party', *Hong Kong Tatler*, 1 (February 1978), at 26–7.

14 *Hong Kong: A Case to Answer* (London: The Research Project; Nottingham: Spokesman Books, 1974), pp. 12–13, 16, 19 (quotation at p. 19). On Walter Easey, see 'Obituary: Walter Easey', *Independent*, 2 April 1998.

15 John Gordon Davis, *Typhoon: A Novel* (New York: Dutton, 1979), pp. 11–13 (quotation at p. 12). le Carré, *The Honourable Schoolboy*, p. 187.

16 *Hansard*, 17 April 1969, 1333, in FCO 40/226, TNA.

17 Duncan Campbell, 'A Secret Plan for Dictatorship', *New Statesman*, 100 (12 December 1980), 8–9, 12.

18 Peter Bauer, 'The Lesson of Hong Kong', *Spectator* (19 April 1980), 10.

19 H. J. Lethbridge, *Hard Graft in Hong Kong: Scandal, Corruption, the ICAC* (Hong Kong: Oxford University Press, 1985), p. 25.

20 Gina Macdonald, *James Clavell: A Critical Companion* (Westport, CT: Greenwood Press, 1996), pp. 1–16 (quotation at p. 3). Macdonald describes Clavell as the type of Australian who was more British than the British. Not all Australians were of this type.

21 Ed Sheehan, 'Clavell: Each Moment is Precious', *Honolulu Advertiser* (March 1966); James Clavell Collection, 45, box 13, Howard Gotlieb Archival Research Center, Boston University.

22 James Clavell, *Tai-Pan: A Novel of Hong Kong* (London: Michael Joseph, 1966), p. 75. Not everything about Chinese culture meets with Struan's approval. For example, he is disgusted by the chief mandarin of Macao, Wang Chu, who has four-inch fingernails; he pretends to beat his concubine so that she can maintain face with the servants listening on the other side of a closed door, but he does not actually beat her, as he believes it is barbaric. See *Tai-Pan*, pp. 53, 433–6.

23 Luckily, 'British justice, though quick and harsh, did not seem cruel to the Chinese'. Clavell, *Tai-Pan*, p. 440. Nor was Clavell alone in celebrating Hong Kong's origins in the drug trade; in the 1960s, Jardine Matheson ran a print advertisement with a full-page depiction of William Jardine, the notorious opium smuggler; it is reproduced in Far Eastern Economic Review, *Telling Asia's Story for Fifty Years* (Hong Kong: Review Publishing Co. Ltd., 1996). In the early 1980s, even as the future of Hong Kong was under negotiation, Margaret Thatcher rather tactlessly celebrated the nineteenth-century taipans at a banquet. Felix Patrikeeff, *Mouldering Pearl: Hong Kong at the Crossroads* (London: George Philip, 1989), p. 124.

24 Jessie Kitching, undated pre-publication review circulated by Atheneum. James Clavell Collection, 45, box 13, Howard Gotlieb Archival Research Center, Boston University.

25 Clavell, *Tai-Pan*, p. 153. See also pp. 13–14 for the reflections of Struan's rival, Brock, on how poor a choice Hong Kong is for a colony. Writing in the 1960s, Clavell conveys that prosperous Hong Kong was created from virtual nothingness.

26 James Clavell, *Noble House: A Novel of Contemporary Hong Kong* (New York: Delacorte Press, 1981), pp. 47–8.

27 Clavell, *Noble House*, p. 31.

28 Clavell, *Noble House*, pp. 226–7.

29 Clavell, *Noble House*, pp. 164–5.

30 Clavell, *Noble House*, pp. 521–2.

31 See, e.g., David Clayton, 'The Riots and Labour Laws: The Struggle for an Eight Hour Day for Women Factory Workers, 1962–71', in Robert Bickers and Ray Yep (eds), *May Days in Hong Kong: Emergency and Riot in 1967* (Hong Kong: Hong Kong University Press, 2009), pp. 127–44.

32 *The Australian*, 30 January 1975, ANA A1533 1957/ 2133, National Archives of Australia, Canberra.
33 Elsie Elliott, *Crusade for Justice: An Autobiography* (Hong Kong: Heinemann Asia, 1981), p. 175.
34 Marjorie Topley, 'The Role of Savings and Wealth', in Topley, *Cantonese Society in Hong Kong and Singapore: Gender, Religion, Medicine and Money*, ed. and intro. Jean DeBernardi (Hong Kong: Hong Kong University Press, 2011), pp. 275–329, at pp. 294, 305.
35 F. D. Ommanney, *Fragrant Harbour: A Private View of Hong Kong* (London: Hutchinson & Co., 1962), p. 44.
36 James Pope-Hennessy, *Half-Crown Colony: A Hong Kong Notebook* (London: Cape, 1969), p. 98. Work by David Clayton supports this view; in the late 1960s, he argues, 'many female workers colluded with employers to undermine the spirit' of a newly-passed eight-hour workday. Clayton, 'The Riots and the Labour Laws', 127.
37 Jan Morris, *Hong Kong: Epilogue to an Empire* (New York: Random House, 1997), p. 179.
38 John Cooper, *Colony in Conflict: The Hong Kong Disturbances, May 1967–January 1968* (Hong Kong: Swindon, 1970), pp. 304–5. This passage is also quoted in J. Walker, *Under the Whitewash* (Hong Kong: 70s Biweekly, 1972), p. 131.
39 Alexander Grantham, interview by D. J. Crozier, 21 August 1968, p. 16. Mss. Brit. Emp. Si 288, Rhodes College, Oxford. For attempts by the British government in 1962 to find countries willing to accept Hong Kong's refugees, see the documents in 'Assistance for Chinese refugees in Hong Kong – Policy', ANA A1209 1962/ 538.
40 le Carré, *The Honourable Schoolboy*, p. 371.
41 James Epstein, *Scandal of Colonial Rule* (Cambridge: Cambridge University Press, 2012), pp. 211–12; Sascha Auerbach, *Race, Law, and 'The Chinese Puzzle' in Imperial Britain* (Basingstoke: Palgrave Macmillan, 2009), p. 30. For the wider context of Chinese labour within the empire, see Rachel Bright, 'Asian Migration and the British World', in Kent Fedorowich and Andrew S. Thompson (eds), *Empire, Migration and Identity in the British World* (Manchester: Manchester University Press, 2013), pp. 128–49.
42 Edward Szczepanik, *The Economic Growth of Hong Kong* (Westport, CT: Greenwood Press, 1986), pp. 4–5.
43 Topley, 'The Role of Savings and Wealth', 280.
44 Lau Siu-kai, *Society and Politics in Hong Kong* (Hong Kong: The Chinese University Press, 1983).
45 See, e.g., Kaye Webb's account in Seven Stories: National Centre for Children's Books, Newcastle, KW/14/01/119, 'Webb 1) Interviews 2) Firecrackers', KW/14/01/119, n.d., but ca. 1964; Zara Holt, Letter #1, September 1960, ANA M2608/10; 'Mr. Harold Holt's Travel Diary', Installment No. 1, p. 2, 2 September 1960, ANA M2608/9.
46 Walker, *Under the Whitewash*, p. 131.
47 Robin Porter, *Child Labour in Hong Kong* (Nottingham: Bertrand Russell Peace Foundation for the Hong Kong Research Project and The Spokesman, 1975), p. 10.
48 Anthony Shang, *Living in Hong Kong* (London and Sydney: Macdonald, 1985), p. 26.
49 Nigel Cameron, *Hong Kong: The Cultured Pearl* (Hong Kong: Oxford University Press, 1978), p. 194; Feng Chi-shun, *Diamond Hill: Memories of Growing up in a Hong Kong Squatter Village* (Hong Kong: Blacksmith Books, 2009), p. 43.
50 Leo Goodstadt, *Profits, Politics and Panics: Hong Kong's Banks and the Making of a Miracle Economy, 1935–1985* (Hong Kong: Hong Kong University Press, 2007), p. 124.
51 John Gordon Davis, *The Years of the Hungry Tiger* (London: Michael Joseph, 1974), pp. 110–11.
52 Davis, *The Years of the Hungry Tiger*, pp. 198–9.
53 Davis, *Typhoon*, pp. 25–6, 134.
54 Law Wing Sang, *Collaborative Colonial Power: The Making of the Hong Kong Chinese* (Hong Kong: Hong Kong University Press, 2009); John Carroll, *Edge of Empires: Chinese Elites and British Colonials in Hong Kong* (Cambridge, MA: Harvard University Press, 2005), pp. 12–13.

55 le Carré, *The Honourable Schoolboy*, p. 168.

56 Murray Sayle, 'Red Flags, Running Dogs and Air Conditioned Horses', *New Statesman* (26 May 1978), 702.

57 E.g., Mark Hampton, 'British Legal Culture and Colonial Governance: The Attack on Corruption in Hong Kong, 1968–1974', *Britain and the World*, 5 (2012), 223–39, at 238.

58 Clayton, 'The Riots and Labour Laws', 141–2.

59 Porter, *Child Labour in Hong Kong*, pp. 3, 4, 7, 20.

60 On the context of the emergence of anti-Keynesian think-tanks, see Richard Cockett, *Thinking the Unthinkable: Think-Tanks and the Economic Counter-Revolution 1931–1983* (London: HarperCollins, 1995).

61 Quoted in 'The Economics of Sir Fu Manchu', *New Statesman* (19 January 1979), 67.

62 Keith Joseph, 'Address by the Rt. Hon. Sir Keith Joseph: To Members of the Hong Kong General Chamber of Commerce, 21st September, 1981'. *The Bulletin* (November 1981), 31–3, http://sunzi1.lib.hku.hk/hkjo/view/17/1700951.pdf (accessed 23 April 2011).

63 Richard West, 'Livingstone's Hong Kong', *Spectator* (31 October 1981), 9.

64 See David Clayton, 'From "Free" to "Fair" Trade: The Evolution of Labour Laws in Colonial Hong Kong, 1958–62', *Journal of Imperial and Commonwealth History*, 35 (June 2007), 263–82; Clayton, 'Trade-offs and Rip-offs: Imitation-led Industrialisation and the Evolution of Trademark Law in Hong Kong', *Australian Economic History Review*, 51 (July 2011), 178–98.

65 See, e.g., 'Statement issued by Mr. T. Y. Wong, Chairman of the Hongkong Cotton Spinners Association, and Mr. N. C. Chang, Chairman of the Federation of Cotton Weavers', n.d. but late 1960, ACS/6/6/19 Cotton Board: Imports, John Rylands Library, Manchester.

66 Government Information Services, *An Introduction to Hong Kong* (Hong Kong: Government Printer, 1983), p. 16.

67 George Edinger, 'Hong Kong, the Chance We Missed', *Spectator* (21 June 1957), 805–6, at 805.

68 George Edinger, letter, *Spectator* (9 August 1957), 190.

69 Quoted in Cooper, *Colony in Conflict*, p. 309.

70 Jordanna Bailkin, *The Afterlife of Empire* (Berkeley, CA: University of California Press, 2012).

CHAPTER NINE

Scrutiny abroad: literary criticism and the colonial public

Christopher Hilliard

At least since Gauri Viswanathan's *Masks of Conquest* (1989), literary scholars have argued that the logic of teaching English literature in a colonial setting was a logic of displacement – the substitution of a 'single shelf of a good European library' for 'the whole native literature of India and Arabia', to use Macaulay's notorious terms.[1] Alternatively, in the settler colonies, teaching the literary canon could be regarded as a means of shoring up the colonists' sense of Britishness. This chapter examines a different aspect of literary criticism's involvement in the cultural construction of the British Empire: the application of modern critical approaches not to canonical 'English literature' but to the products of colonial literary cultures – usually with a view to understanding their inadequacy. When the famously stringent Cambridge literary critic F. R. Leavis recommended a thesis topic to a New Zealand post-graduate student, it was, a third party reported, 'The Reason Why There is No Literature in New Zealand'.[2]

Leavis, the driving force behind the journal *Scrutiny* (1932–53), had former students running English departments at the universities of Ceylon, Melbourne and, briefly, Sydney, and he had supporters at Natal.[3] The imperial history of literary criticism is bound up with the history of the imperial academic networks and institutions examined by Tamson Pietsch.[4] Colonial English departments tended to base their curricula on the Oxford and London models, which placed a premium on textual and historical scholarship and the study of Anglo-Saxon, rather than on Cambridge's example, which placed more emphasis on 'critical' responses to literary texts. 'Leavisites' appointed to universities in the empire usually set about dismantling the local version of the Oxford–London orthodoxy and installing a new curriculum inflected by Leavis's variety of 'Cambridge English'.[5] Less well known than their attempts to reshape the colonial teaching of canonical literature are the efforts of Leavis's followers to analyse the emergence of national literatures on the peripheries of English literature. Leavisian ideas about literature and its conditions of possibility proved flexible enough to be useful in settings as different as 1930s New Zealand, a settler colony with a large white majority whose younger writers often deplored the culturally suffocating effects of calling Britain 'Home', and the much more complex situation of post-independence India.

For the *Scrutiny* group, it was a basic principle that criticism had a constitutive relationship with literature. Both F. R. Leavis and his wife, Q. D. Leavis, approved of Eliot's dictum that the 'important critic' was 'absorbed in the present problems of art, and ... wishes to bring the forces of the past to bear upon the solution of these problems'.[6] Eliot's own career was exemplary: his recasting of tradition in his poetry was undertaken in a reciprocal and dialectical relationship with his reinterpretation of literary history and the nature of criticism. Exemplary in a different way was W. H. Auden, whose poetic development was stunted by the uncritical acclaim lavished on him.[7] Writing in 1933 on the invention of the poetic movement with Auden at its centre, F. R. Leavis framed his discussion around the role of critical journals and little magazines in bringing together an 'intelligently responsive public' for artists.[8] *Scrutiny*'s opening manifesto declared: 'in spite of the romantic conception of the poet as a bird (preferably a skylark) singing to please himself in glorious isolation, the artist does depend in large measure on the prevailing standard of taste'.[9] Those standards in turn depended on a critical minority whose influence was out of proportion to its size.[10]

F. R. Leavis's idea of 'minority culture' has become notorious, but it was not simple snobbery. It was, rather, a conception of concatenated publics. 'In any period', Leavis wrote, 'it is upon a very small minority that the discerning appreciation of art and literature depends: it is ... only a few who are capable of unprompted, first-hand judgment. They are still a small minority, though a larger one, who are capable of endorsing such first-hand judgment by genuine personal response.'[11] Beyond that, there was (in the inter-war period) the public that sought guidance from reviews in the Sunday newspapers; a '*Listener* public' whose sensibilities were attuned to that publication; and so on.[12] In a healthy culture, each of these larger publics would be connected, at some remove, to the 'critically adult public'. In this way, the judgements of a 'very small minority' were transmuted into 'standards' governing a wider community of taste. Leavis, like Virginia Woolf in her collection of literary essays, invoked Samuel Johnson's 'common reader', who was not an 'ordinary' reader but an unusually 'competent' and 'cultivated' one. Eighteenth-century culture, so the story went, was sufficiently unified, its various publics sufficiently articulated, that an elite figure could also represent and shape the collective, the 'common'.[13]

By the early twentieth century, this tradition was dead.[14] The minority was embattled, and communications between it and a mass readership (still a comparative novelty, at least in this reading of British cultural history) had been blocked. In the past, argued Q. D. Leavis, it had been possible for diligent readers to climb the ladder of taste. Nineteenth-century periodicals serialised 'the "better" fiction' alongside trashy stuff, whereas twentieth-century reviewers pandered to anti-intellectualism and promotional vehicles such as the Book Society played on readers' fears that they might not be clever enough to enjoy Virginia Woolf or other 'highbrows', a word that became common in the 1920s and whose currency was, the Leavises believed, a sign of the further fragmentation of the reading public.[15] Q. D. Leavis's *Fiction and the Reading Public* repeatedly cites eighteenth-century working-class autobiographies, and for a time she worked on a study of the autodidact tradition.[16] The idea of a ladder that autodidacts could climb complements the Johnsonian idea of a common reader. This tradition was not as exhausted as the Leavises believed it to be. BBC programming under John Reith was predicated on a comparable ladder-climbing principle, which was one reason lighter entertainment was not cordoned off from more 'difficult' music (though it was later, after Reith's departure).[17] Q. D. Leavis was unimpressed by the BBC, but, as she was writing only a few years after the corporation had assumed its nationalised form, it would have been surprising if she had been aware of this policy.

The publishing business and the reviews and reviewers that had become part of the same commercial apparatus were governed by the logic of mass production, standardisation and levelling-down. This complex of metaphors, fundamentally industrial rather than (as in some other interpretations of modern culture) commercial, structured the *Scrutiny* movement's cultural criticism.[18] Writing about short fiction, or 'magazine stories', a boom genre in the first few decades of the twentieth century, Q. D. Leavis observed: 'To achieve as large a circulation as possible (to secure the advertiser) the editor sets out to satisfy the common measure of taste, and he cannot (or thinks he cannot) afford to publish any story which fails to conform to type.' She gained an understanding of the relevant formulae from her own reading of periodical fiction, from the questionnaires best-selling authors completed for her and from a study of the many guidebooks with titles such as *How to Write Saleable Fiction* and *Short Story Writing for Profit*.[19]

Like her husband, Q. D. Leavis contended that commercially produced popular fiction was a variant of advertising or publicity as much as it was a complement to it. It constituted the 'environment' that militated against genuine 'culture' – as in the opposition in the title of the inordinately influential school book that F. R. Leavis wrote with Denys Thompson, *Culture and Environment: The Training of Critical Awareness* (1933). The Leavises and Thompson insisted that 'culture' did not mean only high art: it also encompassed more organic social relations and customs that survived until advanced capitalism. These modes of living – those of the so-called 'organic community' – were described resonantly in *Change in the Village* (1912) and *The Wheelwright's Shop* (1923), George Sturt's elegies of rural Surrey on the eve of suburbanisation. The Leavises and Thompson took from Sturt's rural workers and village artisans a teachable illustration of the undivided life: a life in which work was not estranged from leisure, workers not estranged from their work, the sensual not estranged from the mental: a life unaffected by the compartmentalisation associated with many accounts of modernity, whether it be the shift from *Gemeinschaft* to *Gesellschaft* or Eliot's 'dissociation of sensibility'. The organic community functioned in *Scrutiny* both as an analogy for literary tradition and as a complement to it.[20]

So while *Scrutiny* stood for 'close reading' and the primacy of 'the words on the page', its literary criticism was bound up with social criticism. At the beginning of the journal's life, in the early 1930s, F. R. Leavis went as far as describing the approach of some of the research students clustered around the journal as 'anthropologico-literary', following the precedent of his wife's *Fiction and the Reading Public*.[21] Q. D. Leavis invoked sociology more than anthropology, though she believed that there was an affinity or compatibility between what she did and what social anthropologists did.[22] Although she and others in *Scrutiny*'s inner circle read the work of sociologists (especially Americans), their idea of social science was an ethnographic one that could be compared meaningfully with the sorts of explorations contemporary novelists engaged in. Robert S. Lynd, co-author of the American community study *Middletown* and one of *Scrutiny*'s favoured social scientists, made such a comparison himself.[23]

Q. D. Leavis's exemplary practitioner of 'the sociology of literature' was far from a professional sociologist. She recommended Leslie Stephen's *English Literature and Society in the Eighteenth Century* (1904) to a research student as 'a stimulating model for handling the sociology of literature in a given period'.[24] Stephen's 'critical credo', she wrote in *Scrutiny* in 1939, 'corresponds generally to the position we' – the *Scrutiny* we – 'hold to-day'.[25] To illustrate, she quoted several passages from his work, including this one: 'Briefly, in talking of literary changes [...], I shall have, first, to take note of the main intellectual characteristics of the period; and secondly, what changes took place in the audience to which men of letters addressed themselves, and how the gradual extension of the reading class affected the development of the literature addressed to them.'[26] Here Stephen's position – Leavis's position – intersects with *Scrutiny* conceptions of the functioning of criticism: the relationship between creative writer and reading public provides an analytical opening for the literary historian as well as the rationale for the critic.

It was a position that held some promise for students of colonial or national literatures other than 'English literature'. The student to whom Leavis commended Stephen's book was David Craig, a graduate of the University of Aberdeen who was embarking on a thesis at Cambridge on Scottish literature. Examining Scottish literature before and after Walter Scott, she told Craig, would confront him with a fundamental question: 'What conditions are necessary to produce & maintain a literature?' Why did Ireland produce an Anglo-Irish literature and drama, with Scotland producing nothing comparable? Why did nineteenth-century Scotland produce nothing to rival the accomplishments of American literature at the same time? Why did Scott not, like Nathaniel Hawthorne, 'turn the inherited theological seriousness into a comparable literary activity'? The absence of a Scottish Hawthorne, Herman Melville or Henry James prompted reflection on 'how Scotland then differed from New England at the same date'.[27] Referring in a subsequent letter to the published doctorate of an American who had studied at Cambridge and contributed to *Scrutiny*, she remarked: 'Marius Bewley's argument is that the tension of the Americans' "complex fate" produced the literature; but the Scots suffered from the same tension as a society, why no literature therefrom?'[28] Researching the conditions necessary for a national literature would mean 'dealing with the Press, Religious institutions, Education, Printing & the visual arts, Political institutions, History, Economics, & the Autobiographies of Eminent Scots as well as Fiction, Poetry & Polite Letters'.[29] Craig's finished book was of course not a clear reflection of these initial ideas from his de facto supervisor, and it unsurprisingly shies away from emphatic conclusions about these fundamental questions. But it does include material on the institutions of literature (one chapter is entitled 'Fiction and the Scottish reading public'). And, harking back to Q. D. Leavis's suggestions and the work of another *Scrutiny* editor, L. C. Knights, on Jacobean drama and society, Craig's book dwells on the significance in changes in the vernacular and on the urban contexts of the literature under examination.[30]

Craig's *Scottish Literature and the Scottish People, 1680–1830*, and his experience of working with Q. D. Leavis and her husband, serves as a corrective to the common assumption that the Leavises were concerned exclusively with things English. More than two decades before Craig started his doctorate, they had guided another study of a 'national literature' (or the absence of one worth the name). This was E. H. McCormick's study of New Zealand writing. Here, too, the question of the conditions necessary for a literature of significance was in play.

McCormick had come to Cambridge after studying at Victoria University College in Wellington, where he had written a master's thesis on New Zealand literature. In Britain he was going to work in a more reputably scholarly field, doing research on a Tudor compilation, *The Mirrour for Magistrates*. He won a travelling scholarship that was not tied to a particular institution: once in Britain, he had to find a university to admit him. Staying in London near University College, he thought of applying there, with C. J. Sissons as a supervisor, 'for no better reason than that he was author of a booklet on the Elizabethan dramatists in Benn's sixpenny library'.[31] Then a New Zealander with a Cambridge PhD in history, who lived in London editing a newspaper for expatriates, encouraged him to apply to Cambridge, which he did successfully.[32]

The Leavises invited McCormick to their weekly afternoon teas.[33] (Alienated from the Cambridge English Faculty, the couple worked to establish an independent intellectual community.) McCormick recalled their house in the early 1930s as 'a gathering place for the vaguely rebellious and the questing'. One of the other students from the empire who went to the Leavises' Friday parties was Iqbal Singh, who later became the London correspondent of several Indian newspapers. Singh and McCormick began kicking around ideas for a little magazine, *The Phoenix*, which 'would publish stories, poems, and articles in sympathy with the views of D. H. Lawrence'. [34] As the plans evolved, F. R. Leavis was drawn in, and the magazine envisioned became more literary-critical. McCormick remembered: 'Neither Singh nor I was much interested in the idea of a critical quarterly – to be called *Scrutiny* – which grew out of the original proposal, and we soon withdrew.'[35]

In any case, both of them were having difficulties with their university studies.[36] McCormick had discovered how unprepared he was for work on the Tudor period. He found it hard to make progress – and to muster much enthusiasm. He turned to F. R. Leavis for advice about whether to continue with his thesis. Leavis advised him to revisit his MA thesis and write about New Zealand literature, 'with greater emphasis now placed on cultural and historical forces'. The English faculty approved the new topic. McCormick hoped that Leavis would be his new supervisor, but as Leavis did not hold a faculty position (or a tenured college fellowship) at this time, this was unlikely. The faculty appointed the intellectual historian Basil Willey instead. Leavis and his wife nevertheless remained McCormick's 'chief friends and unofficial mentors at Cambridge'.[37]

Leavis alluded to McCormick in the first number of *Scrutiny*: 'I know someone who is enquiring why New Zealand has developed nothing in the nature of a distinctive literature.' Leavis made this remark in the course of a devastating review of H. G. Wells's *The Work, Wealth, and Happiness of Mankind*. Wells's faith in material progress and the experts who would keep its machinery ticking over blinded him to other conceptions of value and the good life. Wells had remarked that 'The story of New Zealand is particularly interesting'; as a country with a high average standard of living and an expansive state, New Zealand had long been of interest to Fabians and other reformers overseas.[38] Wells's aside about New Zealand pointed, Leavis said, to the limitations of his mind. The question of why a land of material abundance and 'state socialism' had not produced much in the way of literature was the sort of question that would not occur to Wells.[39]

The cultural narrowness of the New Zealand experiment did trouble some observers, however, most notably the French political scientist André Siegfried in *La démocratie en Nouvelle-Zélande* (1904).[40] (The Tocqueville of New Zealand, Siegfried also wrote books on Britain and Canada: the lack of attention paid to him by historians of the empire is surprising.) Siegfried's critique of settler '*snobbisme*' is woven through McCormick's account of New Zealand poetry and prose. Siegfried assumes something of the role of ethnographer-cum-moralist guide through the New Zealand cultural landscape that Robert and Helen Lynd do in *Culture and Environment*'s tour of modern urban life. When Leavis advised McCormick to emphasise 'cultural and historical forces', he was recommending the approach he called 'anthropological'. The finished thesis sported some of the social-scientific features of Q. D. Leavis's research, such as questionnaire responses and a theoretical appendix on the problem of relating individual texts to wider cultural structures; McCormick's answer, which revolved around what he called the culture of the individual author, arguably had more in common with Eliot's 'Tradition and the Individual Talent' than it did with any of the anthropological theory he discussed.[41]

Yet McCormick's thesis and the book he turned it into in 1940 were not straightforwardly Leavisian interpretations of New Zealand literary and cultural history. The core argument remained that of McCormick's first study of the topic, completed in 1929 before either of the Leavises had published anything much.[42] The central problem was the failure of the colonists to adapt their British literary tradition to local surroundings. The adaptation trope was common in the cultural criticism written in settler colonies. In McCormick's narrative, the literary inheritance of English writers – extracted from the contexts that kept it alive as a tradition – acted as a dead weight on the colonial imagination, frustrating the growth of a national spirit in some cases, and in others depriving an emerging spirit of an authentic voice. The most pernicious of these outdated literary modes was 'a debased and senile Romanticism' – imitations of Wordsworth, Coleridge, Keats and Shelley, their late nineteenth-century reincarnations such as Swinburne and their Georgian successors.[43] The New Zealand novel was blighted by emotionalism, didacticism, melodrama and other Victorian ailments.

It will come as no surprise that the majority of the novels and poems in question were by women. This was, among other things, an argument about the femininity of colonial literature. After quoting at length from a 1930 anthology of New Zealand poetry in the Georgian mode, McCormick concluded: 'These corner-stones of a national literature have been unearthed not to illustrate the effeminacy of certain male versifiers (we could not legitimately expect any poet to stamp the mark of virility on every line of his work) but rather the general nature of the modern New Zealand poetic world, frequented in common by men and women.'[44] The protestation scarcely qualifies the judgement that the poetry in question was feminine. It was also foreign, 'completely remote' from the 'natural and social environment' of New Zealand.[45]

Here a gender politics with its origins in local, acutely homosocial literary-nationalist circles – not *Scrutiny* – was being elaborated and historicised through a Leavisian theory of the relationship between serious literature and its 'social environment'.[46] There is a clear echo of F. R. Leavis's poetry criticism in McCormick's complaint that nineteenth-century New Zealand poets had no 'vital relationship with the life about them'. McCormick's wistful comparison of the politician-cum-poet Alfred Domett's crowded life and his epic poem of cross-cultural romance, *Ranolf and Amohia* – 'how little of this [life] has crept into the interminable cantos of his "South-Sea Day Dream"' – runs parallel with Leavis's judgement of William Morris: 'who ... would guess from his poetry that William Morris was one of the most versatile energetic and original men of his time, a force that impinged decisively in the world of practice? He reserved poetry for his day-dreams.'[47]

The discussion of the later 1930s that McCormick wrote for the published version of his Cambridge thesis announced the beginnings of a literature in tune with its surroundings: a literature whose exemplar was Frank Sargeson, who made his name with short fiction that examined a subculture of itinerant male labourers, the proletariat of what one indignant reviewer called a rural slum.[48] As feminine melodrama was ill-adapted to the colonial scene, so was an authentic New Zealand literature one preoccupied with comically or poignantly undemonstrative men. Sargeson had an unparalleled feel for Pakeha (white settler) popular speech and, McCormick thought, intuited an 'underdog' worldview that sometimes manifested itself in that local idiom. McCormick concluded:

> Despite their kinship with American analogues, there is in Frank Sargeson's Kens, Toms, and Neds and in their outlook something that is deeply rooted in this country. Its origins may be imperfectly seen in the letters of labouring immigrants of the forties and in goldfields literature, though it has rarely reached the printed page. None the less, modified by each turn of events in the past century, it has had a continuous history, passing from each generation to the next, largely by way of popular speech. Thus, paradoxical as it may seem, Frank Sargeson is traditional to a greater degree than any other writer of to-day; he is the exponent of a local tradition that has hitherto been inarticulate.[49]

The understanding of the relationship between literature, language and a living culture in this passage is heavily indebted to F. R. Leavis's *Mass Civilisation and Minority Culture* and Leavis and Thompson's *Culture and Environment*. The latter declares: 'our spiritual, moral and emotional tradition', the distillate of 'the "picked experience of ages"', is '[l]argely conveyed in language'.[50] Language was a force for 'continuity', a key term for Leavis, and one echoed in this passage from McCormick. Both the literary tradition and popular-cultural traditions such as those of organic rural communities kept the past and its store of experience and knowledge alive in the present. Although the two sorts of tradition were described in *Scrutiny* as analogous, sometimes a more direct relationship was asserted. Denys Thompson wrote in an early number that Thomas Hardy's success as a novelist had much to do with rural traditions such as those recorded by Sturt: 'the pleasure derived from reading Hardy's novels results not, as is commonly assumed, from literary art – his literary technique is naïve and clumsy – but from contact with the rich traditional country round of life'.[51] In McCormick's reading, the richness of Sargeson's work draws on the richness and authenticity of the unlettered tradition of his subjects. Literary language owes its strength to the robustness of a genuinely popular culture, not a self-contained and half-foreign literary discourse.

Practising 'cultural criticism', examining 'New Zealand literature' as a cultural formation, allowed McCormick to do something more diagnostic and prognostic than simply demolish wobbly novels or second-rate poetry, of which there was a good deal. After reading McCormick's book, his Cambridge friend – and one of the editors of *Scrutiny* – D. W. Harding told him that he must have exercised self-control 'in refraining from destructive criticism as much as you did'. (He recognised that McCormick's omissions must have constituted further, implicit criticism.)[52] All the same, McCormick's book did have some of the astringency associated with *Scrutiny* – an astringency rare in New Zealand criticism up to that time, certainly outside the more trenchant little magazines of the 1930s. He told a correspondent of his 'distaste' for the 'meaningless lists of names and compliments which so often pass under the name of criticism in New Zealand'.[53] In her *History of New Zealand Fiction*, published in 1939 and apparently written altogether independently of McCormick's book, despite the smallness of the New Zealand intellectual milieu, E. M. Smith entreated local critics to be more critical.[54] Referring explicitly to *Fiction and the Reading Public*, she pleaded for standards that would turn a reading public into 'a reading and a thinking public'. There were civic reasons for wanting a thinking public, but there were also colonial-nationalist reasons: 'a possible literature in the future' depended on the establishment of critical standards.[55]

Some of these *Scrutiny* arguments received a late airing at the conference on 'Fiction and the Reading Public in India' held at the University of Mysore in the mid-1960s. The organiser was C. D. Narasimhaiah.[56] He had attended F. R. Leavis's seminars as a student at Cambridge in the late 1940s and became a promoter of *Scrutiny* approaches in India, where Leavis's school had not been well known. Between 1945 and 1949, only three bookstores on the subcontinent bought copies of *Scrutiny*: a shop in Calcutta and one in Delhi took out a single subscription each; the Minerva Bookshop in Lahore bought five or six copies of each new issue between 1945 and 1948.[57] Narasimhaiah lamented the absence of the journal from 'the catalogues of many university libraries' in India in subsequent decades.[58] On his return to Mysore, Narahsimhaiah attempted to reform the university's examinations so as to make them more in tune with *Scrutiny* values. He launched a journal, the *Literary Criterion*, to which Leavis contributed an essay. Narasimhaiah resorted to Leavis's critical idiom, and worked outward from – or worked around – his presuppositions in his own explorations of Indian writing in English.[59]

The conference did not quite live up to its Leavisian title. Critics offered readings of novels or introduced novelists from a variety of language communities, and novelists, including R. K. Narayan and Raja Rao, spoke about their craft. Only a few contributors addressed Q. D. Leavis's book. Though often apologetic about Indian fiction, especially in English, the seminar's participants showed little inclination to treat their subject matter as documents of an Indian 'environment' rather than as 'literature' worthy of criticism. Many treated 'fiction' as a neutral category, not an implicitly sub-literary one as it was in *Fiction and the Reading Public*. The contributors that nodded most to Q. D. Leavis and her husband were those who supplied the introductory and framing papers, Narasimhaiah and Balagopal Varma.[60] Narasimhaiah hit a succession of *Scrutiny* notes: the loss of the organic community, the degradation of leisure, day-dreaming, substitute-living, the threat posed by book societies and their 'choices', the need to inculcate standards.

Yet the application of *Scrutiny* to Indian conditions was not indiscriminate. While 'affluence and boredom' drove Westerners to substitute-living, 'in our country and in the economically backward countries of Asia and Africa the stimulus to writing no less than reading fiction might be poverty, social injustice, governmental inefficiency, exploitation by the rich and powerful – these have led us to seek refuge in fiction'.[61] (Here Narasimhaiah *was* using 'fiction' in something like Q. D. Leavis's sense.) While Indian writers and readers needed standards, as their British counterparts did, how those standards were constituted necessarily varied from place to place. The Mysore conference was attended by speakers of Hindi, English, Kannada, Telugu, Tamil and Malayalam, and the organisers hoped it would be possible to arrive at 'some sort of general agreement and shared assumptions among all of us reading fiction in different languages'.[62]

Ka Naa Subramanyam's essay on the world of 'slick magazines in Tamil' does not mention Q. D. Leavis, but his flair for passing judgement on folly makes his writing occasionally resemble a deliberate imitation of hers. Subramanyam's chapter was also the one that addressed itself in the most sustained way to the questions Q. D. Leavis explored in *Fiction and the Reading Public*. He wrote novels and short stories as well as criticism, and he grounded his argument in a knowledge of the Tamil-language publishing industry. Subramanyam emphasised the peculiarly strong influence that Tamil periodicals exerted in the writing of novels as well as short fiction in the language. Feeding the periodical machine put writers in a position subservient to their readers. '[T]he reader expects his writer to be conscious of what he expects from him', and the 'reader–writer relationship' degenerates into 'a sort of fan-mail'. This situation made it difficult to establish literary standards; authors could come in for criticism, but not productive criticism. Tamil authors and the public – Subramanyam used that word – lacked 'a critical training in literature and literary appreciation'. One remedy would be to 'insist ... on standards', though Subramanyam did not suggest how this might be done. He also said that Tamil academics were 'afraid for some reasons of their own of a critical look at their literature'. Another solution would be to expose Tamil readers to translated examples of 'the novel as practised in the other languages of the world' – something that 'Tamil insularity ... militates against'.[63] Subramanyam's piece was by no means a direct application of a *Scrutiny* template to a colonial or post-colonial situation, but it did take as an organising principle one of *Scrutiny*'s premises, the importance of the relationship between creative writers and a critical public that articulated and enforced standards.

If Q. D. Leavis's approach proved suggestive to these writers debating the function of criticism in India, it was most useful to literary historians: to those interpreting colonial or – in the Scottish case – marginalised national literary cultures. It provided them with a way of tackling literatures as entities or formations. It also enabled them to deal with 'lesser' writing *as critics*, without devolving into 'mere' bibliographers or antiquarians. *Fiction and the Reading Public* disappoints readers who justifiably expect it to contain more information about popular reading practices than it does. Raymond Williams remarked in 1957: 'It is fair to say of Mrs Leavis's admirable book that the reading public is really only present in the title.'[64] There was more to it than that, though. If Leavis's 'public' was sometimes empirically elusive, it was always necessary as an analytical fiction, a posited variable in her cultural equation. She was interested in the ways writers and critics envisioned their publics and sought to cater to them, and the relationship between writers and public provided a way of interpreting writing in context – 'anthropologically' or 'sociologically'. Given the use that colonial critics made of her approach, and given that her husband theorised the public as deliberately as any of the literary figures who are the focus of the accumulating Habermasian scholarship on modernism, the Leavises' thinking about publics is one of their most underestimated contributions.[65]

Notes

1 Gauri Viswanathan, *Masks of Conquest: Literary Study and British Rule in India* (New York: Columbia University Press, 1989). See also Simon Gikandi, 'Globalization and the Claims of Postcoloniality', *South Atlantic Quarterly*, 100 (2001), 627–58, at 651; Francis Mulhern, 'English Reading', in Homi K. Bhabha (ed.), *Nation and Narration* (London: Routledge, 1990), pp. 250–64, at pp. 253–5, 259–60.

2 Keith Sinclair, *Halfway Round the Harbour: An Autobiography* (Auckland: Penguin, 1993), p. 140.

3 On Natal see Derek Attridge, *Joyce Effects: On Language, Theory, and History* (Cambridge: Cambridge University Press, 2000), pp. 1–2. I discuss Australia and Ceylon in *English as a Vocation: The 'Scrutiny' Movement* (Oxford: Oxford University Press, 2012), ch. 8.

4 Tamson Pietsch, *Empire of Scholars: Universities, Networks and the British Academic World, 1850–1939* (Manchester: Manchester University Press, 2013).

5 Hilliard, *English as a Vocation*, ch. 8.

6 T. S. Eliot, 'Imperfect Critics', in Eliot, *The Sacred Wood: Essays on Poetry and Criticism* (1920; London: Methuen, 1934), pp. 17–46, at pp. 37–8; F. R. Leavis, *How to Teach Reading: A Primer for Ezra Pound* (Cambridge: Gordon Fraser, 1932), p. 38. See also F. R. Leavis, 'Criticism and Literary History', *Scrutiny*, 4, no. 1 (June 1935), 96–100, at 97; Q. D. Leavis, *Fiction and the Reading Public* (London: Chatto & Windus, 1932), p. xv.

7 Doughty Society Minute Book, p. 98 (31 October 1952), DCCS/4/4/1/1, Downing College Archives, Cambridge.

8 F. R. Leavis, '"This Poetical Renascence"', *Scrutiny*, 2, no. 1 (June 1933), 65–76, at 65–7.

9 'Scrutiny: A Manifesto', *Scrutiny*, 1, no. 1 (May 1932), 2–7, at 4.

10 F. R. Leavis, 'Mass Civilisation and Minority Culture', in Leavis, *For Continuity* (Cambridge: Gordon Fraser, 1933), pp. 13–46, at p. 14; F. R. Leavis, '"Scrutiny": A Retrospect', *Scrutiny*, vol. 20, *A Retrospect, Indexes, Errata* (Cambridge: Cambridge University Press, 1963), 1–24, at 24.

11 Leavis, 'Mass Civilisation and Minority Culture', p. 14.

12 Leavis, '"This Poetical Renascence"', p. 69.

13 Leavis, *How to Teach Reading*, pp. 3–4; Leavis, 'What's Wrong with Criticism?' *Scrutiny*, 1, no. 2 (September 1932), 132–46, at 145–6; Virginia Woolf, 'The Common Reader', in Woolf, *The Common Reader* (London: L. & V. Woolf, 2nd edn 1925), pp. 11–12. Woolf's use of Johnson is significantly different from Leavis's: she distinguishes the 'common reader' from the scholar, but does not say that the common reader possesses a superior level of cultivation.

14 Leavis, *How to Teach Reading*, p. 4.

15 Leavis, *Fiction and the Reading Public*, pp. 22–6, 158–9; Leavis, 'Mass Civilisation and Minority Culture', p. 38. On the language of 'brows' in the inter-war decades, see Stefan Collini, *Absent Minds: Intellectuals in Britain* (Oxford: Oxford University Press, 2006), pp. 110–19.

16 On this research, see her husband's comment in 'What's Wrong with Criticism?', 145.

17 See Jonathan Rose, *The Intellectual Life of the British Working Classes* (New Haven, CT: Yale University Press, 2001), pp. 436–7, which reports instances of working-class listeners appreciatively stumbling across classical music on the BBC.

18 F. R. Leavis and Denys Thompson, *Culture and Environment: The Training of Critical Awareness* (London: Chatto & Windus, 1933), pp. 42–4; Leavis, *Fiction and the Reading Public*, p. 271; Leavis, 'What's Wrong with Criticism', p. 137.

19 Leavis, *Fiction and the Reading Public*, pp. 27–32. On these guidebooks see Christopher Hilliard, *To Exercise Our Talents: The Democratization of Writing in Britain* (Cambridge, MA: Harvard University Press, 2006), pp. 20, 83–4, 91–2.

20 See Hilliard, *English as a Vocation*, ch. 2. See also Stefan Collini, 'Where Did It All Go Wrong? Cultural Critics and "Modernity" in Inter-War Britain', in E. H. H. Green and D. M. Tanner (eds), *The Strange Survival of Liberal England: Political Leaders, Moral Values and the Reception of Economic Debate* (Cambridge: Cambridge

University Press, 2007), pp. 247–74; David Gervais, *Literary Englands: Versions of 'Englishness' in Modern Writing* (Cambridge: Cambridge University Press, 1993), ch. 4.

21 Ian MacKillop, *F. R. Leavis: A Life in Criticism* (London: Allen Lane, 1995), pp. 142–4.

22 Q. D. Leavis to Craig, 23 November 1955, Q. D. Leavis Papers, GCPP Leavis 2/1/7, Girton College Archives (GCA).

23 Robert S. Lynd, *Knowledge for What? The Place of Social Science in American Culture* (1939; sixth printing, Princeton: Princeton University Press, 1948), pp. 91 n, 178.

24 Q. D. Leavis to David Craig, 24 May 1955, Q. D. Leavis Papers, GCPP Leavis 2/1/7, GCA.

25 Q. D. Leavis, 'Leslie Stephen: Cambridge Critic', *Scrutiny*, 7, no. 4 (March 1939), 404–15, at 412.

26 Leavis, 'Leslie Stephen', p. 414; Leslie Stephen, *English Literature and Society in the Eighteenth Century* (London: Duckworth & Co., 1904), p. 26. The brackets denote an ellipsis of Leavis's: in the original, after 'literary changes', Stephen says: 'considered as implied in the whole social development'.

27 Q. D. Leavis to Craig, 21 May [1955], Q. D. Leavis Papers, GCPP Leavis 2/1/7, GCA.

28 Q. D. Leavis to Craig, 24 May 1955, Q. D. Leavis Papers, GCPP Leavis 2/1/7, GCA.

29 Q. D. Leavis to Craig, 21 May [1955], Q. D. Leavis Papers, GCPP Leavis 2/1/7, GCA.

30 David Craig, *Scottish Literature and the Scottish People, 1680–1830* (London: Chatto & Windus, 1961), chs 1, 2, 7, 8; L. C. Knights, *Drama and Society in the Age of Jonson* (London: Chatto & Windus, 1937).

31 E. H. McCormick, untitled MS note, c. 1980, E. H. McCormick Papers, MS Papers 5598–31, Alexander Turnbull Library (ATL), National Library of New Zealand, Wellington.

32 E. H. McCormick, *An Absurd Ambition: Autobiographical Writings*, ed. Dennis McEldowney (Auckland: Auckland University Press, 1996), p. 108.

33 On which see L. C. Knights, untitled essay, *Cambridge Quarterly*, 25 (1996), 357; Frank Whitehead, 'F. R. Leavis and the Schools', in Denys Thompson (ed.), *The Leavises: Recollections and Impressions* (Cambridge: Cambridge University Press, 1984), pp. 140–52, at p. 143.

34 Eric McCormick, 'In the 1930s: Cambridge to New Zealand', in Ian MacKillop and Richard Storer (eds), *F. R. Leavis: Essays and Documents* (Sheffield: Sheffield Academic Press, 1995), pp. 227–37, at p. 230.

35 McCormick to Mr Morgan, 15 August 1968, McCormick Papers, MS Papers 5598–31, ATL.

36 McCormick to Mr Morgan, 15 August 1968, McCormick Papers, MS Papers 5598–31, ATL.

37 McCormick, 'Cambridge to New Zealand', pp. 231–2.

38 D. A. Hamer (ed.), *The Webbs in New Zealand, 1898: Beatrice Webb's Diary with Entries by Sidney Webb* (Wellington: Price Milburn & Co., 1974); Henry Demarest Lloyd, *A Country without Strikes: A Visit to the Compulsory Arbitration Court of New Zealand* (New York: Doubleday, Page & Co., 1900). Many of New Zealand's 'state experiments' of the 1890s were the handiwork of William Pember Reeves, who was later director of the London School of Economics. H. G. Wells had an affair with Reeves's daughter Amber, which was the basis of Wells's novel *Ann Veronica*. See Keith Sinclair, *William Pember Reeves: New Zealand Fabian* (Oxford: Clarendon Press, 1965).

39 F. R. Leavis, '"Babbitt Buys the World"', *Scrutiny*, 1, no. 1 (May 1932), 80–3, at 82.

40 André Siegfried, *La démocratie en Nouvelle-Zélande* (Paris: A. Colin, 1904); André Siegfried, *Democracy in New Zealand*, trans. E. V. Burns with introductions by William Downie Stewart and David Hamer (Wellington: Victoria University Press, 1982).

41 E. H. McCormick, 'Literature in New Zealand: An Essay in Cultural Criticism' (Cambridge University thesis, 1935), copy in E. H. McCormick Papers, MSX-4250, ATL; T. S. Eliot, 'Tradition and the Individual Talent' (1919), in Eliot, *Selected Essays* (London: Faber & Faber, 1951), pp. 13–22.

42 E. H. McCormick, 'Literature in New Zealand', MA thesis, Victoria University College, 1929, copy in McCormick papers, MSX-4251, ATL. This thesis has the same title as the later Cambridge one; all subsequent references are to the Cambridge thesis.

43 McCormick, 'Literature in New Zealand', p. 192.

44 McCormick, 'Literature in New Zealand', pp. 223–4.

45 McCormick, 'Literature in New Zealand', p. 224.

46 On that local tradition see Kai Jensen, *Whole Men: The Masculine Tradition in New Zealand Literature* (Auckland: Auckland University Press, 1996).

47 Donal Smith, 'Eric McCormick's Cambridge', in James Ross, Linda Gill and Stuart McRae (eds), *Writing a New Country: A Collection of Essays Presented to E. H. McCormick in His 88th Year* (Auckland: James Ross, 1993), pp. 38–50, at pp. 49–50.

48 See generally Lawrence Jones, *Picking Up the Traces: The Making of a New Zealand Literary Culture, 1932–1945* (Wellington: Victoria University Press, 2003).

49 E. H. McCormick, *Letters and Art in New Zealand* (Wellington: Department of Internal Affairs, 1940), pp. 181–2.

50 Leavis and Thompson, *Culture and Environment*, p. 81.

51 Denys Thompson, 'A Cure for Amnesia', *Scrutiny*, 2, no. 1 (June 1933), 2–11, at 5–6; Leavis, 'Mass Civilisation and Minority Culture', p. 15; Leavis and Thompson, *Culture and Environment*, pp. 76, 81.

52 D. W. Harding to E. H. McCormick, 21 February 1941, D. W. Harding papers, box 26, Emmanuel College Library, Cambridge.

53 McCormick to J. W. Heenan, 2 October 1940, J. W. Heenan papers, MS Papers 1132–1134, ATL.

54 On the New Zealand scene, see Chris Hilliard, *The Bookmen's Dominion: Cultural Life in New Zealand, 1920–1950* (Auckland: Auckland University Press, 2006), chs 1, 3.

55 E. M. Smith, *A History of New Zealand Fiction from 1862 to the Present Time with Some Account of Its Relation to the National Life and Character* (Dunedin: A. H. and A. W. Reid, 1939), pp. 75–6.

56 On Narasimhaiah see C. D. Narasimhaiah, *'N for Nobody': Autobiography of an English Teacher* (Delhi: B. R. Publishing, 1991); Staish C. Aikant, 'Obituary: C. D. Narasimhaiah (1921–2005)', *Journal of Commonwealth Literature*, 41 (2006), 145–8, at 145.

57 *Scrutiny* trade sales ledger, 1945–49, pp. 7, 79, 87, Deighton, Bell and Co. Archives, Add. 9453, B5/1, Cambridge University Library.

58 Narasimhaiah, *'N for Nobody'*, p. 60.

59 Narasimhaiah, *'N for Nobody'*, pp. 128–31, 177–91, 256; C. D. Narasimhaiah, 'Indian Writing in English: An Area of Promise', *Journal of Commonwealth Literature*, 9 (1974), 35–49, at 37, 38–9, 47.

60 C. D. Narasimhaiah, 'Introduction', in Narasimhaiah (ed.), *Fiction and the Reading Public in India* (Mysore: University of Mysore, 1967), pp. vii–xv; Balagopal Varma, 'Some Thoughts on English Fiction and the Reading Public', in Narasimhaiah, (ed.), *Fiction and the Reading Public in India*, pp. 1–7.

61 Narasimhaiah, 'Introduction', pp. ix–x.

62 Narasimhaiah, 'Introduction', p. xi.

63 Ka Naa Subramanyam, 'Slick Magazines in Tamil', in C. D. Narasimhaiah (ed.), *Fiction and the Reading Public in India*, pp. 112–25, at pp. 122, 124, 125.

64 Raymond Williams, 'Fiction and the Writing Public' (1957), in John McIlroy and Sallie Westwood (eds), *Border Country: Raymond Williams in Adult Education* (Leicester: National Institute of Adult Continuing Education, 1993), pp. 106–10, at p. 106.

65 Mark S. Morrisson, *The Public Face of Modernism: Little Magazines, Audiences, and Reception, 1905–1920* (Madison: University of Wisconsin Press, 2001); Patrick Collier, *Modernism on Fleet Street* (Aldershot: Ashgate, 2006).

CHAPTER 10

Mr Hickey's pictures: Britons and their collectibles in late eighteenth-century India

Tillman W. Nechtman

If we are to believe John Scott Waring, the often-feckless political agent to Warren Hastings, Governor-General of India from 1773 to 1785, 'There is not such a set of vermin in England as our Custom House Officers.'[1] Waring's complaint stemmed from the treatment Hastings' wife, Marian, had received at the hands of customs officials at Portsmouth upon her return from India in 1784. Because of customs laws prohibiting the importation of 'foreign textiles', the officers seized all of Hastings' silk gowns 'as well as a velvet riding-habit worked with pearls, and various dresses, curtains, and stuffs containing gold and silver thread'. She was, she later noted, 'virtually threatened with the loss of her entire wardrobe but for those [items] she had hand carried onto shore'.[2]

Like Marian Hastings, William Hickey was stripped of a small fortune's worth of property when he returned from a thirty-year career as an attorney in Calcutta in 1808. He was outraged that the customs officers buffeted his belongings, confiscated his treasures and seized his paintings under regulations that forbade the importation of foreign art.[3] Hickey considered the loss of his paintings to be 'the most infamous part of the transaction'. What, he asked, made the paintings *foreign*? They had, after all,

> been executed in a British settlement, by different artists, but all of them Englishmen constantly living under English law. The persons represented were all subjects of Great Britain, holding offices of trust under our government, and these paintings were executed for and paid for by me who am likewise a Briton born and bred. Moreover, every canvas upon which the paintings were made, the colours, oils, and even the very hair pencils used in the work were all of British manufacture, and after all they were conveyed to Europe in an English East India Ship. Nothing foreign from beginning to end in the whole transaction! Under such circumstances is it not preposterous, is it not most unreasonable, to pronounce such pictures to be foreign![4]

Setting aside our pleasure at Hickey's feud with the taxman, there is something significant about his sense of Britishness, a geographically complex argument that late eighteenth-century India (or at least the parts of it controlled by the East India Company) ought to be included as part of Britain. Such a claim, made, as it was, only a century after the Act of Union formed Great Britain out of the kingdoms of Scotland and England, could hardly have been received as 'ideologically neutral', to borrow a phrase from Beth Fowkes Tobin.[5] Between Hickey and his enemies at the Customs House, there existed a very real contest over the definition of Britishness.

On the one hand, there were imperial Britons like Hickey and employees of the East India Company who began returning to metropolitan Britain in greater numbers in the last half of the eighteenth century. These men, famed for their rapacious mismanagement of the Indian subcontinent, were labelled by their contemporaries as 'nabobs', a term of derision that brought with it connotations of lax morality and criminal greed. On the other hand, there were those like the erstwhile revenue men whose sense of the national self revolved around much more nativist cultural sensibilities. To connect India and Britain as Hickey sought to do unsettled this nativist vision, suggesting as it did that the Company's mercantile-imperial activities in South Asia had inscribed themselves into the character of the relatively young British state.

Historians from Holden Furber to Peter Marshall have written extensively on Company employees. These studies have linked the political debates over how to manage eighteenth-century British India to attacks made against nabobs.[6] Hickey's claim for a material fluidity between what was Indian and what was British seems, though, to be a call to re-read the brouhaha that surrounded nabobs not as a purely political battle but as a broader cultural struggle to define the boundaries between nation and empire, a struggle that has been richly explored through the East India Company at Home project hosted by University College, London.[7] Rather than arguing that the nabobs found themselves the subjects of anti-imperial attitudes as a result of political hostility articulated by political elites and directed against imperial mismanagement, Mr Hickey's paintings focus our attention on popular claims made against nabobs, claims that – as we shall see – brought the politics of Indian administration to the attention of a wider domestic public by binding them directly to questions of material culture.

If we take Hickey's logic seriously, and there is no reason why we ought not, we find that nabobs saw their material possessions as a means by which to narrate their imperial biographies. Like modern travellers, eighteenth-century British nabobs came back from India with material objects that helped to describe their time – in some instances time that spanned decades – in South Asia. Contemporary tourism, though, takes modern travellers away from home for only a short span of time, and the souvenirs we bring back from vacation serve specifically to mark the difference we have encountered in our travels. Who, after all, would need a refrigerator magnet, a snow globe or a postcard of something they could see just outside their front door?

A nabob's collection functioned on a more complex register, for, as Hickey suggested, the things that nabobs collected in India were (arguably) *British* goods, purchased in British settings and indicative of British culture, albeit set against a South Asian context. These collections, then, manifested Britain's increasingly hybrid identity in a display of concrete material artefacts at a moment when neither the British nation nor the British Empire were clearly articulated entities.

For all of its military and economic might, the British Empire as Hickey experienced it was a global cultural system. Within this system the geography of the British state *per se* was only part of what shaped the boundaries of Britishness. By Hickey's logic, a life spent in Calcutta could still be distinctively British. Investigating late eighteenth-century hostility towards nabobs and imperial agents like William Hickey as a matter of material culture illuminates previously unnoticed popular protests at a significant historical juncture when the domestic British public attempted, but eventually failed, to articulate a strictly nativist identity in the face of an emergent and hybrid model of Britishness that was taking shape as a result of the country's interaction with the wider world. William Hickey eventually paid his taxes to reclaim his art, but Hickey's larger argument would ultimately win the day. By the nineteenth century, Britain and its empire were so fully equated one with the other that it would seem foolish to try to articulate the kinds of finely wrought binaries that the customs officials did when they classified Mr Hickey's paintings as foreign art in 1808.

To begin, we have to acknowledge that the experience of India was something that was integral to the lives of Company employees. Take Warren Hastings, for example. When Hastings first left for India in 1750, he was only eighteen years old. Across his career with the Company, Hastings spent two tours of duty in South Asia, totalling more than thirty years, in all more than a third of his life. As Mildred Archer has suggested, many Company employees recorded this intense connection to India in portraiture.[8] Not only did portraits fill the empty walls of newly built British houses in India, they may rightly be taken as visual autobiographies. Archer's work cataloguing the portraits of Company servants now held at the British Library suggests just how often East

India Company employees and their families appear in explicitly Indian settings or with explicitly Indian symbols in their portraits – clear indications that Company employees were eager to memorialise the time they spent in India and to commemorate that portion of their lives – lives that might fruitfully be described as 'braided' narratives.

Company employees were a prime market for portrait artists in the eighteenth century. As art historians have noted, London's portrait market was glutted in the second half of the century, and many talented artists found that they simply could not make ends meet in the city's competitive atmosphere. Tilly Kettle, Johan Zoffany, Arthur William Devis, John Thomas Seton and William Hodges all sought permission from the Company's directors to travel to India, recognising that the market for portrait painters was less crowded in South Asia than it was in metropolitan Britain. Hodges, of course, was best known for the art he produced while sailing on Captain James Cook's second Pacific voyage, but by reflecting that he painted in *both* South Asia *and* the South Pacific, we are reminded that the visual history of eighteenth-century material culture need not be limited to any one geographic field.

In India, these artists painted portraits of the Company's most affluent employees, frequently filling the paintings with Indian servants, Indian flora and fauna, Indian statues and other distinguishing markers that clearly situated the works as having been set in South Asia. When the famed Orientalist, Sir William Jones, commissioned a portrait of himself from Arthur William Devis, he asked to be shown at a desk. On the desk, Devis painted a large statue of the elephant-headed Hindu deity Ganesha, symbolic of Jones's life's work translating South Asia's religious, linguistic and legal traditions.[9] The portraitist Charles Smith, who himself toured India and painted the portraits of many Company employees, likewise represented his Indian sojourn by depicting himself dressed in a turban.[10]

Portraits, then, opened a window into the lives of late eighteenth-century nabobs. They allowed outsiders to peek into the domestic interiors of nabobish life and witness the degree to which Company employees indulged in the foods and fashions of South Asian life, how richly served they were by Indian domestic workers and how committed they were to Indian intellectual culture. As we have seen, William Hickey would have been hard pressed to identify anything foreign about the life-style he and other Britons were living in India in these years. That life in Calcutta looked different than life in London, he would have conceded, but that difference did not, to his mind, negate the fact that Calcutta remained 'a British settlement … under English law'.[11] To domestic audiences, though, the fact that some nabobs adopted South Asian cultural ways while on the subcontinent was only confirmation that India had changed them – rendered them less British than a Briton who never left the three kingdoms, and the notion that Britons could be corrupted by the tempting influences of South Asian culture was deeply troubling to these domestic critics. To celebrate difference as part of a heterogeneous spectrum of Britishness was a direct challenge to the assumptions about nationality and identity put forward by men like David Hume, who had theorised that the 'same set of manners will follow a nation, and adhere to them over the whole globe'.[12]

As William Dalrymple has noted, smoking a hookah pipe was 'the height of fashion' among British residents of South Asia by the 1780s.[13] Many Company servants also brought pipes home with them as decorative reminders – souvenirs of their time in India. In Britain, the foreign pipe was a central object for those who sought to define nabobs as alien. Those who continued to smoke upon their return were thought to be addicted to South Asia. Though they were home, they could not let go of India. The hookah pipe was, though, but one of the many cultural practices that marked Company servants as alien in domestic Britain. Dalrymple has suggested that many of the Britons who survived their stay in South Asia adopted hygienic practices indigenous to the subcontinent – a fact that may, in part, have contributed to their survival. 'Those who returned home and continued to bathe and shampoo themselves' with the same regularity that was customary among the people of the subcontinent 'found themselves scoffed at by their less hygienic compatriots'.[14] As Michael Fisher has noted, the very word shampoo came into usage in Europe from the Hindi *champi*, 'meaning to knead the flesh in therapeutic massage'.[15] Britons who adopted the practice of bathing and shampooing were viewed askance by domestic observers, thought, so the cliché held, to have become 'effeminate'.[16]

If cultural practices tinged nabobs with a hint of foreignness to domestic Britons, material artefacts from South Asia were even more problematic, for they made this air of difference plainly visible. Fashions from the subcontinent were clearly the foremost visible means of identifying difference. As Roxann Wheeler has argued, clothing and religion were the two most powerful categories of difference in the early modern period, and they persisted as categories into the eighteenth century.[17] Clothes, quite literally, made the man. South Asians wore turbans; Britons did not. And yet, as we have seen, nabobs were not above being pictured in explicitly Indian settings and, as was the case in Charles Smith's self-portrait, in explicitly Indian fashions, marking what Wheeler has called a cultural, if not a completely racial, 'makeover'.[18]

Mildred Archer has rightly argued that most Company servants who retired back to Britain in the late eighteenth century refrained from wearing South Asian fashions in metropolitan settings.[19] At the same time, nabobs did (even if unintentionally) make Indian fashions more present in domestic Britain, positioning themselves to function as conduits for a cultural exchange (of ideas, habits and material goods) that was inevitable on the colonial frontier. Eastern clothing styles became the metaphoric means by which to represent a nabob. On the late eighteenth-century stage, nabobs were always costumed in orientalised fashions. Governor Anderson of Mrs Griffith's 1772 *A Wife in the Right* appeared in a 'loose Indian Habit'.[20] When asked to change into proper dinner attire, the Governor protests. 'Dress! What silly fops you Europeans are! – Why can't a man sit down and eat his victuals, in a comfortably easy habit, instead of being cased up in a strait waistcoat?' Indeed, at one point in the play, Anderson demands that once he has a seat in Parliament, 'I will endeavour to have an act passed, that ... there shan't be a button worn in all England'.[21]

It was not only on the stage that Eastern costumes came to symbolise nabobs and the dangers they posed to domestic British society. Political cartoons and satirical etchings used South Asian dress as an indicator. James Gillray's political satires of the impeachment trial of Governor-General Warren Hastings always show Hastings dressed in Indian styles. He always wears a turban. He always dresses in loose-fitting pyjamas. He always has fanciful shoes with curled toes. He always wears a flowing cape. Though Hastings never clothed himself in any of this apparel in reality, the stereotypical costume of an Eastern potentate became the public means of representing him, his Indian career and the decadence, indolence and rapacity of his administration in British South Asia. Only when he was made to dress the part of Montesquieu's oriental despot could Hastings evoke the fear that nabobs were normalising oriental despotism in metropolitan settings.

The visual jousting here is obvious. If nabobs used South Asian material culture to braid the Indian portions of their lives in biographical narratives being told in their portraits, domestic observers who were suspicious of nabobs, their foreign manners and their South Asian styles used that same material culture to highlight just how different nabobs had become while living in the Indian empire. Eyes that had never looked upon India directly, like people who had never left the three kingdoms, could not appreciate that one life might span such diversity. Those who tried to bridge such an unbridgeable gap had to be playing at some pernicious game. It was precisely this lesson that the anonymous artist of the cartoon *Court Cards, the best to Deal With* hoped to make.[22] In the scene, Warren Hastings, who by the time the cartoon appeared in 1788 was being impeached for malfeasance in office, is dressed in eastern robes and a large turban. He genuflects between Lord Thurlow, the Lord Chancellor, and King George, represented on suitless playing cards as a jack and a king respectively. Ever the faithful imperial servant, Hastings supplies the two unidentified cards with their appropriate suit – large, shining diamonds, no doubt from the mines at Golconda. Hastings appears in the etching as a supplicant subject, but his is a poker face. He is playing a game. Hastings will not be impeached, the illustration seems to suggest, because the former Governor-General holds all the right cards and will eventually play his ace – or rather, in this instance, his Lord Chancellor and his King.

If, as Homi Bhabha has argued, the process of imperialism resulted in hybrid cultures in the colonised world, nabobs turned the paradigm on its head.[23] They offered the possibility of a second hybrid identity within the imperial system – a hybrid identity located at the very heart of empire, Britain itself. Material culture – the very things nabobs used to narrate their global biographies – served also as markers of this cultural borrowing. The ideological implications of such imperial collectibles were, then, hardly neutral, for, in the hands of a nabob, they actually suggested that domestic 'British' culture was itself one of the by-products of various global interactions. Let us take Indian animals as a case study.

While it is difficult to establish a concrete sense of how many Indian animals lived in late eighteenth-century Britain, newspaper accounts from the period indicate that it would not have been hard to see an elephant, exotic birds, tigers and other large cats, Indian oxen and other exotic mega-fauna in Britain itself, particularly in London, other urban centres and at the estates of Company employees. The Tower of London had been home to the royal family's menagerie since the thirteenth century, and by the eighteenth century it had been opened to the public as an early zoo. Lady Mary Coke went to the Tower in March 1768. In her diary, Lady Coke recorded that she, Lord and Lady Stafford and Lord Bessborough all ventured to the Tower. For Lady Coke, who had been previously, nothing was new. The menagerie, though, impressed her companions.[24] Like Coke, the Reverend James Woodford recorded in his diary that he and his family went to the Tower in May 1782. 'Nancy, myself, and Will', he recorded, 'took a coach and went to the Tower and saw the Horse Armory, the small Armory, the Artillery, the Regalia, and the wild beasts.'[25]

As the Royal Menagerie became an increasingly profitable tourist destination in the late eighteenth century, the nation's growing empire became a logical resource for filling the zoo's pens, cages and stalls.[26] As Daniel Hahn has written, 'the constant to-ing and fro-ing of traders meant that for a time the Tower seemed to have a white fleet of procurers of animals for His Majesty's collection'.[27] The activity of the East India Company in this period and the Company's concomitant interest in the natural sciences resulted in what Hahn has called 'a shift in the kinds of animals represented in the Tower collection, a sharp bias towards those to be found on the Indian subcontinent'.[28]

In addition to the imperial animals that domestic audiences could see at the Tower of London, the India House on Leadenhall Street itself housed a remarkable collection of South Asian animals and other oddities. The Company's headquarters were, one observer noted, 'full of rare and curious things … birds of paradise, a serpent whose size is most remarkable … and many other animals and curiosities which came from India and are being kept there to gratify the curiosity of the public'.[29] Opening its doors to the public and displaying examples of the growing Indian empire to domestic Britons was a clever move on the Company's part, on two fronts. First, as Hahn has argued, it showed the Company to be a responsible manager of the Indian empire, concerned enough to learn about and study the subcontinent and its inhabitants. Second, the Company's directors 'saw the practical benefit of harnessing scientific knowledge for massive potential gain (scientists could help them transplant Chinese tea to India, Himalayan cashmere goats to Scotland, and so on)'.[30]

By the end of the eighteenth century, then, there were multiple opportunities for British citizens in London to see and study living specimens from South Asia. As a 1773 guidebook of the city proclaimed, London had 'Lions, Tygers, Elephants, &c. in every street in town'.[31] Though the 1773 guidebook undoubtedly exaggerated the prevalence of Indian animals in London, the fact remained that such animals were increasingly common in this period. Because they were indigenous to India, these animals appeared in Britain as physical manifestations of South Asia, and because the East India Company and its servants had imported them, they increasingly became symbolic of the Company's role as a link between the nation and the empire.

The first such animal to gain widespread fame in the late eighteenth century was the so-called 'Shah Ghost'. The animal, which had been a gift to Robert Clive from the Nawab of Bengal, had been shipped to London by Clive as a gift for William Pitt. Pitt, who seems to have wanted the beast about as much as Clive did, re-gifted it to King George in 1759. The 'Shah Ghost' proved to be 'too fierce and ungovernable' to be a pet and was sent to the Tower to be locked in a cage.[32] The strange beast, most probably a caracal, was immediately celebrated. In November 1759, *The London Magazine* noted that

> a very beautiful and uncommon animal ... is lodg'd in the Tower ... It is called, in the Indostan language a Shah Goest [sic], and is even in that country esteemed an extraordinary rarity, there having been never known more than five in those parts.[33]

Not everyone was so impressed by the animal. In March 1760, Horace Walpole, ever the curmudgeon, quipped in a letter to Horace Mann that 'there is some big news from the East Indies. I don't know what, except that the hero Clive has taken Mazulipatam and the great Mogul's grandmother. I suppose', he continued, 'she will be brought over and put in the Tower with the Shahgoest [sic], the strange Indian beast that Mr Pitt gave to the King this winter.'[34]

That Indian animals were locked in the Tower of London while rapacious nabobs roamed free on the city's streets was a bit of irony that others appreciated as well. In 1786, Warren Hastings imported six tropical birds for King George III and a hyena for the Prince of Wales. *The English Chronicle* suggested that the gifts were intended to purchase the royal family's good graces in the face of Hastings' upcoming impeachment trial, and it mocked his attempts at bribery. Of all of Hastings' gifts to the royal family, it was his hyena that merited the most elaborate media coverage. The hyena was, it was written, 'an obscene and solitary animal', a creature so demonic that, 'when destitute of other provisions, it scraped up the graves; and devours the dead bodies'.[35]

Hyenas were the worst kind of scavengers, but late eighteenth-century observers who read about the hyena would surely have noticed that much of the language used to describe the ravenous hyena had already been used to describe nabobs and their rapacious behaviour in India. 'It is rather remarkable', *The English Chronicle* noted wryly, 'that of all the voracious animals, and strange creatures brought over from India, the poor Hyaena [sic] is the only one which has been sent to the Tower.'[36] Like the hyena, then, Hastings and his fellow Company servants were scavengers, but, unlike the caged animals at the Tower, they roamed loose on the streets of the nation.

Domestic concerns aside, Indian animals abounded in late eighteenth-century Britain. In September 1763, one Captain Sampson of the East India Company followed Clive's example when he brought an elephant home and gave it as a present to the King.[37] In 1765, Sir George Pigot, the former Governor of Madras, ordered a painting of an Indian cheetah he had brought from South Asia, a stag and the cheetah's two Indian keepers from the painter George Stubbs. The cheetah was later given as a gift to George III, who handed the difficult animal off to his brother, the Duke of Cumberland. Throughout the rest of his career, Stubbs, not unlike Noah, waited at the foot of the Company's ships and chronicled the animals that passed onto its docks. His works include a monkey and a rhinoceros as well as a yak that Warren Hastings allowed to graze on his estate at Daylesford and a zebra that the Company had given to Queen Charlotte as a gift.[38]

As Stubbs's paintings suggest, animals from around the empire were appearing more and more often in domestic Britain in the last half of the eighteenth century. Domestic curiosity was aroused by a desire to see these fabled beasts, in the case of some species, for the first time. *The London Chronicle* reported that the Indiaman *Ponsborn* brought 'a most beautiful tyger [sic], a curious hyena, and a civit cat' back from India in June 1772.[39] In June 1784, *The Public Advertiser* wrote of the arrival of a 'remarkable fine young lion', and in July of that year the paper reported on the ceremony at which the King received the lion as a present from William Hornby, the former Governor of Bombay.[40] In July 1784, the Queen received a bull from India as a gift from Lord Southampton.[41] In January 1786, *The Nottingham Journal* celebrated the arrival of a 'hart-beast, or gazle [sic]' from India, noting that the animal, with its 'fine cinnamon colour', its 'pair of beautiful black twisted horns', its yellow hoofs and its black stripes, 'occasioned many disputes among the writers of natural history' who tried to classify it.[42] The Edinburgh-based *Caledonian Mercury* likewise celebrated the arrival of a new elephant in London in March 1795. The paper trumpeted the beast as 'a most wonderful' surprise, and crowds flocked to see the new arrival for the price of one shilling. Many, the paper noted, would not have seen a living elephant at the Tower, as the one presented by Captain Sampson in 1763 had died some twenty years before.[43]

From London to Nottingham and from Nottingham to Edinburgh, Indian animals imported to Britain by the Company and its agents caused nothing short of a minor sensation in late eighteenth-century Britain. These animals marked the presence of India as part of the British imperial world, but they also marked the presence of India within the British national landscape. Because they were linked to the Company, these animals also exposed the Company's role in promoting the growing relationship between the nation and the empire, and Company employees were seen to be the prime movers behind this growing imperial presence in domestic Britain. Company servants could be accused of being addicted to India, and there was no reason to suspect that they were not equally partial to its exotic animals. Robert Clive's granddaughter, Charlotte Florentia Clive, later the Duchess of Northumberland, confessed that she was deeply in love with an Indian gazelle she had received as a gift while living in India during her father's tenure as the Governor of Madras. The 'beautiful gazelle', she reported in her journal, 'became attached to me, travelled in my palaquin, and slept by my bed-side', and Clive felt 'a sad grief' the day her beloved pet, eager to graze on the front lawn of the Madras Governor's Mansion, plunged to his death from her third-floor balcony.[44]

If nabobs felt partial to South Asia and a partiality for its animal inhabitants, domestic critics did not always view that partiality as benign. The non-human inhabitants of Britain's overseas empire were not always docile, caged and safe. *The Sheffield Register* gave its readers good reason to fear imperial animals in July 1793, when it published the story of the death of Sir Hector Munro's son. The young Munro, along with his friends Mr Downey and Lieutenant Pyefinch, had been hunting tigers on Saugur Island in December 1792 when 'an immense royal tyger [sic] sprang upon the unfortunate Munro, who was sitting down; in a moment', the article continued, 'his head was in the beast's mouth, and he rushed into the jungle with him, with as much ease as I could lift a kitten; tearing him through the thicket bushes and trees, every thing yielding to his monstrous strength'. Munro survived the attack and 'lived for twenty-four hours in the extreme of torture; his head and skull were all torn and broke to pieces, and he was wounded by the claws, all over his neck and shoulders'. His friends could only be thankful that they had been able to recover their unfortunate colleague's body at all rather 'than leave him to be devoured limb by limb'.[45]

News of Munro's death must have raised the public's curiosity towards the animals at the Tower, and also their suspicions and fears. It was not unknown for the wild beasts at the Tower to escape into the streets of London. Rumours and children's storybooks alike told of a leopard that had escaped from the Tower.[46] Such stories gained credence when the *Reading Mercury and Oxford Gazette* reported in June 1785 that a keeper of the King's wild animals at the Tower had forgotten to latch one of the cages properly. As a result, the 'lion got out and continued banging about the yard for upwards of an hour, and tearing a table and stool to pieces'.[47] Animals from India had the potential to be a pestilence in domestic Britain. They were not unlike the 'large swarm of rats' that infested the city of Peterborough in the summer of 1784. The rats, it was supposed, had 'come from India in some of the ships'. They plagued the town and its inhabitants, burrowing into the walls of people's homes, destroying supplies of grain, fruits and poultry. 'They get into peoples [sic] houses', *The Public Advertiser* reported, 'and do much mischief'.[48]

Imperial animals were representatives of the untamed forces of imperialism, symbols of the perils inherent in Britain's becoming an imperial nation. The corrupted behaviours of British nabobs too closely mirrored the necrophagic tendencies of the imperial hyena. On the surface, imperial animals were just a collection of higgledy-piggledy souvenirs from India brought back by servants of Britain's growing empire. To the nativist eye, though, they were tainted, living, material artefacts from South Asia, markers of a new imperial presence in the British metropole. They were visible signs that becoming an imperial power was changing the emergent face of the British nation. The contest over how to understand the nabobs and their imperial pets was itself a popular subject in late eighteenth-century Britain, as demonstrated in the plays, operas and political cartoons of the period. But the debate was also something deeper, indicating as it did a cultural connection that spanned and integrated the British world. Dread them as they might, nativist Britons could not avoid Indian animals in domestic Britain, animals that functioned as cultural markers of an empire that was otherwise imagined in purely institutional, political and economic terms.

Indian food served a similar role as East India Company servants brought home the new imperial flavours they had discovered in South Asia and threatened to change the types of food that filled the plates across the nation. George Grey, who retired from India after serving the Company for twenty-two years, found that he missed the flavour of his favourite mango punch, and he asked his friends still serving in South Asia to try to find a way to send him some.[49] Newspaper advertisements of the period sought to capitalise on nabobs' new-found tastes for South Asian foods. In December 1773, *The Public Advertiser* listed an advertisement for a 'True Indian Curey [sic] Paste' that was 'so well compounded with rare and choise [sic] ingredients, that purchasers have no other Trouble than to mix a piece the size of a walnut of the paste with the gravy intended making a curey [sic]'. The paste was available, the advertisement continued, for the rather expensive price of two shillings and sixpence per pot at the Norris Street Coffee House, Haymarket. For those who could not be bothered to mix the simple curry paste with their home-cooked gravy, the mistress of the Norris Street Coffee House would send 'ready dressed curey [sic] and rice, also Indian pilaws [sic], to any part of the town' at 'the shortest notice'.[50]

In May 1784, *The Morning Herald and Daily Advertiser* ran a listing that specifically targeted nabobs as the prime purchasers of Indian foods. Curry powder 'brought from the East Indies', the advertisement began, was available at Sorlie's Perfumery Warehouse at Piccadilly 'to persons of Rank, Traders to all Nabobs, and Servants'. For others who were unfamiliar with curry powder, the advertisement went on to explain that the powder was instrumental in making 'celebrated East-India Dishes, and most sumptuous sauces'. It was 'exceeding pleasant and healthful – renders the stomach active in digestion – the blood naturally free in circulation – the mind vigorous, and contributes most of any food to an increase of the human race'.[51] The advertisement, thus, listed nabobs as the primary target audience for curry. It labelled them as the community to blame for curry's presence in Britain, but it also encouraged other Britons to sample the powder, to enjoy its medicinal qualities, to savour its dynamic flavour and to indulge in its sexual side-effects. Curry was not just a food. It was an experience that shaped a person's health and a person's sexual behaviour. It changed a person, the advertisement argued, and nabobs were responsible for introducing it to their nation and their compatriots.

As had been the case with South Asian fashions, Indian culinary tastes became a symbol for nabobs at large. Governor Anderson, who refused to dress for dinner in proper English fashions in Mrs Griffith's *A Wife in the Right*, also objected to the traditionally bland English meal that he faced when he reached the dinner table. Not only, he exclaimed, would he pass a law banning buttons once he won a seat in Parliament, he would also push through legislation that would make 'curry and pellow [sic] ... the common food' of Great Britain.[52] As the authors of *The Rolliad* feared, nabobs' predilections for South Asian cuisine were replacing Britain's traditional fare. 'Mighty beef, bedew'd with potent ale', the poem suggested, had once 'rous'd' the Saxons 'at early dawn'. A diet of beef had made the Saxons a race of champions. It had made them 'a sturdy, bold, rebellious race, strength in the frame, and spirit in the face'. Imperial foodstuffs, though, were making the nation a collective population of weaklings who indulged in luxurious novelties beneath 'gilded roofs' and on 'polish'd tables'.[53]

To the authors of *The Rolliad*, imperial foods were responsible for a change in the British nation and its people's character. Nowhere, though, were these changes more evident than in the architectural styles nabobs employed in the construction of their homes, buildings with the power to remake the British landscape. In part, the mythology surrounding what were popularly known as 'nabobs' palaces' grew out of the fact that many returning nabobs invested their savings in a traditionally British way – they bought landed estates. Many of these men believed that an estate was their only sure path to political power. Most purchased and lived in typical country homes, Georgian estates with neo-classical or Palladian façades, but a select group of returning nabobs followed a different path, constructing homes using Eastern architectural flourishes that quickly earned the opprobrious appellation 'the Indian style'. It was this smaller group whose houses came to symbolise the community of nabobs as a whole, and it was their homes that came to suggest a cultural threat to the British nation.

In 1767, Captain John Gould built a home for himself at Margate that was designed 'in imitation of a house in Calcutta'. William Hornby, the former Governor of Bombay, likewise modelled his home on the Government House at Bombay.[54] Sir Hector Munro built a Hindu temple on his estate at Novar in 1777.[55] As well, on the summit just above the estate, he built faux ruins replicating the ancient gates of the city of Negapatam.[56] In 1793, James Forbes constructed an Indian temple in the gardens of his estate in Middlesex. Surrounding the temple, he placed a group of statues he had brought back from South Asia which 'were said to be the only specimens of Hindoo sculpture in England'.[57] John Osbourne constructed a similar temple in the gardens surrounding his estate, Melchet Park in Wiltshire, in 1800. The temple's exterior was decorated with religious figures representing the principal incarnations of Vishnu. Rather than filling the temple with Indian gods, though, Osbourne placed a bust of his mentor, Warren Hastings, inside the edifice.

In 1787, Hastings purchased his family's ancestral estate at Daylesford and commissioned the architect Samuel Pepys Cockerell, the architect to the East India Company, to design a new main house. Cockerell's design for the new building incorporated a large dome, derived from Islamic architectural influences, over the central entry hall. The house had a conservatory with Eastern-styled windows, and in the park surrounding the estate Cockerell peppered the landscape with Hindu temples and other garden follies based on South Asian themes.

Samuel Cockerell also designed Sezincote House for his brother, Charles, who returned from Calcutta in 1800. Sezincote, like Hastings' neighbouring estate, was fitted with arched windows and an Eastern dome. Cockerell's bedroom was distanced from the main house by a long colonnade designed to give the bedroom the effect of a tented palace. Its landscaping was designed to reflect an Eastern garden, and Cockerell commissioned Humphrey Repton, who would later work with the Prince Regent on the designs for the Royal Pavilion at Brighton, to design a series of garden follies that included a bridge guarded by two sacred cows, a Hindu temple and a mock ruin designed to replicate a snake pool.[58]

It was not just façades and parks that nabobs decorated in the 'Indian style'. Rather, the interiors of their homes were often filled with markers of their lives in South Asia. In South Asia, nabobs were known to spend lavishly on decorating their homes. William Hickey recorded that he and his wife, Charlotte, spent more than 12,000 rupees on decorating their first home in Calcutta.[59] When he returned to Britain more than two decades later, Hickey, now a widower, hoped to import most of this furniture home with him. It was thus possible for even those nabobs who lived in typically Georgian estates in domestic Britain to surround themselves with the accoutrements of life in South Asia.[60]

At Daylesford, Hastings commissioned architects and artists to fill the estate with reminders of his past in India. He called in the sculptor Thomas Banks to design a fireplace for him. The result, which still exists in the house today, was a marble mantel balanced on the heads of two South Asian women between whom Banks carved a series of scenes representing Hastings' accomplishments as Governor-General. The house was filled with other paraphernalia and memorabilia from Warren and Marian Hastings' travel across the subcontinent. The reminders served as a comfort to Hastings as he endured the final years of his long impeachment trial, and perhaps even as a retreat from the world after his acquittal in 1795. To Hastingses, living with such reminders must have seemed natural and fitting. They had met on their way to India, and Hastings had spent three decades of his life there. For domestic British critics, though, Daylesford and other nabobish homes posed a significant problem on several levels. First, these homes reversed the process of imperial colonisation by building what appeared to be Indian settlements across the British nation. Second, they served as the nabobs' bold refusal to re-domesticate themselves to living in Britain; they were an insistent declaration that the process of empire made Britain and India equally home to Company servants.

Nabobs returned to Britain and refused to settle into a life-style that was domesticated and British because such a singular narrative could not contain their global biographies. They brought home fashions, pets and architectural styles, all of which forced domestic audiences to come face to face with the material reality of the South Asian empire. They built micro-Indias in the British landscape. They surrounded themselves with products from the empire that were not 'ideologically neutral'.[61] As a result, nabobs were ostracised and insulted. David Hare, a Scottish watchmaker and a founding member of the Hindu College at Calcutta, was 'denied a Christian burial when he died of cholera, on the grounds that he had become more Hindu than Christian'. Francis Gillanders, a Company tax-collector at Bihar, was chastised for 'administering heathen rites' when he donated a bell to a Hindu temple in 1798.[62]

To men like Hare or Gillanders, the fluid movement from India to Britain made sense at a biographical level. There was nothing, as William Hickey might have said, 'foreign' about their lives. But, to metropolitan Britons, the nabobs were not arbiters of an imperial national identity. Such an idea was mere pablum. They were different.

They dressed differently, they had strange pets, they lived in unusual houses and they seemed to be domesticating all of this foreignness on British soil. They brought home strange and unusual items that belonged to India, and they used them, as a matter of daily course, in domestic British settings. Attacks against the nabobs that highlighted their involvement in bringing South Asian animals, clothing and architectural styles home with them to domestic Britain were rooted in intrinsically xenophobic fears of outside people and unknown cultures.

Nabobs brought all of India's difference home with them; they argued that it was hardly difference at all. They attempted to domesticate empire as part of the national experience. Their lives, in short, suggested that the 'symbolic barrier' between nation and empire could, in fact, be permeable. They insisted that Britain was more than the island, more than the landfall. They suggested that British history and British imperial history could not be distinguished one from the other, and they were met with resistance from a domestic public that rejected the notion of ever being 'at home with the empire'.[63]

Notes

1 Sydney C. Grier (ed.), *The Letters of Warren Hastings to His Wife* (London: William Blackwood and Sons, 1905), p. 394.

2 Grier (ed.), *The Letters of Warren Hastings*, p. 394.

3 For more on Hickey's departure from India, see Peter Fryer, *Staying Power: The History of Black People in Britain* (London: Pluto Press, 1984), p. 77.

4 William Hickey, *The Memoirs of William Hickey*, ed. Alfred Spencer (London: Hurst and Blackett, 1925), pp. iv, 470–1.

5 Beth Fowkes Tobin, *Picturing Imperial Power: Colonial Identity in Eighteenth-Century British Painting* (Durham, NC: Duke University Press, 1999), p. 33.

6 The most recent such study is Nicholas Dirks, *The Scandal of Empire: India and the Creation of Imperial Britain* (Cambridge, MA: Harvard University Press, 2006). See also Percival Spear, *The Nabobs: A Study of the Life of the English in Eighteenth-Century India* (Oxford: Oxford University Press, 1932); and James Holzman, *The Nabobs in England: A Study of the Returned Anglo-Indian, 1760–1785* (New York: Columbia University Press, 1926). A short list of other such studies would include, Anna Clark, *Scandal: The Sexual Politics of the British Constitution* (Princeton: Princeton University Press, 2004), pp. 84–112; William Dalrymple, *White Mughals: Love and Betrayal in Eighteenth-Century India* (London: Harper Collins, 2002); Michael Edwardes, *The Nabobs at Home* (London: Constable, 1991); Holden Furber, *John Company at Work: A Study of European Expansion in India in the Late Eighteenth Century* (New York: Octagon Books, 1970); Holden Furber, *Private Fortunes and Company Profits in the India Trade in the Eighteenth Century* (Brookfield, VT: Ashgate, 1997); Philip Lawson and James Phillips, '"Our Execrable Banditti": Perceptions of Nabobs in Mid-Eighteenth-Century Britain', *Albion*, 16 (1984), 225–41; P. J. Marshall, *East India Fortunes: The British in Bengal in the Eighteenth Century* (New York: Oxford University Press, 1976); P. J. Marshall, *The Impeachment of Warren Hastings* (London: Oxford University Press, 1965); P. J. Marshall, *Trade and Conquest: Studies on the Rise of British Dominance in India* (Brookfield, VT: Ashgate, 1993); and P. J. Marshall, *Problems of Empire: Britain and India, 1757–1813* (New York: Barnes and Noble, 1968).

7 See, *The East India Company at Home, 1757–1857*, http://blogs.ucl.ac.uk/eicah/about/ (accessed 8 December 2014).
8 Mildred Archer, *India and British Portraiture, 1770–1825* (New York: Philip Watson, 1979), p. 57.
9 This portrait is now held at the British Library. Arthur William Devis, *Sir William Jones* (Calcutta, 1793), Oriental and India Office Collection, British Library (hereafter OIOC) F840.
10 For a copy of this self-portrait, see Archer, *India and British Portraiture*, p. 183.
11 Hickey, *The Memoirs of William Hickey*, ed. Spencer, pp. iv, 470–1.
12 David Hume, 'Of National Characters', in *Essays Moral Political and Literary*, 2 vols (London: Longmans, Green, and Co., 1875), Vol, I, p. 250.
13 Dalrymple, *White Mughals*, p. 33.
14 Dalrymple, *White Mughals*, p. 36. For more on the practice of bathing in British South Asia, see Fryer, *Dr. Fryers Travels*, p. 200. See also Mark Harrison, *Climates and Constitutions: Health, Race, Environment, and British Imperialism in India, 1600–1850* (New York: Oxford University Press, 1999), pp. 84–6.
15 Michael Fisher, *The First Indian Author* (Oxford: Oxford University Press, 1996), p. 173. See also Michael Fisher, *The Travels of Dean Mahomet* (Los Angeles: University of California Press, 1997), p. 148. See also, Harrison, *Climates and Constitutions*, pp. 84–6.
16 See Dalrymple, *White Mughals*, p. 36.
17 Roxann Wheeler, *The Complexion of Race: Categories of Difference in Eighteenth-Century British Culture* (Philadelphia: University of Pennsylvania Press, 2000), p. 17.
18 Wheeler, *The Complexion of Race*, p. 289.
19 Archer, *India and British Portraiture*, pp. 412–13.
20 Mrs. Griffith, *A Wife in the Right* (London, 1772), p. 11.
21 Griffith, *A Wife in the Right*, p. 13.
22 The cartoon is available at the British Library. Anonymous, *Court Cards, the Best to Deal With* (London, 1788), BL P1772.
23 Homi Bhabha, 'Signs Taken for Wonders: Questions of Ambivalence and Authority Under a Tree Outside of Delhi, May 1817', in *The Location of Culture* (New York: Routledge, 1994), pp. 102–22, at p. 122.
24 Lady Mary Coke, *The Letters and Journals of Lady Mary Coke*, 4 vols, ed. J. A. Home (Edinburgh: David Douglas, 1889–96), Vol, II, p. 208.
25 James Woodford, *The Diary of a Country Parson: The Reverend James Woodford*, 5 vols, ed. John Beresford (Oxford: Oxford University Press, 1924–31),Vol. II, p. ii, 31 May 1782.
26 For more on the nineteenth-century display of imperial animals, see Helen Cowie, *Exhibiting Animals in Nineteenth-Century Britain: Empathy, Education, and Entertainment* (New York: Palgrave, 2014).
27 Daniel Hahn, *The Tower Menagerie* (London: Simon and Schuster, 2003), pp. 182–3.
28 Hahn, *The Tower Menagerie*, p. 182.
29 Quoted in Hahn, *The Tower Menagerie*, p. 140.
30 Hahn, *The Tower Menagerie*, p. 185.
31 Quoted in Hahn, *The Tower Menagerie*, p. 224.
32 Hahn, *The Tower Menagerie*, pp. 182–3 and 205–6.
33 *The London Magazine* (November 1759), p. 603.
34 Quoted in Nirad C. Chaudhuri, *Clive of India: A Political and Psychological Essay* (Bombay: South Asia Books, 1977), pp. 323–4.
35 *The General Evening Post*, 11–13 July 1786, and *The Morning Chronicle and London Advertiser*, 14 July 1786.
36 *The English Chronicle*, 8 July 1786.
37 *The Gentleman's Magazine* (September 1763), p. 464.
38 See Jeremy Osborn, 'India, Parliament, and the Press under George III: A Study of English Attitudes towards the East India Company and Empire in the Late Eighteenth and Early Nineteenth Centuries' (unpublished D.Phil. thesis, Oxford University, 1999), p. 32.

39 *The London Chronicle*, 9–11 June 1772.
40 *The Public Advertiser*, 28 June 1784 and 14 July 1784.
41 *The Public Advertiser*, 12 July 1784.
42 *The Nottingham Journal*, 7 January 1786.
43 *The Caledonian Mercury*, 28 March 1795.
44 *Voyages to the East*, OIOC WD.4235, 185.
45 *The Sheffield Register*, 12 July 1793. See also *The Sheffield Register*, 11 July 1793.
46 See Hahn, *Tower Menagerie*, p. 158.
47 *The Reading Mercury and Oxford Gazette*, 13 June 1785.
48 *The Public Advertiser*, 5 August 1784.
49 George Gray to Harry Verelst, May 11, 1763, OIOC Mss Eur D691.
50 *The Public Advertiser*, 6 December 1773.
51 *The Morning Herald and Daily Advertiser*, 4 May 1784.
52 Griffith, *A Wife in the Right*, p. 13.
53 Anonymous, *The Rolliad* (London: J. Ridgway, 1795), pp. 56–8.
54 See Raymond Head, *Sezincote: A Paradigm of the Indian Style* (unpublished MA thesis, Royal College of Art, London, 1982), p. 7.
55 I thank Andrew Mackillop for suggesting Munro, his family and his estate at Novar to me.
56 See Head, *Sezincote*, p. 10.
57 Head, *Sezincote*, p. 10.
58 Head, *Sezincote*, pp. 39–47.
59 William Hickey, *The Memoirs of William Hickey*, ed. Peter Quennell (London: Routledge and Kegan Paul, 1960), p. 435.
60 Nathaniel Middleton, for example, built a classical home at Town Hill Park in South Stoneham, Hampshire, where he kept his collections of Indian miniatures and Persian manuscripts. See, Head, *Sezincote*, p. 8.
61 See Tobin, *Picturing Imperial Power*, p. 33. See also, Louis Landa, 'Of Silkworms and Farthingales and the Will of God', in *Studies in the Eighteenth Century*, ed. R. F. Brissenden (Toronto: University of Toronto Press, 1973), Vol. II, pp. 259–77. See also J. G. A. Pocock, *The Machiavellian Moment: Florentine Political Thought and the Atlantic Republican Tradition* (Princeton: Princeton University Press, 1975); David Solkin, *Painting for Money: The Visual Arts and the Public Sphere in Eighteenth-Century England* (New Haven, CT: Yale University Press, 1993).
62 Dalrymple, *White Mughals*, pp. 49–50.
63 See Catherine Hall and Sonya O. Rose, 'Introduction: Being at Home with the Empire', in Catherine Hall and Sonya O. Rose (eds), *At Home with the Empire: Metropolitan Culture and the Imperial World* (New York: Cambridge University Press, 2006), pp. 1–31, at pp. 22–5.

CHAPTER ELEVEN

Material culture and Sierra Leone's civilising mission in the nineteenth century

Bronwen Everill

The British world has long been synonymous with the 'white settler neo-European world' in imperial history.[1] Although this was originally an important cultural corrective to the idea of a purely military or financial empire, the limitations of this group of colonies and colonists as a frame for understanding the operations of imperial culture are extensive. As numerous historians have pointed out, the impact of the empire on British life 'at home' both drew on an imaginary tropical empire and on real connections to the colonies.[2] British connections to India wove through British language, education, literature, career paths and national imagination. Family connections in Canada, Kenya or New Zealand tied together the imagined geography of greater Britain.[3]

But the British settler world was not exclusively white and those participating in the imagining of Britain's imperial geography were not only based in Australia, New Zealand, South Africa and Canada. Expanding understandings of the British world have begun to incorporate the United States because of the high levels of British immigration to that country in the nineteenth century.[4] And cultural – rather than ethnic – understandings of British identity in the empire further complicate the story of the British world. Black loyalists who fought with the British in the American Revolution and were resettled in Nova Scotia and then Sierra Leone; black South Africans who fought with the British in their imperial wars; 'Afro-Victorians' who served in colonial administrations and ran the empire in Africa; and the 'creole elite' who believed they would benefit from a shared, non-ethnic British cultural identity: all of these challenge the image of a British world made up exclusively of the British diaspora.[5]

It is clear that empires have a much wider impact on material culture than an examination of exclusively white settler colonies would suggest. The 'footprint' of empire is often seen in the physical landscape as well as the imagination, and it is important to consider what kind of impact material culture has on how empire is being lived on the ground. Material culture was an important part of defining the British world, as it was in all empires.[6] Settlers – both white and black – used that reliance on material culture (both as signifiers and in terms of actual trade) to make claims on the empire.[7] As Susan Lawrence has written, 'ethnicity consists of traits believed to be shared with others, but the constellation of those traits is fluid and actively negotiated according to circumstance'.[8] In the case of Sierra Leone, those material culture claims were tied up with the metropolitan argument over the success of legitimate commerce and the civilising mission in replacing the slave trade from Africa.

Founded in 1787, the British colony of Sierra Leone was established to provide a home for the 'Black Poor' of London. After the initial founding in 1787, Freetown subsequently became a destination for black loyalist refugees from the American Revolution, Maroons from Jamaica and slaves freed from the West African slave trade – 'recaptives' or Liberated Africans – after its abolition in 1807. The colony was an important site of utopian imperial experimentation that yielded lessons both for the British in administering a number of its African colonies from the late nineteenth century and for the anti-slavery movement that founded the colony. In the 1810s and 1820s, Governor Charles MacCarthy worked with the Church Missionary Society (CMS) to establish a system for integrating and 'inculturating' arriving Liberated Africans. This process involved apprenticeship, church membership and education provision in the village parishes set up throughout the Freetown Peninsula. The scheme was ultimately phased out by budget-conscious governors, but many of the means for assimilating Liberated Africans were carried on by the first generation of Liberated Africans themselves in the establishment of schools, colleges, churches and companies. Although it is difficult to quantify settler identification, by the 1840s, large groups of Sierra Leoneans in Freetown who had never lived in London, in Britain or even in other parts of the British Empire wrote petitions as British subjects, joined British societies or societies modelled on British institutions, made purchases, dressed and lived in ways that would have been recognisable in other parts of the British world, and wrote and thought of themselves as part of a broader British culture.[9]

Sierra Leoneans' identification with British values was in fact a fundamental part of the experiment in anti-slavery colonisation. Britishness – as a package of both material and ideological identifications – was formative to the creation of Sierra Leone's settler identity.[10] Values of 'civilization, commerce and Christianity' promoted by the various metropolitan organisations involved with the running of the colony over the course of the late eighteenth and early nineteenth centuries helped to shape what it meant to be Sierra Leonean as well as shaping how such civilising projects were viewed, planned and executed by imperial organisations as the century wore on.[11]

This accords with Donal Lowry, Vivian Bickford-Smith and Timothy Parsons' accounts of the creole elite in British Africa in the mid-nineteenth century. As Parsons writes, 'The Krios and other West African coastal élites also adopted English names, Victorian dress, and sent their children to British mission schools.'[12] Bickford-Smith notes that the Sierra Leone 'Krio' experienced cultural change in 'religious belief, dress, agricultural practices, domestic architecture, privately owned objects, diet, and the sense of self in relation to society'.[13] As Mariana Candido has noted for the creation of Luso-Atlantic culture, 'Identity should not be read as synonymous with ethnicity ... but as related to kin, lineage, and connections with political alliances.'[14] Catherine Hall has called the creation of imperial identities discursive, and this certainly seems to be the appropriate understanding of identity in Sierra Leone.[15] 'British' in Sierra Leone was an identity of continual self-definition, expressed through material culture and ideology. The settlers had to construct new identities on their arrival in the colonies, taking into account their new relationships with indigenous Africans, the countries they left behind and the other colonial residents. Andrew Walls writes that 'the only identity possible for the recaptives was a new identity.'[16]

Black identification with British values and culture was not uncommon in the British African colonies.[17] Donal Lowry singles out allegiance to the monarch as another unifying symbol under which all subjects could identify as equally British, and in their petitions to the government, Sierra Leoneans regularly singled out their shared subjecthood with those in the metropole.[18] As Timothy Parsons points out, '"Afro-Victorians" held senior positions in local civil services and played a willing role in the expansion of British influence because they assumed they would be its primary beneficiaries.'[19] Although Sierra Leoneans numbered among the most influential 'Afro-Victorians', they also differed from other 'creole elite' Africans because the founders were settlers who brought experience of British cultural life from other parts of the empire (Jamaica, Nova Scotia, Virginia, New York, the Carolinas). For these settlers, as for white settlers in the empire, the 'British World' was a material world as well as a set of values and connections. The adoption of recognised cultural trappings gave Sierra Leoneans a shorthand to identify as British subjects.[20] Choice of clothing, development of relationships, political engagement, civic involvement and participation with institutions and associations were part of the process that helped to announce settler culture and identity in dealing with the metropole.

Frequently classified as a 'tropical' 'periphery' colony for the post-Scramble period, Sierra Leone is often thought of as a resource-extractive colony, rather than a settler colony. Although by the first half of the twentieth century the economy of Sierra Leone had shifted to a focus on extraction from the hinterland, for most of the nineteenth century, the relationship of Sierra Leone to the empire was much more that of a trading port or entrepot. Settlers from North America, the Caribbean, Britain and other parts of West Africa were brought to the Freetown peninsula. Here they took on a variety of occupations: some took up trade with the interior; others began farming for domestic consumption; a minority became wealthy and had their children educated in colonial private schools or sent to England, from where they returned to become lawyers, civil servants, real estate moguls and politicians.

In general, Sierra Leone can be seen to differ from other Anglophone settler colonies because the settlers were a mixed group both from other parts of the British Empire (Nova Scotia, the American colonies, Jamaica, England, the Gold Coast and Senegambia) and from African societies along the coast. This led to a level of hybridity rarely seen in the white settler colonies, where racial boundaries prevented total hybridisation.[21] The hybridity of Sierra Leone's settler population has most frequently been noted with regard to the development of the Krio language. It also persisted in the development of culture more widely, including eating habits, living arrangements, religious ideology, attitudes toward careers and provision for death. In this way, it fell between the white-settler colonial experience, the African experience and the experience of other colonial 'auxiliaries' like the Lebanese.[22]

Sierra Leone's contested role in the formation of British ideas of its own humanitarian imperial culture largely rested in the early to mid-nineteenth century on the debate over Sierra Leoneans' industriousness and their ability to exemplify and spread British values and goods in Africa. As the anti-slavery movement's *cause célèbre* in the late eighteenth and early nineteenth centuries, the colony came under repeated attacks from the pro-slavery lobby, which portrayed the colonists as dissipated, as lazy, as slave traders themselves and at the very least as incapable of 'civilization'.[23] Others, such as the first colonial Governor, Thomas Perronet Thompson, or the colony's former Chief Justice, Robert Thorpe, cited mismanagement in the colony and claimed that there was profiteering in the abolition movement, or a continuation of slavery under the designation of 'apprenticeship'.[24]

As these debates took place in Parliament and in public discourse, participants in the popular anti-slavery movement – the largest philanthropic movement of its kind – were exposed to the arguments for Sierra Leone (and against) and for the type of British civilisation that Sierra Leone represented in Africa.[25] Although the colony was not initially very successful in abolishing the slave trade along the whole coast of West Africa (the vision promoted by some rather overly enthusiastic advocates), as the century progressed and a 'legitimate commerce' replacement for the slave trade was found in palm oil, Sierra Leone was increasingly seen in a favourable light. Tellingly, even when the colony's detractors had the upper hand in metropolitan discourse, their 'alternative' plans frequently called for moving the location of the colony (to Fernando Po; to the Niger) rather than for disrupting the fundamental idea of a settlement of black colonists who would promote British culture – material and ideological – in the region.[26]

Rather than seeing the Sierra Leoneans as simply 'assimilating' to British culture, they were in fact involved in developing the imperial ideals of modernity and Britishness as connected to material culture. The Sierra Leone project was in the public eye throughout the early nineteenth century, as anti- and pro-slavery campaigners debated its success, and as pro- and anti-expansionist parliamentarians debated public expenditure on the colony. The spread of legitimate commerce throughout West Africa provides a frame for understanding the role of Sierra Leoneans as cultural mediators for *both* West African *and* British publics. This in turn allowed Sierra Leoneans to benefit from metropolitan support for their own expansionist agenda in the mid to late nineteenth century. Those Sierra Leoneans who participated in British imperial culture transformed British expectations about what could and could not be achieved in a British West African empire. Sierra Leoneans' use of legitimate commerce and British material culture *created* the image of modern 'civilised' West Africans and gave metropolitan Britain hope that civilising – particularly through economic means – worked.

Sierra Leoneans were important in developing the imperial ideals of civilisation and ideas of imperial citizenship connected to material culture through their use of petitions, anti-slavery rhetoric and their purchases and sales of imperial goods. Sierra Leoneans' use of material connections, participation in commerce and emphasis on these as factors of 'civilisation' in opposition to 'native' backwardness encouraged the perception of the success of Britain's civilising mission, but also defined what 'success' looked like in the nineteenth-century British development project.

Sierra Leone had a unique role in Britain's African empire. With the settlers and resettled Africans as consumers of British material culture and participants in British ideological projects and institutions, many in Britain saw Sierra Leone as an ideal place from which to spread British culture in West Africa. Productive and 'civilised' African economies would buy manufactures from Britain and other parts of the empire. Sierra Leone's governors and other officials encouraged this emphasis on legitimate commerce. The Sierra Leone Company's governors reported 'that all the most valuable productions of the tropical climates seem to grow spontaneously at Sierra Leone; and that nothing but attention and cultivation appear wanting, in order to produce them of every kind, and in sufficient quantities to become articles of trade'.[27]

Legitimate commerce was important in the establishment of Sierra Leonean 'British' civilisation for two main reasons. First, the success of the anti-slavery project – and, therefore, Britain's role in ending the slave trade and promoting its own conception of civilised society – was tied to the replacement of the slave trade with legitimate commerce.[28] The size of trade to and from the colony acted as a proxy for the success of the civilising project and the replacement of the slave trade. Although it took a number of years for Britain's philanthropic community to agree what 'legitimate commerce' should look like (commercial agriculture in the form of plantations? black yeoman farmers? trade with African producers?) Sierra Leone's ultimate success in fostering trade and spreading demand for British and British imperial goods along the West African coast and in the Sierra Leonean hinterland helped to define how commerce in the post-slave trade Atlantic would operate.

A number of important raw goods were exported from West Africa in the period after the abolition of the slave trade. These 'legitimate' commercial products included camwood, ivory, coffee, palm oil and palm kernels. In 1824, for instance, the value of exports from Sierra Leone to Britain was £68,525, with African teak, ivory, camwood, palm oil and hides making up 92 per cent of the value. By 1837, the value had increased to £108,257, with timber alone making up 72 per cent of the value. By the 1850s, the value of exports from Sierra Leone was regularly above £200,000.[29] Sierra Leone's traders also spread along the coast in the 1840s and 1850s, expanding British commercial reach and the demand for British material culture.

Second, legitimate commerce was important because British imports into Sierra Leone also grew over the period.[30] In public debates over expenditure on the colony, Sierra Leone's advocates consistently pointed to the colony's ability to spread British manufactures as well as to export exotic goods.

> Placed in the centre of the most valuable part of the Western Coast of Africa, it will eventually become the grand emporium of its Commerce. Its name, and the superior advantages of its trade, have become known among the Natives of the richest countries of the interior, whose anxiety

> to bring their valuable produce to our market is best shewn by the perseverance with which they have overcome the difficulties of the path ... The vast field which this Continent opens for the consumption of British manufactures, will, ere long, equal any market in the world – the Natives preferring them, in their barters for produce, to any others that can be offered.[31]

The commissioner of the Mixed Courts at Freetown reported to the Parliamentary Select Committee in 1842 that goods from Manchester and India were traded by Sierra Leone merchants for the legitimate commerce exports, while 'for colonial use and consumption' 'spirits, tobacco, salt, beads, hardware and common crockery-ware' as well as 'many articles of British dress, necessaries and luxuries' were imported.[32] The success of the colony's trade was an important argument for Sierra Leone's abolitionist allies in Britain: with a few exceptions, most years saw revenue exceed expenditure.[33]

The growth of imports and exports led to the growth of a merchant class in Sierra Leone. One account reported that 'Many of them have realized considerable sums of money. Peter Newland, a liberated African, died a short time before I left the colony, and his estate realized, in houses, merchandise, and cash, upwards of £1,500.'[34] Imports in 1830, for instance, included thirty-nine trunks of apparel, worth £890; beads worth £6,311; 'India Goods' worth £12,305; 'Manchester Goods' worth £5,392; 1,027 tons of salt; 1,041 boxes of soap; £1,429 worth of boots and shoes; £870 worth of hats; £16,335 worth of molasses; 159 pipes; 425 boxes of cigars; and 10,000 bricks.[35] For a population totalling roughly 30,000 people, these goods demonstrated a sizeable impact of British material culture on their purchasers.[36] This merchant class actively participated in the civic life of the colony, promoting free trade, challenging taxation policies, demanding representation, developing credit networks both in Africa and in Britain and encouraging the legal protection of property rights. In debates with colonial and metropolitan authorities, they pointed to their civic engagement and promotion of these values as indicative of their civilisation, their 'Britishness'. Together, these two side-effects of the legitimate commerce project helped to define how the trade connections between Britain and Sierra Leone would be associated with the civilisation project in Africa.

Like 'settler capitalists' elsewhere in the empire, Sierra Leone's elite were 'self-consciously "European" in their attitudes and aspirations, pursued export-led growth to considerable material advantage' and were 'dependent on Britain for both capital and markets'.[37] Lieutenant Governor William Fergusson wrote to British anti-slavery activist Thomas Fowell Buxton describing the rise of Freetown's middle-class Victorians, with the same material culture and values as their metropolitan counterparts (and white settlers elsewhere). Aside from building houses on Dundas Street, attending services at St George's Anglican Cathedral and owning real estate in Wilberforce (a village on the Freetown peninsula), Fergusson pointed out that 'In several of them are to be seen mahogany chairs, tables, sofas, and four-post bedsteads, pier glasses, floor cloths, and other articles indicative of domestic comfort and accumulating wealth.'[38] These Liberated Africans were not only becoming wealthy, but were using that wealth to purchase the trappings of material culture associated with Britain. The most important factor, though, for this argument, was the type of employment undertaken by these Liberated Africans: 'They are almost wholly engaged in mercantile pursuits, and are to be found in nearly fitted-up shops on the ground-floor of their respective dwelling-houses.' These 'Afro-Victorians' had developed a creolised British settler society that occupied positions of prestige within the commercial, Christian and civic realms of Sierra Leone life, and they believed themselves to represent British interests in West Africa.

This emphasis on the material aspect of 'civilisation' was further enhanced by the sometimes explicit rejection of ideological aspects of Britishness. Not all of those Africans living in and around Freetown were convinced of the superiority of British culture or civilisation. Some explicitly chose to remain animists or return to traditional religions, marriage practices and Poro societies. Others affiliated with the Muslim populations of West Africa, who entered Freetown as traders or who lived in nearby regions. Since much of the Sierra Leone population was made up of recaptives, many were themselves first-generation converts to Christianity. With as many as 15,000 'pagans' in the colony out of a total population of 45,000 in the late 1840s, it is not surprising that there was some ambiguity in the colonists' dealings with the groups they called the 'Timmany', 'Ibo' and 'Aku'.[39] An equivalent number of the Sierra Leone population retained their Muslim religion or converted after coming into contact with the Mandinka and Fula. Governor Pine estimated in 1848 that 'the number of persons attending Christian and Mahomedan worship is about 23,000'.[40] Despite their rejection of British Christian ideology (and even anti-slavery ideology, in some cases), Muslim traders and converts still served an important commercial and material purpose in the colony. For many, British civilisation could come with a rejection of Christianity, which left a particularly material definition of 'Britishness': one associated with the rights and protections to trade.

In the on-going discourse between the colonists, indigenous African groups and the British metropole, appeals to shared material culture were used to promote the colony and champion policies or colonial officials that they felt were particularly beneficial to their own success. In a published book of petitions in support of former Governor Campbell, a group of Liberated Africans listed the cultural values they associated with British civilisation that they felt they were promoting outside of the colony: 'since Governor Campbell has located the young liberated Africans among them, and established large schools, they are enabled to sell their produce on the spot, and the circulation of money which has taken place in consequence, has acted as a stimulus to their industry, and enabled them to clothe themselves, and to purchase those comforts'.[41] These appeals to shared material values were connected to claims of Britishness. In 1829, one group wrote to the metropolitan government,

> That your memorialists deem it an act of duty toward themselves to recall to the recollection of His Majesty's Government that this Colony has become their home and that they have embarked all their means in adding to its respectability, and appearance, that their whole fortunes have been expended in furtherance of such objects and they have hitherto contributed their full share to the increase of its revenue, cheered they must confess by the hope that they would at some no distant period, be permitted to participate in those favors, so exclusively bestowed on their European, British fellow subjects.[42]

Here, the petitioners explain their claim as British subjects, equal to their fellow 'European, British' subjects, as being based on their exertions in contributing to Sierra Leone's 'respectability and appearance' and the increase in its revenue. Industriousness, success in legitimate commerce and the crafting of a 'civilised' settlement on the coast of West Africa meant that Sierra Leone's settlers felt they should be considered worthy of equal treatment by the British Empire.

The material success of the colonists led to repeated calls for representation as the wealthy petitioned against taxes, import duties and the arbitrary restrictions they felt that their lack of representation in colonial government yielded.[43] A group of petitioners in 1835 argued that the Governing Council should be made up of members 'chosen from the community by the inhabitants, under such restrictions as may make persons of the highest reputability and freehold proprietors only' and in this way, 'insure the economical expenditure of the colonial revenue, its proper application and also prevent any laws but those calculated for the public welfare being in future passed by the board of the Governor and the Council'.[44] Governor Findlay specifically noted in response to one such petition that 'the pride and presumption of the persons of colour who have got money into their hands … is such, that if not checked there will be no leverage with them in the colony'.[45] To colonial officials, material success was directly equated with increased leverage in the claims made upon the colonial government and the metropole.

Although they could reject certain cultural values, material connections and the strength of legitimate commerce helped the settlers to demonstrate their value, and helped them support claims to other cultural values, such as representation in colonial decision making, positions in government and expanded educational opportunities. Material success could lead not only to the purchase of more British manufactures, but also to an expanding cultural connection to Britain. In describing the successful merchants of Freetown, one governor wrote that 'Many of them at the present moment have their children being educated in England at their own expense.'[46] In turn, these cultural connections fostered further material connections, whether through the development of business contacts or through increased demand for the British goods encountered while studying in Britain.

As a result of Sierra Leone's on-going material links to Britain and, in particular, Sierra Leoneans' increasing use of those links to establish claims on 'civilisation' and the promotion of 'native' legitimate commerce, they were able from the 1840s to 1860s to make advances towards more representative government in the colony and to pursue their own expansionist aims outside of the colony. In this period, there were two governors, briefly, of West African descent; one Nova Scotian Colonial Secretary and member of the governing council; and one mayor of Freetown of African descent. In particular, as Gustav Devenaux wrote about the period, 'in Freetown, the civil and mercantile communities, predominantly African, were strong advocates of the acquisition of political control, and the pressure they were able to exert on the local colonial administration did much to circumvent the official directives from Whitehall' when they were not able to extract their demands from metropolitan allies of the civilising and anti-slavery missions.[47]

As an example of the Sierra Leoneans' use of material claims to Britishness, in the 1840s and 1850s they were able to push the frontiers of the colony outward and expand ideas of British subjecthood by claiming British property rights outside of the colony. In 1848, settlers petitioned Acting Governor B. C. C. Pine because they had been robbed or attacked while trading outside of the colony. Pine responded forcefully, promising protection for the Sierra Leone subjects. For instance, Pine directed two ambassadors to seek an audience with Stephen Caulker, the Eurafrican trader and a chief on Sherbro Island, to reprimand him for plundering 'a large amount of property belonging to the following Sierra Leone people, viz. Isaac George, Richard Johnson, Jim

Macaulay, John Johnson, Richard Quashie, and Jack Repeyarn'. Pine requested that 'he will for the future carefully abstain, and cause his people to abstain from interfering with Sierra Leone Subjects, whilst pursuing their lawful trade', under threat of severe punishment if he did not comply.[48] In another example, Pine wrote to King Canreba of Bonthe to inform him that 'I will not permit the property of any of the Sierra Leone people to be taken from them or their trade up the Sherbro to be interfered with, unless it can be clearly proved that they have been guilty of bad conduct.'[49] Worse still, 'some of your people have robbed and beaten William Thomas and William Meheul belonging to this Colony, and ... they at the same time grossly insulted the Flag of England by tearing it to pieces'.[50] When Canreba failed to respond to Pine's demands for satisfaction, Pine felt he was 'obliged to destroy the places where these wrongs were done'.[51]

As a result of Sierra Leoneans' repeated assertions of a shared British culture and their influence in spreading that culture along the West African coast, parliamentary reports continually supported the colonists throughout the later nineteenth century. Although the early debates in Parliament had centred on the colony's efficacy in suppressing the slave trade, by the 1840s Sierra Leoneans' success in promoting legitimate agriculture and spreading British culture was practically undisputed. In 1841, Dr Robert Madden's report to Parliament indicated the potential for the growth of the palm oil trade in the Sierra Leone region. In 1839, Sierra Leone exported £7,993 of palm oil, as compared with the Niger delta's £50,000. Explaining that palm oil, whose import into Britain had grown exponentially between the beginning of the century and 1840, was primarily imported directly from indigenous traders in the Niger region, Madden concluded that British interest in West Africa should concentrate on commerce as the best means of effecting the civilisation of Africa and the abolition of the slave trade.[52]

In recognition of the contributions of Sierra Leoneans to growing West African trade, Colonial Secretary Earl Grey wrote to Governor Macdonald in 1851 authorising treaties that recognised the jurisdiction of the British Government over British subjects when they were outside of the colony.[53] When Sierra Leoneans were ultimately recognised as British 'natural born subjects of Her Majesty' in 1853, it was because they continued to push the boundaries of the colony in pursuit of willing trading partners for the import of British goods and the export of 'legitimate' commercial produce.[54] Freetown's merchants had amassed a good deal of wealth, with upcountry trade growing to five times its 1830 levels by the 1880s, and these merchants still sought to use commerce as a civilising, anti-slavery tool. In 1874,

Freetown businessman William Grant argued for annexation of the interior in order to create stability amongst warring peoples, which 'hampered the progress of commerce and religion, and civilization, which are indispensables in every land'.[55] The arguments for Sierra Leone's civilising mission were intimately connected to that conflation of civilisation and commerce; colonisation and material culture.

As the strength of legitimate commerce in creating a Sierra Leonean middle class with shared British values became more obvious as the century progressed, others praised its success. Sierra Leoneans were involved in expanding British commerce and missionary work to Nigeria and Cameroon, as well as to the immediate vicinity of the colony.[56] Their work there drew praise from Palmerston, who authorised the occupation of Lagos in 1851 in response to Sierra Leonean requests.[57] An 1865 report to Parliament noted of Sierra Leone that 'the position and influence she exercises over so considerable a portion of the country, coupled with her prosperous and peaceful state, would prevent any thought of her abandonment'.[58] This conclusion was supported with evidence of the value of British imports into the colony and the small expenditure of the metropolitan government in supporting the colony. Sierra Leone's merchants were successful in spreading British material culture in the region, and thereby bolstering manufacturing imports into West Africa.

Even detractors in the latter part of the century had to recognise the influence of this strain of argument on perceptions of West Africa. In his report on an 1881 expedition to the interior, an administrator reported that 'a great deal has been spoken, and a good deal has been written, in an exaggerated strain as to the capabilities and resources of the West Coast of Africa, and the interior thereof, and the possibility, and indeed probability, of the country becoming a sort of second India, and the last hope of the British manufacturer', which, he believed, was all 'a fiction' that did not account for 'an extremely sparse population' on the coast.[59] The fact that this 'fiction' had survived into the 1880s testifies to the perception of Sierra Leone's success in the metropolitan imagination. Sierra Leoneans' perceived ability to carry British manufactures and material culture to their immediate hinterland as well as to the areas they colonised in Nigeria and Cameroon was probably based more on rhetoric than reality. But the success of an elite Sierra Leonean settler class to adopt and adapt the messages of civilisation and material culture helped to shape thinking about the spread of the British Empire in West Africa until at least the 1880s. The *Sierra Leone Gazette*'s assertion in the 1820s that 'The vast field which this Continent opens for the consumption of British manufactures, will, ere long, equal any market in the world' was carried forth by colonists in their claims on the British Empire, and by their humanitarian allies in debates over the colony's role in that empire.[60]

The colony also had an impact on perceptions of the model necessary to carry the civilising mission and British material culture to the world. By the 1820s, the London Missionary Society was attempting to replicate the success of the CMS's civilising mission in Sierra Leone with its own settlements in South Africa.[61] Because of the on-going metropolitan debates over Sierra Leone's success or failure, people in humanitarian networks were aware of it as a model, and promoted anti-slavery, missionary and civilising plans based on the arguments for Sierra Leone's success. Sir Stamford Raffles, in setting up Singapore, wrote to his colleague William Wilberforce to suggest that a missionary settlement in Borneo might help to combat the slave trade.[62] In 1819, Raffles wrote again requesting the oversight of the African Institution, the body responsible for directing Sierra Leone policy from London: 'Can you not take us under your parental wings, or could you not make the Eastern Islands a branch of the African Institution under some other designation?' He believed that 'our objects and principles are the same, and the field for improvement is at least as wide and important'.[63] He continued, pointing out that 'the station which has been established at Singapore, at the southern extremity of the Malayan Peninsula has given us the command of the Archipelago as well in peace as in war: our commerce will extend to every part and British principles will be known and felt throughout'.[64] Sierra Leone's success as a model for tying together the civilising mission, humanitarianism, colonisation and commercial expansion may have been debated throughout the early nineteenth century, but advocates were clearly convinced that this model was applicable in the wider imperial project.

In 1840, anti-slavery campaigner Thomas Fowell Buxton published his plan for spreading 'civilization, commerce, and Christianity' in West Africa, citing, reluctantly, the fact that 'The only glimmer of civilization; the only attempt at legitimate commerce; the only prosecution, however faint, of agriculture, are to be found at Sierra Leone.'[65] Based largely on the same ideas of legitimate commerce and Christian education that had been applied in Sierra Leone, Buxton's plan proposed that 'civilization, commerce and Christianity' were the only effective ways of abolishing the slave trade. He wanted to use Sierra Leone as a model on which to base a new and improved colonisation project on the Niger River.[66] When that expedition failed, as a result largely of disease, British humanitarian interest settled firmly into the idea that Sierra Leone was the best place – and Sierra Leoneans the best agents – for spreading British values and British commerce in West Africa.

Finally, in dealing with the slave trade in East Africa, which replaced that of West Africa in metropolitan debates of the later nineteenth century, anti-slavery proponents pointed directly to the successes of Sierra Leone as a model for establishing a similar settlement in East Africa. At the meeting of the East African Slave Trade Committee in 1874, a new settlement was discussed and the group concluded that 'The results which had followed the work in Sierra Leone were a great encouragement to do this and why should they not have a second Sierra Leone on the Eastern Coast, where the liberated slaves might be taught the arts of civilization.'[67] David Livingstone's suggestion for following the Sierra Leonean model struck a chord with Sir Bartle Frere and his East African campaigners as well, and a new settlement was established with his name (Freretown).[68] Sierra Leoneans' self-identification with British material culture and the values associated with British civilisation made them strong examples of the 'civilising mission' for campaigners, missionaries and parliamentarians in the metropole.

Black settler identification with British culture in the nineteenth century helps to explain the belief in the promise of the 'civilising mission' as well as the profound disappointment of colonial subjects, described by Bickford-Smith as the 'betrayal of creole elites', in Britain's hardening racial attitudes at the end of the century. The place of Sierra Leone within British-world scholarship reflects the colony's changing role after the scramble for tropical colonies at the end of the nineteenth century. What was once an important part of British imperial culture and metropolitan debates was relegated to a rather unimportant place in the history of empire. But Sierra Leone had played an important role in the mid-nineteenth-century empire, shaping metropolitan debates about humanitarianism, economic expansion and sub-imperialism. Largely, this outsized role was due to the identification of a vocal group of Sierra Leonean settlers with British culture.

Sierra Leone's settler population carried British values to other parts of West Africa, replicating the material culture of empire and spreading British cultural influence. The British world in West Africa was defined in part by a common material culture which stood for the common values of legitimate commerce, industriousness and merchants' civic participation. The place of Sierra Leone at the nexus of a variety of philanthropic and colonial experiments meant that its influence – and correspondingly the influence of the settlers – in shaping the culture and practice of empire was more widely felt than its size would suggest. On-going mission projects in East and Southern Africa, New Zealand and the West Indies; company projects in Singapore; ideas of the civilising mission in India: all were influenced, to some degree, by Sierra Leoneans' perceived success in spreading British cultural influence ('civilisation, commerce, and Christianity') in West Africa.

Notes

1 Carl Bridge and Kent Fedorowich, 'Mapping the British World', *Journal of Imperial and Commonwealth History*, 31 (2003), 1–15; Carl Bridge and Kent Fedorowich (eds), *The British World: Diaspora, Culture and Identity* (London: Routledge, 2003); Tamson Pietsch, *Empire of Scholars: Universities, Networks and the British Academic World 1850–1939* (Manchester: Manchester University Press, 2013); Bernard Attard and Andrew Dilley, 'Finance, Empire and the British World', *Journal of Imperial and Commonwealth History*, 41 (2013), 1–10.

2 Catherine Hall (ed.), *Cultures of Empire: A Reader* (Manchester: Manchester University Press, 2000); John Mackenzie, *Imperialism and Popular Culture* (Manchester: Manchester University Press, 1986).

3 See Robert Bickers (ed.), *Settlers and Expatriates* (Oxford: Oxford University Press, 2010).

4 Andrew Thompson and Gary Magee, *Empire and Globalisation* (Cambridge: Cambridge University Press, 2010); James Belich, *Replenishing the Earth* (Oxford: Oxford University Press, 2010).

5 Maya Jasanoff, *Liberty's Exiles* (London: HarperPress, 2011), pp. 279–309; Stephen Braidwood, *Black Poor and White Philanthropists: London's Blacks and the Foundation of the Sierra Leone Settlement, 1786–1791* (Liverpool: Liverpool University Press, 1994); Bill Nasson, 'Why They Fought: Black Cape Colonists and Imperial Wars, 1899–1918', *International Journal of African Historical Studies*, 37 (2004), 55–70; Timothy Parsons, 'African Participation in the British Empire', in Sean Hawkins and Philip D. Morgan (eds), *Black Experience and the Empire* (Oxford: Oxford University Press, 2006), pp. 257–85; Vivian Bickford-Smith, 'The Betrayal of Creole Elites, 1880–1920', in Hawkins and Morgan (eds), *Black Experience and the British Empire*, pp. 194–227; David Killingray, '"A Good West Indian, a Good African, and, in Short, a Good Britisher": Black and British in a Colour-Conscious Empire, 1760–1950', *The Journal of Imperial and Commonwealth History*, 36 (2008), 363–81.

6 Chris Gosden, *Archaeology and Colonialism* (Cambridge: Cambridge University Press, 2004), p. 3; Susan Lawrence (ed.), *Archaeologies of the British: Explorations of Identity in the United Kingdom and Its Colonies 1600–1945* (London: Routledge, 2013), p. 7; J. Daniel Rogers, 'Archaeology and the Interpretation of Colonial Encounters', in Gil J. Stein (ed.), *The Archaeology of Colonial Encounters* (Oxford: James Currey, 2005), pp. 331–54, at pp. 338–9.

7 Derek Peterson, 'Introduction', in Derek Peterson (ed.), *Abolitionism and Imperialism in Britain, Africa and the Atlantic* (Columbus: Ohio University Press, 2010), pp. 1–37, at pp. 21–3.

8 Lawrence (ed.), *Archaeologies of the British*, p. 4.

9 Bronwen Everill, *Abolition and Empire in Sierra Leone and Liberia* (Basingstoke: Palgrave, 2013).

10 And Black Victorian identity elsewhere too: see Elizabeth Elbourne, 'Early Khoisan Uses of Mission Christianity', *Kronos*, 19 (1992), 3–27.

11 Arthur T. Porter, *Creoledom: A Study of the Development of Freetown Society* (Oxford: Oxford University Press, 1966); Christopher Fyfe, *A History of Sierra Leone* (London: Longmans, 1962).

12 Timothy Parsons, 'African Participation in the British Empire', in Philip D. Morgan and Sean Hawkins (eds), *Black Experience and the Empire* (Oxford: Oxford University Press, 2006), pp. 257–85, at p. 258.

13 Vivian Bickford-Smith, 'The Betrayal of Creole Elites, 1880–1920', in Philip D. Morgan and Sean Hawkins (eds), *Black Experience and the Empire* (Oxford: Oxford University Press, 2006), pp. 194–227, at p. 196.

14 Mariana Candido, *An African Slaving Port and the Atlantic World: Benguela and Its Hinterland* (Cambridge: Cambridge University Press, 2013), pp. 12–13.

15 Catherine Hall, 'Culture and Identity in Imperial Britain', in Sarah Stockwell (ed.), *The British Empire* (Oxford: Wiley-Blackwell, 2008), pp. 199–217, at p. 203.

16 Andrew Walls, 'A Colonial Concordat: Two Views of Christianity and Civilization', in Derek Baker (ed.), *Church, Society, and Politics*, vol. 12 of *Studies in Church History* (Oxford: Wiley-Blackwell, 1975), pp. 293–302, at p. 295.

17 Elizabeth Elbourne, *Blood Ground: Colonialism, Missions, and the Contest for Christianity in the Cape Colony and Britain, 1799–1853* (Montreal: McGill-Queen's University Press, 2002), pp. 155–96; Kristin Mann, *Marrying Well: Marriage, Status and Social Change among the Educated Elite in Colonial Lagos* (Cambridge: Cambridge University Press, 1985) pp. 16–25; Killingray, '"A Good West Indian"'.

18 Donal Lowry, 'The Crown, Empire Loyalism and the Assimilation of Non-British White Subjects in the British World: An Argument against "Ethnic Determinism"', in Carl Bridge and Kent Fedorowich (eds), *The British World: Diaspora, Culture and Identity*, pp. 96–120, at p. 99. The National Archives (hereafter TNA) CO 267/99, received 29 January 1830.

19 Timothy H. Parsons, 'African Participation in the British Empire', in Philip D. Morgan and Sean Hawkins (eds), *Black Experience and the Empire* (Oxford: Oxford University Press, 2006), pp. 257–85, at p. 258; see also Vivian Bickford-Smith, 'African Nationalist or British Loyalist? The Complicated Case of Tiyo Soga', *History Workshop Journal*, 71 (2011), 74–97.

20 Catherine Hall, 'Introduction', in Hall (ed.), *Cultures of Empire*, p. 11.

21 Lorenzo Veracini, *Settler Colonialism* (Basingstoke: Palgrave, 2010), pp. 16–52.

22 Robert Bickers, 'Introduction: Britains and Britons over the Seas', in Bickers (ed.), *Settlers and Expatriates* (Oxford: Oxford University Press, 2010), pp. 1–17, at p. 14.

23 James Macqueen, *The Colonial Controversy ... with a Supplementary Letter to Mr. Macaulay* (Glasgow: Khull, Blackie & Co., 1825); Parliamentary Papers, 1865 (170) West Coast of Africa. Copy of the report of Colonel Ord, the commissioner appointed to inquire into the condition of the British settlements on the West Coast of Africa; David Lambert, 'Sierra Leone and Other Sites in the War of Representation over Slavery', *History Workshop Journal*, 64 (2007), 103–32.

24 Robert Thorpe, *A View of the Present Increase of the Slave Trade* (London: Barnard and Farley, 1818); Zachary Macaulay, *A letter to the Duke of Gloucester ... occasioned by a pamphlet lately published by Dr. Thorpe ... entitled 'A letter to William Wilberforce'* (London: Ellerton and Henderson, 1815); Padraic X. Scanlan, 'The Rewards of Their Exertions: Prize Money and British Abolitionism in Sierra Leone, 1808–1823', *Past and Present*, forthcoming; Michael J. Turner, 'The Limits of Abolition: Government, Saints and the "African Question", c. 1780–1820', *The English Historical Review*, 112 (1997), 319–57.

25 For instance, *The Royal Gazette and Sierra Leone Advertiser*, 24 July 1824, 323; *The Royal Gazette and Sierra Leone Advertiser*, 31 December 1825, 622–3. The *Sierra Leone Gazette* was circulated amongst supporters of the African Institution.

26 TNA, ADM 1/4242, Croker to Hay, 29 January 1827; Parliamentary Papers, 1827, VII (312), Report of the Commissioners of Inquiry, Liberated Africans 29 June 1827, 45–7; Robert T. Brown, 'Fernando Po and the Anti-Sierra Leonean Campaign: 1826–1834', *The International Journal of African Historical Studies* 6 (1973), 249–64, at 252–3; see also Lambert, 'Sierra Leone and Other Sites in the War of Representation', 103–32.

27 *Substance of the Report of the Court of Directors of the Sierra Leone Company, 19th October 1791* (London: James Phillips, 1792), 12.

28 Bronwen Everill, '"The Colony has made no progress in Agriculture": Contested Perceptions of Agriculture in the Colonies of Sierra Leone and Liberia', in Robin Law, Suzanne Schwarz and Silke Strickrodt (eds), *Commercial Agriculture, the Slave Trade and Slavery in Atlantic Africa* (Oxford: James Currey, 2013), pp. 180–202.

29 TNA, CO 272/1–38.

30 TNA, CO 272/1–38; Everill, 'Contested Perceptions of Agriculture', p. 190.

31 *Sierra Leone Gazette and Royal Advertiser*, 21 December 1825, 622–3.

32 Parliamentary Papers, 1842, (551) Report from the Select Committee on the West Coast of Africa, 338.

33 Everill, *Abolition and Empire*, p. 88.

34 Letter from William Fergusson to Thomas Fowell Buxton in Buxton, *The Slave Trade and Its Remedy* (London: John Murray, 1840), 371–3.
35 TNA, CO 272/7, Sierra Leone Blue Book, 1830.
36 TNA, CO 272/7, Sierra Leone Blue Book, 1831.
37 Magee and Thompson, *Empire and Globalisation*, p. 41.
38 Letter from William Fergusson in Buxton, *The Slave Trade and Its Remedy*, 371–3.
39 TNA, CO 267/204, 27 October 1848, The Temne, Igbo, and Yoruba.
40 TNA, CO 267/204, 27 October 1848, The Temne, Igbo, and Yoruba.
41 *Addresses, Petitions, &c. from the Kings and Chiefs of Sudan (Africa) and the Inhabitants of Sierra Leone, to his Late Majesty, King William the Fourth* (London: Gilbert & Rivington, 1838), 11.
42 TNA CO 267/99.
43 TNA, CO 267/118; CO 267/129.
44 TNA, CO 267/129, Lt. Gov. Campbell, 10 November 1835.
45 TNA, CO 267/118, 10 February 1833.
46 Letter from William Fergusson in Buxton, *The Slave Trade and Its Remedy*, 371–3.
47 Gustav Kashope Deveneaux, 'Public Opinion and Colonial Policy in Nineteenth-Century Sierra Leone', *The International Journal of African Historical Studies*, 9 (1976), 45–67, at 64.
48 Sierra Leone Archives, Governor's Local Letters 1846–48, B. C. Pine to R. A. Oldfield and W. Saukey, 17 July 1848.
49 Sierra Leone Archives, Governor's Local Letters 1846–48, B. C. Pine to Tom Coubak Bonthe, April 1848.
50 Sierra Leone Archives, Governor's Local Letters 1846–48, B. C. Pine to Canreba King of Bonthe, 2 May 1848.
51 Sierra Leone Archives, Governor's Local Letters 1846–48, to Fourry Bundo, 27 June 1848.
52 TNA, CO 267/172, Commissioner Dr Madden's Report, 1841.
53 TNA, CO 267/225, Grey to Macdonald, 28 June 1851.
54 Parliamentary Papers, 1855, XXXCII (383), 36.
55 TNA, CO 806/36, October 6, 1874.
56 Bronwen Everill, 'Bridgeheads of Empire? Liberated African Missionaries in West Africa', *Journal of Imperial and Commonwealth History*, 40 (2012), 789–805; John Kopytoff, *A Preface to Modern Nigeria: The 'Sierra Leonians' in Yoruba, 1830–1890* (Madison, WI: University of Wisconsin Press, 1965).
57 Lamin Sanneh, *Abolitionists Abroad: American Blacks and the Making of Modern West Africa* (Cambridge, MA: Harvard University Press, 1999), p. 127; TNA, FO 84/858, Palmerston to Beecroft, 18 February 1851.
58 Parliamentary Papers, 1865 (170) West Coast of Africa. Copy of the report of Colonel Ord, the commissioner appointed to inquire into the condition of the British settlements on the West Coast of Africa.
59 Administrator V. S. Gouldsbury: Report of the Futa Jallon Expedition, June 1881, Parliamentary Papers, 1881, LXV, 30–4.
60 *Sierra Leone Gazette and Royal Advertiser*, 21 December 1825, 622–3.
61 Bronwen Everill, 'Freetown, Freretown and the Kat River Settlement: Nineteenth-Century Humanitarian Intervention and Precursors to Modern Refugee Camps', in Bronwen Everill and Josiah Kaplan (eds), *The History and Practice of Humanitarian Intervention and Aid in Africa* (Basingstoke: Palgrave, 2013), pp. 23–42, at pp. 29–31; Alan Lester, *Imperial Networks: Creating identities in nineteenth century South Africa and Britain* (London: Routledge, 2009).
62 Sir Stamford Raffles to William Wilberforce, 23 October 1817, in Robert Isaac Wilberforce and Samuel Wilberforce (eds), *The Correspondence of William Wilberforce, Vol 2* (London: John Murray, 1840), pp. 386–7.
63 Letter from Sir Stamford Raffles to W. Wilberforce, Esq., September 1819, in Lady Stamford Raffles, *Memoir of the life and public services of Sir Thomas Stamford Raffles, vol 2* (London: J. Duncan, 1835), p. 53.
64 Letter from Sir Stamford Raffles to W. Wilberforce, Esq., September 1819, in Lady

Stamford Raffles, *Memoir*, p. 54.

65 Buxton, *The Slave Trade and Its Remedy*, p. 365.

66 Howard Temperley, *White Dreams, Black Africa: The Antislavery Expedition to the River Niger 1841–1842* (New Haven, CT: Yale University Press, 1991).

67 East African Slave Trade Committee, *First Report of the Proceedings of the East African Slave Trade Committee* (London, July 1874), p. 17. For more on this settlement, see Everill, 'Freetown, Freretown and the Kat River Settlement', pp. 29–31; Lindsay Doulton, 'The Royal Navy's Anti-Slavery Campaign in the Western Indian Ocean, c.1860–1890: Race, Empire, and Identity' (unpublished PhD thesis, University of Hull, 2010), p. 219.

68 Sir Bartle Frere, *Articles on the East African Slave Trade &c. 1872–83, The Quarterly Review*, vol. 133 (1872), 521–56, at 552.

INDEX